GREEK STUDIES

GREEK STUDIES

BY

GILBERT MURRAY

O.M., D.C.L., Litt.D., L.L.D.

FORMERLY REGIUS PROFESSOR OF GREEK
IN THE UNIVERSITY OF OXFORD

OXFORD
AT THE CLARENDON PRESS

Oxford University Press, Amen House, London E.C. 4

EDINBURGH GLASGOW NEW YORK TORONTO MELBOURNE
WELLINGTON BOMBAY CALCUTTA MADRAS CAPE TOWN

Geoffrey Cumberlege, Publisher to the University

FIRST EDITION 1946
REPRINTED JUNE 1947

PRINTED IN GREAT BRITAIN

PREFACE

THE studies contained in this volume form a rather mis-
cellaneous collection: three come from a course which
I gave at Cambridge for the Gray classical foundation on the
subject of that deliberate rejection of accepted values which
Diogenes the Cynic called *Paracharaxis* or 'Defacing the
Coinage'; three are taken from my own contributions to a
course popularly known in Oxford as 'The Seven against
Greats', 'Greats' being the name commonly given to the
final examination in classical history and philosophy. In the
'Seven' a number of eminent scholars from this University
and others were good enough to give lectures 'for the Professor' about excavations, inscriptions, papyri, philology,
anthropology, and various historical or philosophical subjects,
with the idea of giving to students at the start of their Greats
course some conception of the different aspects of Hellenic
study. I only wish I could have included here some of the
lectures I had the privilege of listening to.

The other papers are publications or republications of
lectures given to various learned or literary societies.

The selection and revision by an old man of studies written
many years before is a somewhat nervous work. It is easy to
make a bad selection; it is easy to repeat oneself or even,
horribile dictu, to repeat one's jokes; it is terribly easy to
forget the authority for some familiar statement and consequently to state it wrong. But, after all, dangers of some
kind lie in wait for all who are rash enough to write books.

G. M.

BOAR'S HILL, 1946.

CONTENTS

I

HELLENISM

IT is surely a remarkable occurrence that Hellenism, a
particular civilization which existed for its moment of
history and passed away, should have remained so long for
after ages and for utterly foreign nations something like an
ideal, or at least an inspiration. It is common enough for a
nation to look back with pride and longing to its own time
of greatness. But through most of antiquity and again since
the Renaissance, Greek civilization of the classical period
has rightly or wrongly been something like a Golden Age to
the imagination of very different nations, or at least to the
more intellectual elements in them, without any illegitimate
support from mere national pride or interest. Like all ideals
this ideal Hellenism is very different from the reality on
which it is based; and the present lecture is meant to make
a comparison between the ideal and the reality in a number
of separate domains.

Our own western civilization of the nineteenth and early
twentieth centuries is to a marked degree both Hellenic and
un-Hellenic. Historically we are, to a greater extent than
we ever realize, the children of Greece in literature, in art,
in thought, in ethics, in politics, and notably in religion; on
the other hand, we are, to a degree unparalleled in history,
a rich, highly organized material civilization in control—or
shall I say under the control?—of material possessions and
inventions; an age of machinery, of mass production, of
economic complexity and terrific governmental strength. The
civilization of the Greeks was conspicuous for the very opposite qualities. The arm of their government was neither long
nor strong. Their clothes, however graceful, were little more
than a sleeveless shirt and a blanket. I suspect they went
mostly barefoot. At any rate, they thought the Lydians
luxurious and 'soft-footed' because they habitually wore shoes.

They had no proper roads, such as the Persians had, no drains like those of the Romans or even the Minoans, no palaces to compare with the Persian palaces. Indeed no Greek community in the classical period was at all comparable in size, wealth, population, material splendour, military strength, or steady permanence to—for instance—the great River Civilizations of Egypt and Mesopotamia. By all such standards the Greeks come out as little better than savages. The greatness of Greece depended on quite other qualities.

Writers often try to understand ancient Greece by comparing it with our own civilization, but of course that is quite unhistorical. The best starting-point for a study of Hellenism is to notice the significant differences between Greek civilization and those which preceded or accompanied it.

Now the first thing that strikes us is that in Greece there was no divine 'Great King' in the Babylonian or Egyptian sense, nor even in the Persian or Minoan sense. For one thing, Greek States are on a small scale; for another, Greek potentates are always sharply warned that they are not gods and will only get into trouble if they think they are. They must not put up megalomaniac inscriptions about their own glory; they must not expect to have concubines and attendants sacrificed on their tombs. They must not expect people to kiss the earth on entering into their presence or to walk backwards on leaving it. The law is always above them. They must not put people to death without trial; not seize other men's wives and daughters; not amuse themselves or the dregs of their people with gladiatorial games. Before they accepted such things as that, as the philosopher Demonax put it, they must 'overthrow the Altar of Pity in the market-place'. Even in war, where most moral rules tend to disappear, Greek custom kept a high standard. There must be no triumph, no boasting, no maltreatment of enemy dead, no killing of prisoners of war, no torture. Furthermore, the Greek conqueror must put up no permanent war memorial, only what they called a 'trophy', that is, a wooden pole and

cross-bar with armour upon it to mark the site of the victory;
a monument which the conqueror must never repair and the
conquered never pull down, but both must allow gradually
to break up and sink into the earth as the memory of the old
bitterness faded. The Egyptian or Assyrian put up gigantic
limestone reliefs, still extant after two thousand years, showing himself in superhuman size receiving tribute from his
enemies; or, in the Assyrian case at least, making pyramids of
their skulls and leading their kings into captivity by fish-
hooks stuck through their noses after their eyes have been
put out. How else shall a great king show his greatness? Even
the Romans,[1] long afterwards, had their horrible triumphs,
the conqueror in pomp on his chariot with the spoils; chained
prisoners dragged behind him, and some of them strangled
in the Tullianum. They made permanent sculptures in stone
on triumphal arches afterwards, to keep the memories of
glory and humiliation alive. Roughly speaking, in the Great
Monarchies there was only one duty, *obedience*. 'Except for
one man, all was slavery'; and that one, so far as he had any
duty at all, had merely to obey some Great King in his own
image among the gods. For the Greek there are many duties.
There is a whole system of ethics. He is a citizen, one among
others, whose rights are equal to his. Hellenism, we find,
becomes in the fullest sense a humane civilization.

One can see some of the causes that led to this great
difference. First a geographical cause: Greece is a country
of small, broken valleys, like Switzerland, except for its har-
bours and islands, a place for many independent cities but
not for any one great over-mastering city, like Babylon or
Nineveh or Memphis. Then an historical cause: while Mesopotamia and Crete were both conquered by invaders from
the north and passed through their Heroic Age or 'time of
troubles', the Heroic Age in Greece was quite peculiar in its
action. It resulted in no uniform subjugation of the natives
by the invaders. There was no fixed centre of sovereignty

[1] Cf. 'Greece and England', p. 207 below.

for the conquerors, and there were always the sea and the
islands offering chances of flight and refuge for the defeated.
In the Greek or pre-Greek 'time of troubles', when people
were flying from the invaders or from those whom the invaders were driving before them, there seems to have been
a complete and general collapse of the social structure. Look
at the Book of Leviticus with its meticulous list of taboos
and rules of behaviour, or even at the detailed laws of Hammurabi. Most early tribes had similarly elaborate codes, but
in Greece they were broken up. According to Strabo, nearly
every place of refuge was filled by a σύμμεικτον πλῆθος, a
'mixed multitude', of different origins and traditions. The
tribes had been scattered, and with them the peculiar tribal
taboos and sanctities. The graves of each tribe's ancestors had
been left behind, and with them the religious rites and
customs which had held the old village together.

There was little that the refugees could carry with them
except their memories, their poetry, and perhaps—to some
extent—their dances. There was no social order in which to
put their trust except that created by the circuit-wall or
polis, which they had hurriedly built up to protect them
against a hostile world. That is why the *polis* is so peculiarly
significant in Hellenism. It took the place of clan or kindred.
It was the new centre of loyalty, though the Greeks never
forgot that it was not really the wall but the men behind the
wall that made a city.

If, in Professor Toynbee's phrase, one regards this collapse
of the social order as an ordeal or challenge, one may remark
that it was a challenge almost intolerably severe. Most
peoples would have broken down under it. It is perhaps the
tremendous spiritual effort necessary for meeting successfully
the ordeal of the Heroic Age that launched the Greek *polis*
forward upon its amazing history.

The old rules and taboos and superstitions were gone.
Henceforth men were not tribesmen. They were a mixed
multitude but at least they were πολῖται, citizens, bound to

support the *polis* on which the lives of all depended. They must agree on their νόμοι, their laws or customs, and conform to them; in disputes they must use δίκη, or arbitration, for the other πολῖται were neither subjects nor strangers, but equals before the law and all free. Obviously, all alike must observe 'measure' and be temperate. Life must depend not upon force but upon free speech and persuasion. And after all οὐκ ἐστὶ πειθοῦς ἱερὸν ἄλλο πλὴν λόγος, 'The goddess Persuasion has no temple except the Word.'

It is not surprising that the most characteristic word in the Greek language is '*logos*'. The new Liddell and Scott, severely compressed as it is, takes about 5,500 words to explain its chief meanings. Its history would need a whole book. It seemed to the Greeks to lie at the roots of politics, ethics, and religion, of science, and of philosophy; and of course to us who seek to understand the Greeks, it is 'the word' more than anything else, more even than the art or the history, that acts as interpreter. I wish to consider to-day the kind of *logoi* which the Greeks took the trouble not only to make but to record and keep in remembrance. Their written records differ in so many ways from those of their neighbours and predecessors.

The Hebrews, for instance, have left a splendid literature, though somewhat narrow in range. There is a cosmology, as in Babylonian and Egyptian. There are elaborate and scrupulous collections of laws and taboos, mostly taken from Babylon. There are valuable books of history, consisting first of a few traditions about the early judges, and then of the doings of a whole list of kings, the text carefully edited again and again by the Jahvist priests in the interests of orthodoxy. There is a collection of songs or psalms, all pretty much in the same style and all religious. There is also a great body of literature not extant anywhere else, a collection of the oracles of the orthodox prophets—the unorthodox, the prophets of the Baalim, however numerous and accomplished they may have been, were, of course, suppressed. But the class of

prophets in general was more admired and reached a higher
level of intelligence among the Hebrews than in any other
society known to us. Practically the whole mass of the literature is not only religious; it is sacerdotal. Both the code of
law and the historical record have been made to conform to
the views of the priestly class.

Almost the only exceptions are the Book of Ruth, which—
contrary to all the teaching of Nehemiah—takes for its
heroine a woman of Moab, and the epithalamium of Solomon,
which was perhaps mistaken for an allegory. The Wisdom
literature, and probably the philosophic book about the un-
deserved sufferings of Job, are already under Greek influence.

My knowledge is not sufficient to enable me to speak with
any confidence about Egyptian and Babylonian literatures.
The Babylonian differs from the Hebrew, of course, in having
the characteristics of a Great State. It is polytheistic: as a
rule in antiquity only a small country can confine itself to
one god. When King Josiah was determined to make his
people monotheist, he had to suppress all shrines except
Jerusalem. If you annex neighbouring peoples you must
annex their gods with them. We have to remember also
that the Bible is a careful selection of what was considered
most valuable in ancient Hebrew literature, whereas our
Babylonian remains depend partly on excavations and monuments and partly on innumerable potsherds, unselected and
only preserved by accident. Babylonian literature possesses
all the styles of Hebrew, except that it has not preserved the
oracles of its prophets, and in addition has a vast mass of
laws and treaties, private contracts, letters, and records of
the deeds of individual kings. It has also some very rudi-
mentary epics, some few non-religious stories, and some love
songs. In the main it is dominated by religion, astrology, and
magic in general, by the power of the king and priestly class,
and by a majestic edifice of uniform law. Egyptian literature
is even more completely dominated by magico-religious
texts. The Book of the Dead, for instance, has been found in

more than a thousand tombs. Egypt has less law and less history than Babylon, but it escapes from its bonds of magic and king-worship in its fairly abundant stories and folk-tales. There are no epics, though there are some short stories about gods and a good store of hymns. Prophetic literature is represented by one or two vague Jeremiads about the deplorable condition of the modern world. (The poor thing has always been modern and always deplorable.) There is no legal code, but, curiously enough, there is an account of one lawsuit in which the king was concerned. There is some interesting Wisdom literature; there are five medical treatises and two mathematical.

When we turn to Greek literature the first thing that impresses us is its extraordinary variety. Where Hebrew presented us with one form of poetry, or at most two, the psalm and the prophecy, and those two identical in metrical treatment and in vocabulary, Greek gives us the epic and the mock epic, the didactic or philosophic poem, the choral lyric, and the personal lyric, each class comprising a great many subdivisions; the political poem, like those of the reforming Solon, the disgruntled Theognis, the revolutionary Alcaeus, the patriotic Tyrtaeus; the satire, like those of Archilochus and Hipponax; the drama, both tragic and comic; the love song, elegy, and narrative. And there are not only these different forms of poetry. Every form is apt to have its appropriate metres and even its appropriate dialect.

In prose the variety is even greater, though, curiously enough, the kind of prose that is commonest in Babylonia and Egypt is absent. In the classical period, at least, there are no records of royal megalomania, no magic texts, no books of oracles. Particular oracles are sometimes quoted, and of course magic charms and rituals must have existed. We know that for certain. But they were not considered to be worth preserving, any more than the paroxysms of itinerant prophets. There is no great uniform legal code, like that of

Hammurabi. Instead we find a number of local codes, some-times traditional, sometimes the work of individual law-givers, the result of active and original thinking. There is history of various types; the local chronicles; Hellanicus' collection of such chronicles; Herodotus and his universal *Historiê*, or Inquiry into everything that interested him; Thucydides and his strictly limited and scientific history of a particular war. Then come two forms of literature almost unknown elsewhere, philosophy and oratory. Philosophy takes the most various forms, as it is based on physical science, on mathematics, on astronomy, or on the needs of society, and culminates perhaps in the two schools of ethical thought which still divide modern moralists, the Stoic and the Epicurean. Oratory, business-like argumentative oratory, was a natural growth from free political institutions, for which there was no place in Egypt, Babylon, or Jerusalem. A bye-form of oratory is the mass of occasional writing, like the Old Oligarch's criticism of the Athenian demo-cracy, Xenophon's *Memorabilia* and notes on hunting dogs, Sophron's mimes and their marvellous progeny, the Plato-nic Dialogue. The variety is much greater than that of any literature before or since until we come to quite modern times. Neither Rome nor the Middle Ages came near to it.

The next characteristic which will strike us is the very small part played by superstition or magic; amazingly small when we think of Babylon, Egypt, or India. There was, of course, a great deal of superstition in ancient Greece. There must have been and, as a matter of fact, the evidence for it is abundant. One need only think of Nicias and the eclipse, of the mutilation of the Hermae, of the descriptions of superstition in Theophrastus, Epicurus, Lucretius, and Minucius Felix, and St. Paul's remarks about δεισιδαιμονία.[1] But superstition was evidently looked down upon, and in general the supernatural was not allowed to interfere with serious literature. I suspect that there were innumerable

[1] Acts xvii. 22.

fragments of unauthoritative local religions floating about among the illiterate, but we must leave that question aside for the present. The intelligentsia were emancipated except for one firmly rooted belief which it would be harsh to call superstitious. In poetry, history, and philosophy alike there is an undercurrent of conviction that the natural order of the world is somehow also a moral order: the moral law is real, and transgression is naturally followed by punishment. No one can be unjust with entire impunity. *Dikê* is justice, but is also the way in which things happen. Apart from this undercurrent the historians are remarkably free from superstition. Philosophy emancipates itself from traditional bonds with an ease and completeness which has no parallel before the seventeenth century in France and the eighteenth in England. As for science, it is difficult to read even now without emotion the passages in which Hippocrates, the father of medicine, repudiates all appeal to superstition or magic. His pupils must swear to make no pretensions to magical powers. They must take no advantage of the patient's sufferings or fears, but enter the house in sincerity, as a friend to all who dwell there.

The dethronement of the supernatural in art and poetry is equally remarkable and takes a curious shape. Ancient religion was always local. The god of your home and your fathers was real to you, quite different from these rootless international gods whom Homer and the poets had carried all over Greece. But it was only the international gods that played much part in poetry or in art: the somewhat unreal gods in idealized human form and, if only you can either deny or allegorize the unedifying legends of a more primitive time, with idealized human characteristics. 'It is not fabulous Titans and Giants who rule mankind', cried Pelopidas, 'but one who is a Father of all Gods and men.' The anthropomorphic gods of classical Greece represent not a primitive religion but a reformation against the savagery of such religion. Religion itself was humanized.

It would be presumptuous to try to read the intimate thoughts of people so far distant from us in time and space, but the impression which most scholars receive in this matter would, I think, be something like this: that the poets felt a fairly complete, though tolerant and affectionate, scepticism towards the whole of what the Greeks called θεολογία, the mass of stories, often mutually contradictory, which the poets and chroniclers had picked up from different geographical sources, combined with a serious though formless and undogmatic religious sentiment, attaching itself sometimes to an almost monotheistic Zeus or 'The Divine', sometimes to some particular local shrine or ritual or some special supernatural being or group of beings whose worship in some way came close to them.

But in the main poetry also is emancipated from the paralysing grasp of the supernatural. There are plenty of religious inscriptions and records of peculiar rituals, but one cannot imagine Greek priests going through the Homeric poems and industriously removing all traces of unorthodox worship, as the Jewish priests did with their ancient literature. An expurgation of Homer did occur, but it took quite another shape; it was an expurgation of cruelties or barbarities.

Let us consider for a moment what this dethronement of the supernatural implied and what results flowed from it. Egypt and Babylon filled their papyri and tablets with magic for a solid practical reason, just as they wrote down their contracts and made notes of the moneys they were owed. If by reciting correctly a certain formula and performing correctly a certain ritual you could really ensure good crops, a large haul of fish, recovery from sickness, the softening of a policeman's heart, or prosperity in the next world, it stands to reason that all sensible men would wish to know and use such valuable instruments, and that extreme care must naturally be taken to see that the formulas and the rituals were recorded without any mistake. An error in the title of one among twenty subordinate deities might produce most distressing results; and as for sacrificing theological exactitude in order to make a poem more interesting or a verse more melodious, the very idea would savour of madness. If Hippocrates had believed that magic formulae would really help to cure the patient, he could not have forbidden the use of them. Thus we see that one of the first characteristics of Greek civilization and consequently of Greek literature is scepticism; or in other words, the discovery that man did not know a great many highly important things which he would have liked to know and which in most societies he passionately claimed to know.

Hence comes the third striking characteristic of the Greek record: the absence of authoritative orthodoxy and censorship. In the Old Testament the ancient polytheism of the Semites has been drastically censored and amended till it conformed to the conditions of orthodox Jahvism. All other opinions are, of course, wrong and are therefore suppressed. But in Greece from the very outset we find divergent schools and divergent historical traditions. In the heroic tradition we find remnants of legend which are contrary to the *Iliad* and *Odyssey*. Herodotus makes a point of collecting and criticizing divergent versions of the stories he relates.[1] Hecataeus, we may remember, started his book with the remarkable outburst: 'I write as seems to me true, for the stories of the Greeks are various and absurd.' Protagoras says boldly: 'About the gods I cannot say either that they are or that they are not, or what like they are.'

In philosophy we find the Ionian school of physicists in general agreement with one another, though not without particular differences, but a completely different outlook in the Pythagorean school and another in those of Parmenides and Empedocles. And there is nothing to prevent Heraclitus of Ephesus from saying roundly that 'much learning does not teach sense; else it would have taught Hesiod and

[1] Cf. 'Greece and England', pp. 200, 210.

Pythagoras, and again Xenophanes and Hecataeus', and
adding that Homer and Archilochus ought metaphorically
to be 'whipped off the course' for their misconduct. Imagine
Jeremiah, or even Habakkuk, who was *capable de tout*, saying
such things about Moses! That is a philosopher, you may
say, speaking against poets and historians; but Xenophanes,
a professional *rhapsode*, who lived by reciting Homer, passes
on him an equally free and almost equally severe criticism.
'Homer and Hesiod attributed to the gods actions that are
disgraceful to men.' 'Besides, their anthropomorphism is
ridiculous. No doubt cows would say God has the form of
a cow. God is a spirit, with no shape.'[1] One sees therefore
what the Greeks meant by proclaiming their devotion to
ἐλευθερία and παρρησία—to freedom, and above all to freedom of speech. Most nations when they demand freedom
really wish to be free to compel other people; but throughout the classical age, with a few rare exceptions, the Greeks
did really let people say what they believed without censorship or punishment. No other nation when engaged in a
serious war has allowed the opponents of the war to speak
in public with anything like the freedom of Aristophanes.
On the other hand, it is the existence of this freedom that
makes the Greek writers so insistent on the need for order,
Cosmos, for *Metron*, measure in all things, for *Sophrosynê*, the
quality which we translate by 'temperance', but which seems
to mean the temper of mind which saves things in peril. If
we are all free in thought and speech, clearly we must
remember proportion, do 'nothing too much', and think the
thoughts that save. There was no need of such warnings
under despotism.

We can go farther. This readiness to let the 'other fellow'
speak developed from a matter of conscientious principle to
a positive taste. We hear a good deal of the pleasure which
in real life the Athenians took in listening to debates or
public trials. Would such debates have been at all possible

---

[1] Cf. 'Prolegomena to Ancient Philosophy', p. 68.

in Jerusalem or Memphis or Babylon ? In literature certainly
there is evidence of something like a passion for hearing
both sides of a case. In the *Iliad*, accepted as the great
national and patriotic epic, one is made to see the Trojan
side of the case as well as the Greek. Indeed there is more
sympathy roused for Hector and Andromachê than for any
of their Greek conquerors. Art and truth are matched
against national pride and easily win the day. In Herodotus,
in spite of his strong Hellenic and democratic instincts, one
feels a continual sympathetic interest in the Scythians and
Persians and Egyptians. He tends not to say, 'These people
are different from us; how wicked they must be!' but rather,
'These people are different from us; what have they discovered about life that we do not know?' The Jews might
shudder at an 'uncircumcised Philistine' or proclaim what
nations should or should not be 'abhorred', but in the Greek
record there was almost none of that instinctive intolerance.
In Thucydides it is a fixed principle on every important
political issue to marshal the arguments on both sides in the
form of speeches, and the work has been done with such
impartiality that modern critics differ as to where the
historian's own sympathies lay. One tends to compare
Thucydides in this matter with the most scientific modern
historians; but to see him in his true historical perspective
one should set him beside the Roman Livy or the authors of
the Book of Kings. Imagine, if you can, two contrary
speeches on the policy of rebuilding the Temple from
Nehemiah and Sanballat, the Horonite, or on foreign policy
from Jehu and Jezebel.

Nay, this pleasure in seeing two sides of a controversy,
and the combined interest in the contest of wits and in the
effort after seeing truth, as it were, in the solid, led directly
towards one of the greatest and most characteristic creations
of the Greek genius, the Drama.[1] Drama has occurred in
many different societies, generally in the form of a religious

[1] Cf. 'Prolegomena to Greek History', p. 54.

ritual, but never has it formed such an important element in civic life, and seldom has it reached such intensity and artistic perfection as in fifth-century Athens. Now it is in the essence of drama that, since the actors represent different characters, they have to make some attempt to enter into the feelings of different characters; but I doubt if this practice of entering into the feelings of both parties to a dispute was ever, until quite modern times, developed to such a degree as in the Attic drama. Even in the Aristophanic comedy there is always an *agôn* or contest; two contrary points of view are at least stated, and stated with some rhetorical force. But in tragedy the psychological effort is much greater. It has been truly said that there are no stage villains in Greek tragedy. There are murderers; there are adulterous wives; there are wicked schemers; but there is never a character without a defence or a plea for extenuating circumstances. Clytemnestra not merely explains herself, but does so with such conviction and such deep feeling that the Elders who came to condemn her without mercy halt and confess themselves bewildered. Reviling, they say, comes easily but judgement is hard. The same is true of the murderess Medea, the mad Orestes, the unscrupulous Odysseus. What other ancient literature—except under Greek influence—ever approached this imaginative fairness, or even desired it? It looks as if the Greek poet actually took an intellectual pleasure in understanding his enemy; the average man thinks enemies are not made to be understood but to be beaten. One can see, indeed, as Professor Cornford has pointed out, that drama has a definite influence on the writing of history in Greece. It led both Herodotus and Thucydides to do two things which are not commonly found outside Greece: to give, either in narrative or direct speech, the views of both contending parties, and secondly, to conceive their subject in a form or pattern derived from tragedy. As the Old Testament writers see all history in the pattern of a desertion of Jehovah, a punishment and a forgiveness, as many modern writers see it in the pattern of biological evolution, the Greeks tended to see it in the form of *Hubris* and retribution, or rather of growth, excess, and downfall. This last point is perhaps historically speaking a weakness; artistically it makes the history not a mere chronicle of events but a story with form and meaning.

Still more visibly the drama has influenced philosophy. The most famous and most intensely characteristic of Greek philosophers, Plato, wrote always in dramatic form, and, what is still more remarkable, seldom or never gave the complete victory to one side in the dialogue. Except on certain moral questions, Plato seems always to conceive of truth not as a proposition to be certainly known and asserted, but as an end or ideal to be approached from this side and that side, to be understood better and better, but never, it would seem, to be certainly and completely attained. At the end of the discussion he generally leaves the conclusion unstated or at best adumbrated through some fable or metaphor. After Plato the dialogue became a common form of philosophical writing. I cannot imagine Jeremiah or Cato or even Confucius rising to that conception, much less any sage from Egypt or Babylon.

So far we have been noticing a series of qualities which are all causally connected: the wreck of ordered tribal traditions and taboos in the Heroic Age, the unsacerdotal and unsuperstitious background, the consequent absence of dogmatism and censorship, the freedom of thought and speech, the consciousness that our enemies have something to say for themselves and ought to be understood, the enjoyment of drama and dialectic, and lastly the use of both as instruments in the search for truth. I want now to consider a quite different property of the Greek written record, which results, I think, from the same causes. It is much more intimate than that of any previous nation and far more intimate than one has any right to expect from a people in such primitive conditions.

Intimacy is a quality difficult to achieve even for the most skilful writer. The writer must have complete command of his instrument and a fair knowledge of himself. He must also be on terms of confidence with his public, and above all not be afraid that any admission he makes will be used against him. These conditions scarcely ever existed in any ancient or medieval civilization, except inside certain privileged aristocratic circles. Life was too dangerous. A man was too much exposed to possible informers and enemies. No writer in the Old Testament takes us into his confidence or chaffs himself. Still less, as far as I know, do those of Babylon or Egypt, with the possible exception, it may be, of some of the popular Egyptian story-tellers.

It is rather wonderful how some of the classical Greek writers, while hardly talking about themselves at all, making no elaborate confessions, and leaving no important correspondence behind them, do contrive to make themselves intimately known to us. The *Memorabilia* of Xenophon are full of intimate and easy touches. The conversations described in Plato are just like glorified versions of the conversations that fourth-year students have on reading parties or in one another's rooms, glorified but not made at all stiff or un-intimate. In reading the *Republic*, no doubt, you sometimes want to break in and pull Socrates up, but you never feel that if you had been there you would not have been free to say what you liked. You may feel that Glaucon and Polemarchus allowed themselves to be hypnotized, but you do not feel that, if they had started to make an objection, there would have been a murmur of 'Hush, do not interrupt the Master'. There is the same feeling of intimacy with Aristophanes. He seems to be saying just what is in his mind—trifling, serious, indignant, poetical, or whatever it may be—without thought of his dignity or fear of being misunderstood. As to private letters, there is no collection of letters in Greek at all comparable in personal detail to those of Cicero, or in volume and business importance with those of Hammurabi. But the few fragments that remain—for example—of Epicurus' correspondence with fellow philosophers, children, and young women, are surprising in their ease and intimacy.[1]

To some friend

25. If you two don't come to me, I am capable of arriving with a hop, skip, and jump, wherever you and Themista summon me.

To Leontion

,32. Lord and Saviour, my dearest Leontion, what a clapping of hands there was, when we read aloud your dear letters!

To Pythocles

33. Blest youth, launch your boat and fly from every form of education.

But here comes a rather curious observation. What does one mean by intimacy? Neither Aristophanes nor Plato nor Epicurus give us much information about material and economic details. Is it not strange, for example, that prominent as ships of all kinds are in Greek literature from Homer to Demosthenes, we do not yet know for certain how a trireme was built? We never hear what anyone's income is, nor his rent, nor his wardrobe, nor what he pays in wages, nor how many hours he works. About all such matters there is far more information to be gathered from the Hammurabi correspondence, and indeed from the innumerable inscribed tablets scattered about Mesopotamia with records of contracts and business dealings. If we want detailed economic information we must turn in quite another direction. The papyri used by Rostovtzeff in his account of *A Large Estate in Egypt in the Third Century*, B.C. or the inscriptions of Delos, Delphi, and the Acropolis give us much more economic and material information about ancient life than do these authors whom I have called 'intimate'. When the friends of

---

[1] *Epicurus*, edited C. Bailey; see Fragments, pp. 127, 129.

Plato and Aristophanes met and talked, I dare say they did much as other people do and talked about their sport and health and business prospects and τοιοῦτον λῆρον, as Plato would say. But the talk that Plato thought worth recording was about quite other subjects—justice and the State and love and the possible immortality of the soul and so on—and it is through their thoughts about these things that they have become intimate to us. After all, you may know all the material facts about a man—his income, his hours of work, his debts, and how often his children have had mumps— without any intimacy at all; intimacy will only come, and may then come with a flash, when he really lets himself go on one of the subjects that Plato talks about. I think this possibility of intimacy is the mark of a very high civilization. It implies not only a high gift of expression, but still more an absence of fear. You can only speak freely and intimately when you are not afraid, afraid of spies, of enemies, of friends who may turn and betray you. Think of life in certain modern countries. Think of most medieval portraits, with never a frank and open countenance among them. Fear, I believe, was the normal condition of society in antiquity and the Middle Ages; a few high civilizations, here and there, for a short time escaped from it and their reward has been the possibility of intimacy.

'Laicity' with its consequences in freedom of thought and speech; drama and the readiness to hear and understand the other side; intimacy and fearlessness in social relations—let me add another quality of the Greek record which is not indeed peculiar to Greece but was carried there to a higher degree of intensity than, as far as I know, in any other part of the world. I mean something which one might call 'artistry' or the pursuit of perfection. It is not entirely a good quality. There were perhaps too many contests and prizes in ancient Greece, prizes for valour, for drama, for music and singing, for athletics of every sort; and the fact that the prize might be merely a crown of parsley or wild

olive and seldom had any pecuniary value, only emphasized
the desire for distinction in itself. It reminds one sometimes
of the spirit of the Napoleonic armies. Such a spirit imparts
to human life sometimes a feverish tension, or even poisons it
with the bitterness of jealousy. But it is after all a wonder
and the mother of wonders.

We are all struck, when we begin to read Plato and Aristotle,
by their underlying and unquestioned assumption that life is
a τέχνη, an art, or a body of τέχναι. There are good ways and
bad ways of making shoes or ships or laws or verses, or perhaps,
strictly speaking, there is one right or best way and innumerable wrong ways. I want to consider this habit of mind
only as it affects the written record, and I would call your
attention to two different points about it. For one thing,
it produces an idealism and an intensity of effort, to which
it appears a complete and satisfying object of life to be very
good at some art, to ἀριστεύειν, to be the best sort of athlete
in the great contests, the best sort of poet in the public
recitations. Besides, as everyone would hate to be a bad
bootmaker or a bad shipbuilder, similarly we must hate the
thought of being a bad father or colleague or a bad citizen.
In every department of life there is *Aretê*, which we translate
by virtue or goodness of quality or perfection, a thing to be
loved, striven for, and possibly to be attained. It is the only
thing in the world worth having, said the Stoics. It is the
thing which Heracles, in his famous choice, chose in preference to wealth, pleasure, and all the material good things
of life. Aristotle, a cool-headed man engaged on an encyclopaedia of the sciences, turned aside to write an Ode to *Aretê*:
'Aretê, longed for by the human race, best prize that life
offers, Virgin for whose beauty it is happiness in Hellas to
die. . . .' Rather strong language in the mouth of a sober man
of science, is it not?

That is the spirit that has made saints and heroes, as it has
made men go to the North Pole or fly across the Atlantic,
the spirit of the idealist, who rejects a multitude of cheap

things for the sake of one that is infinitely precious. It has further the immense merit of making the artist subject to his art, not subjecting the art to the egoism of the artist. Greek tradition does not allow the artist to say, 'I am I; I express myself as I desire and despise all rules', any more than it allows the citizen to say, 'My will is my law; I am superior to the laws of the city.'

And there I stop. This account is very fragmentary. I have said almost nothing of the sculpture and architecture which many consider the greatest achievement of the Greeks, nothing of their political and social failures, or of that despairing quest for *Cosmos* and *Homonoia*, order and concord, which pervades the later centuries of Hellenism. Strangely like the nations of modern Europe, the Greek communities knew that nothing but *Cosmos* and *Homonoia* could save them but found the goal too hard to reach. They failed to abolish war and war ruined them.

The outline of this address was written several years ago, and I have not made any attempt to adapt it to the particular interests of the present day; yet, in reconsidering it, I could not help feeling, in detail after detail, how closely the spirit of ancient Hellenism represents the cause for which this country now stands as champion before the world. We stand for freedom, for man's right to use his supreme gifts of thought, speech, and creative art, as the spirit moves him, not because we are blind to the dangers involved in freedom, but because we have confidence in the general patriotism and social conscience of our community, and know that the human spirit withers if it is not free. We stand for law, law untouched by threats and supreme over the arbitrary will or ambition of any ruler or political party, subservient only to the continual and never completed search for true justice. We want to live and to let all mankind live in such a way as to be able to seek truth, to enjoy and create beauty, and to foster that goodwill between man and man which casts out fear, and is to a great extent the main secret both of political stability and of personal happiness. Above all, we have seen the mortal dangers of *Hubris* and fanaticism and will not for the sake of any national pride or cherished dogma of our own allow the altar of pity to be overturned in our market-place.

1941.

II

PROLEGOMENA TO THE STUDY OF
GREEK LITERATURE

WE have all been struck, in the references to books which we find in Greek and Roman literature, by the habitual treatment of them as texts to be recited or read aloud. Juvenal is not always compelled to read, he is *semper auditor tantum*—compelled to listen.[1] When a new piece of the *Thebais* is finished by Statius there is a run—*curritur ad vocem iucundam*; not a run to the bookshops. Pliny is annoyed when one of the company interrupts the ἀναγνώστης, or slave reader, to correct him; but does not seem to consider the convenience of reading to himself. The very words ἀναγνώστης, ἀναγιγνώσκειν, which we translate 'read' or 'reader', seem to tell the same tale. Γιγνώσκειν is to understand, i.e. to understand the *grammata* or marks on the papyrus; ἀναγιγνώσκειν to understand them 'up' or 'aloud' as in ἀναβοᾶν, ἀνειπεῖν. If we read the account in the earliest extant Greek grammarian of the true grammarian's duties we find that several minor ones lead up to that of ἀναγιγνώσκειν κατὰ προσωιδίαν, reading aloud with the right accent and intonation. Even as late as Photius (ninth century A.D.) we find that his famous *Bibliotheca* is a list of the books that were read aloud in his learned circle during three particular years. In fact, where we moderns think of a book as a thing to read to oneself, or in exceptional cases to read aloud to a circle, the ancients thought of it just the other way. The recitation was normal, the private reading exceptional.

This is only one of several points of difference which have resulted from the invention of printing. One of our first difficulties in dealing with ancient literature is escape from the imaginative domination of the printed book. The books that we use to-day may be in English or Latin or Greek,

[1] Juvenal, i. 1; vii. 82. See Mayor's note on iii. 9, pp. 173 ff.

but they have all had the same general history. They have
been first written and corrected; then set up in type, corrected
again at least twice, and finally printed off in some hundreds
or thousands of identical copies on a given date, and normally
with the author's name on the title-page. The text is, for
that edition at any rate, uniform and definitive. The pages
are numbered, so that reference is easy, and the reader, if he
has missed a point, can look back without trouble. Plagiarism
is easily detected, and literary property is definitely pro-
tected by law.

In the age before printing there was nothing of this kind.
Some few books indeed were copied by a number of skilled
operators from the dictation of a reader; but very few books
called for such treatment; the number of copies in one edition
can seldom have reached double figures in classical Greece or
three figures in Imperial Rome; and even so each copy was
likely to differ in small details from every other, as the scribes
varied in carefulness or in keenness of hearing. In general the
writing of every book was a separate undertaking, and where
exactitude was important a studious man preferred to write
out his Homer, or the particular tragedy or philosophic
treatise that he wanted, with his own hand. That is the
method of which we hear in the fourth and third centuries
B.C., when there was a well-established reading public, but
at the beginnings of Greek literature things were not nearly
so far advanced.

Up to the end of the sixth century B.C. we may assume
that there was throughout most of Hellas no reading public.
Literature, as we call it, was still oral; it was 'told', not
written. There was a *logos*, and those who had the gift might
express the *logos* in stories told, in verses recited or sung, in
vase-paintings, in bas-reliefs, and friezes. When the ladies
of Creusa's suite see the friezes of the temple at Delphi they
immediately recognize Heracles; but who is that with him?
It must be 'he whose story is told beside my loom, Ioläus'.[1]

[1] *Ion* 197, *Iph. Aul.* 788.

They spent their days at the loom, fabling together or sometimes being told a connected story by some specially skilled
person. In this way they evidently had a very wide knowledge of the current *logoi*; they are able, for instance, to say
that 'among all the *logoi* and talks at the loom' they have
never yet heard of love between a mortal woman and a god
ending happily.[1] These, you may say, were women and
illiterate. But the cultivated Xenophon when he quotes
Prodicus' famous Choice of Heracles[2] has evidently no text
to refer to; he says he cannot emulate the eloquence with
which Prodicus told his tale. Herodotus was eminently a
λόγιος ἀνήρ, or man of *logoi*, and his sources are much discussed. He refers freely to Homer and other poets whose
words were *viva per ora virum*, to monuments, war memorials,
and temples, to what was 'said by' the Spartans, Cartha-
ginians, and so on, or to what he was 'told' by certain individuals, but he only mentions one 'book', that of Hecataeus.
A book was still a rarity.

Failure to realize these facts has often led to misinterpre-
tation of passages like *Clouds* 534 ff., where Aristophanes says
that his play 'like Electra in the story, will recognize her
brother's hair'. A modern reader is apt to take this as a
definite reference to the recognition scene in the *Choephori*,
but that is to forget that by the date of the *Clouds*, 423 B.C.,
the *Choephori* was a play thirty years old and not likely to be
in the minds of more than a small fraction of the audience.
It is really a reference to the *logos*, the old and famous *logos*
about Orestes which was 'told at the loom' and known to
everybody, though varying in detail as different poets sang
about it. It was clearly a part of the tradition by the time
of Euripides' *Electra*[3], where it is used with fine psychological
effect.

For centuries after educated people knew how to write,
literature was still oral, a thing to be performed and heard.
A book was not a thing to be given to the public. It was the

---

[1] *Ion* 506.   [2] *Mem.* II. i. 21.   [3] 412 B.C.

private stock-in-trade of the rhapsode or the professional story-teller. It must be kept from the public; above all, it must be kept from the eyes of professional rivals. In that way it secured, as long as it was really kept from others, a sort of exclusive copyright. One of 'Homer's' scrolls, we are told, served as his daughter's dowry; that was the *Cypria*. Another, the *Taking of Oechalia*, was left to his heir.[1] We hear just the same thing, in detail, about certain medieval bards and troubadours.

A book that was kept for its owner's sole use must have been very different from a book meant for the public. In the first place, the owner did not need to go to the labour of writing out the whole thing; he wanted a book to recite from, or to refresh his memory with. Most of his recitation he could probably remember or improvise. In the second place, he emphatically did not want his book to be intelligible to every Tom, Dick, and Harry who might get hold of it. I think perhaps this is one reason why the 'wise man' in antiquity or in the Middle Ages generally has a boy or disciple attached to him. The disciple is shown his master's book, and is taught, as a privilege, to read in it, a thing which he could not do except with the direct help of the master.

With shorter poems, and of course with stories such as we find in Herodotus, it must have been practically impossible for the author to keep his exclusive property. A song sung at a banquet, a story told at a *panegyris*, would soon be remembered more or less correctly by some of those present. Even longer poems might be picked up by clever listeners, as seems to have happened to some of Shakespeare's plays, and copied with alterations. A talented actress of my acquaintance could, I am assured, dictate the whole of a play with almost verbal accuracy after seeing it once. Other

---

[1] See for the dowry Pind. fr. 280 (Aelian, *Var. Hist.* ix. 15). His daughter marries Stasinus of Cyprus (*Vita* iii). Creophylus inherits Οἰχαλίας Ἅλωσις (*Vita* vii). On medieval bards see *Rise of the Greek Epic*, p. 96.

analogies suggest themselves; but of course it is impossible
to guess the particular customs and conventions that may
have surrounded the birth of literary property in an age of
which we have almost no intimate record.

But let us consider some of the extant remains of this
pre-literary epoch.

How can we explain the condition of the so-called *Homeric
Hymns* or, as they are called in the manuscripts, 'Preludes',
Προοίμια? There are thirty-three Preludes, or rather Preludes
and Farewells: i.e. phrases like: 'Sing, O Muse, of Hermes,
son of Zeus and Maia, ruler of Kyllenê and Arcadia rich in
sheep, Messenger of the Gods . . . whom Maia bore,' &c.,
at the beginning, and at the end, 'Fare thee well, Son of
Zeus and Maia, I will remember thee in yet another song.'
Thirty-three of these; evidently a collection, taken perhaps
from some professional's book or perhaps from the memory
of the collector and his friends. But seven of the thirty-three
have other matter in them. There is a lay or story in verse
put in between the Prelude and the Farewell. This makes
the book interesting, and I should imagine that the collector
put in any such lays as he could find written or remembered.
Apparently he could only get hold of seven. We happen to
know of the existence of some others.[1] Yet that is not quite
the whole story, because in the Hymn to Apollo it is clear
that we have a conflation of two lays; and there are less clear
signs of conflation in some of the others. Apparently the
collector, when he came on two versions of a lay, tried to get
in as much as possible of both. He was not a scholar in the
modern sense. It did not occur to him to make a point of
preserving an accurate text or two accurate texts. Like all
ancient booksellers after him he made the fullest text he
could. He made—to use the correct word—a σύγγραμμα; we
have what he collected and wrote down.

Even more instructive is the condition of Hesiod's poems.
The tradition is good. The early papyri which have been

[1] See for example *Berliner Klassikertexte*, v. 1.

found confirm its general trustworthiness. But what a chaos
it gives us! No poet could have composed the *Theogony* or
the *Works and Days* as our collection presents them; no
rhapsode could conceivably have so recited them. They are
συγγράμματα, collections, by—what shall we call him? Perhaps the διαθέτης. In spite of ambiguities I will call him the
bookmaker; they are collections by the bookmaker of what he
could get. He might have some real private book belonging
to an ancient bard; he would certainly have the memories of
living men who had heard the poems or had recited them
themselves. But we can say a little more. He certainly had
before him in some form or other different versions of the
same matter, for the text as we have it is full of doublets.
There are two or perhaps three alternative openings; the
Prometheus folk-tale is inserted at two different places; and
so on. Evidently here also the bookmaker, instead of taking
his different versions and separating them out, preferred to
combine them, however confusedly, into one text. We must
remember that he had no numbered pages, no index, and
no supply of cheap paper. There is another characteristic
which reminds one of the *Prooimia*; there, we remember, the
manuscript gave us again and again regularly the opening
and the closing formula of a lay to some god, without the
lay itself. Similarly in Hesiod's *Theogony* the first 115 lines
are occupied with alternative addresses and farewells to the
Muses, first those of Helicon, then of Olympus. But there
are other transitions also. We know that Hesiod wrote a
Κατάλογος γυναικῶν, i.e. a catalogue of the heroic ancestresses
of various noble houses. The catalogue must have existed in
different forms, for one of them was called the *Eoiai*, and
another *The Great Eoiai*. They were so called because each
ancestress was introduced by the formula ἣ οἵη, *vel qualis*.[1]
He also wrote a poem on Ὀρνιθομαντεία, or Augury. Now

---

[1] Leo, *Hesiodea*, pp. 8 ff., identifies the *Catalogue* and the *Eoiai* while
treating *The Great Eoiai* as different and later. This was the general opinion
of ancient critics.

the Ἡμέραι ends with the transition-line ὄρνιθας κρίνων καὶ
ὑπερβασίας ἀλεείνων and the scholia inform us that, according to some authorities, here followed the Ὀρνιθομαντεία. In
just the same way our text of the *Theogony* at line 963
suddenly says farewell to the Olympian gods and prays the
Muses to tell of all the goddesses who bore children to
mortal men, a rather small list beginning with Demeter and
ending with Calypso; then comes an appeal to the Muses to
'tell of the race of women', Νῦν δὲ γυναικῶν φῦλον ἀείσατε,
ἡδυέπειαι, and there the manuscript abruptly ends. Evidently
the last lines are the transition formula to the *Catalogue of
Women*, but the catalogue itself is not there. Still more
curious, and more obviously a σύγγραμμα, is the one poem
in the Hesiodic corpus that makes any pretence to artistic
unity. I mean the Ἀσπίς, or the Shield of Heracles. It starts
undisguisedly as an Ἠοίη, 'Or as Alcmena left her home and
fatherland', and tells how she gave birth to two sons, Iphicles,
son of Amphitryon, and Heracles, son of Zeus. Here the
Eoiê proper ends; but the poem continues, 'Who also slew
Cycnus, son of Ares', and proceeds to narrate the story of the
fight as far as the arming of Heracles. Here there come two
versions of the arming, one giving him the primitive club and
arrows, the other greaves, breastplate, spear, helmet, and
shield. But the shield takes nearly 200 lines (138 to 316),
and is clearly a lay of the same type as the account of the
Shield of Achilles in *Iliad* xviii. Then comes the rest of the
story of the fight with Cycnus, helped by his father Ares.
An extraordinary mixture, and unintelligible until we realize
that it is a σύγγραμμα of oral elements derived from quite
independent sources! First a regular *Eoiê* about Alcmena,
mother of Heracles; then, added thereto, a lay of one of
Heracles' adventures. In the middle of that a great description of a shield. We do not know whose shield it originally
was, whether it was originally meant for some particular
hero, or—more likely—was simply an independent description of a heroic shield, which could be attributed to what-

ever hero happened to be suitable. It can hardly have been
originally meant for Heracles, since the earlier conception
of Heracles did not make him a hoplite but left him a peasant
hero with no arms beyond a club, or a club and a bow. In
oral poetry these elements can be fitted and transposed as
convenience suggests. And the elements themselves are
equally malleable. For in a papyrus of the first century B.C.
we find a fragment of a description of a shield which for 12
lines agrees—except for one strange line—with the Shield
of Achilles in *Iliad* xviii, and then runs off into the Shield of
Heracles as described in Hesiod's *Aspis*! Quite natural in
oral poetry; quite unintelligible to those who think in terms
of printed books. The bookmaker collected his materials
where he could find them, and chose the versions he preferred, or even rewrote them a little to suit his immediate
purpose: the real difference between the *Aspis* and the other
so-called works of Hesiod is that in the *Erga* and the *Theogony*
the bookmaker seems to have collected in his *Syngramma* all
the matter that he could find, whereas in the *Aspis* he has
set himself to make what we should call a poem, or an artistic
unity. The reason for this difference may become clearer
later on.

Much simpler is the condition of the collection which we
call 'Theognis'. The manuscripts give the heading Θεόγνιδος
Γνῶμαι, or Ἐλεγεῖαι. It is more than a collection of *Gnômai*,
it is certainly not a collection of elegies, unless by that word
we mean simply verses in elegiac metre. It is a collection of
all sorts of short poems, from two lines to about thirty lines in
length, mostly of a hortatory or gnomic character. Poems of
this sort were easily learnt by heart and doubtless sung freely
at banquets and symposia, the verses remembered and the
author forgotten. Hence we find a habit in Theognis,
Demodocus, Phokylides, and others of putting a personal
mark on their poems—σφρηγίς, or 'seal' they call it—to
prevent their being attributed to someone else. Generally
it is the introduction of the writer's name in the body of the

verse: καὶ τόδε Φωκυλίδεω, like Ἑκαταῖος Μιλήσιος ὧδε
μυθέεται; but Theognis—like Hesiod—uses for a 'seal' the
name of the person to whom he addresses the poem, a certain
Kyrnos son of Polypaïs—unless indeed Πολυπαΐδης is a different person—to whom he gives 'the wings of fame' by his verses.
Another 'seal' is the style itself; the hard, disillusioned style,
in part cynical and part over-sensitive, of the wronged and
embittered aristocratic exile. Neither seal of course is very
effective by Yale-lock standards. It was easy enough for one
who wished to write in the character of Theognis both to
imitate his style and put in the name of Kyrnos, and for one
who wished to steal the poems to put some metrically
equivalent name in the place of Kyrnos, say, Glaukos or
Phaidros. But probably it was not meant for a protection
against bad faith, only against the vagueness of popular
memory. Thus our book is a σύγγραμμα of all the elegiac
verses the collector could find current in someone's memory
and attributed to Theognis, or at least like enough to Theognis
to be worth putting in. For here comes another striking
fact. We find in the collection poems, or sets of verses, which
are quoted elsewhere and ascribed by ancient authors not to
Theognis, but to sundry other poets—Tyrtaeus, Mimnermus,
Euênus, and Solon; and, considering how comparatively rare
and accidental it is to find such quotations at all, we may
assume that if our remains of ancient literature were larger,
or again if we had actual manuscripts of Mimnermus, Solon,
and the others, there would be many other passages in our
Theognis collection which were also attributed to other
authors. Does this mean that the passages in question are
'spurious' or really by Solon or Mimnermus rather than
Theognis? No, such a conclusion would be utterly arbitrary.
It only means that the maker of our collection came across
a large number of verses which were too good to lose but
whose authorship was uncertain or forgotten. He put them
into his Theognis collection, but doubtless if he had been
making a collection of the Elegiac *Gnômai* of Solon or

Euênus or Mimnermus he would have put them in just the same. In a similar spirit, when he found a passage in two slightly different forms, he put in both; sometimes indeed he put in by mistake two practically identical versions. It is curious to read Mr. Harrison's extremely clever and scholarly edition of Theognis, published in 1902, and to see the shifts to which the editor is reduced by his failure to realize that an ancient σύγγραμμα, composed before the days of a reading public, was something completely different from a modern printed book. He has, for example, to treat the casual variations of wording which are inevitable in oral poetry, as deliberate and extremely subtle corrections or criticisms of one poet by another.[1]

Modern parallels can never be quite exact, but I imagine we most of us know the lines 'If all the good people were clever, And those that are clever were good, The world would be better than ever We dreamed that it possibly could', &c. But probably most of us do not know that they were written by Miss Wordsworth of Lady Margaret Hall; I have heard them attributed to Mr. Belloc, Maurice Baring, and others. If all printed books were destroyed and people began to write out such poetry as they could find remembered by somebody, I have little doubt that they would appear in the συγγράμματα of many authors, and I need hardly add that the versions would often differ slightly in wording. (Even my own quotation above is, I see, slightly wrong when compared with the original, though I had the original in the next room at the time of writing.)

When we speak of 'the collector' or 'the author of the *Syngramma*' we must not, of course, assume that the act was done once for all and the text so constituted reproduced faithfully from edition to edition. That would be falling again into the misleading analogy of the printed book. We can be fairly sure, in the case of Theognis, that the com-

---

[1] Such a correction does no doubt sometimes occur: Solon 22 corrects Mimnermus 6, but does so explicitly with an apology to Mimnermus by name.

mercial bookseller comes in at some stage or other. The songs were immensely well known, and used—it is instructive to remember—for purposes of education and edification by people who disapproved of democracy. A time consequently came when by a process of expurgation the poems which were against the feelings of the age were secluded in a separate book. The collection is not quoted before the time of Plato, Xenophon, and Isocrates, when it seems to have burst into rather sudden celebrity in anti-democratic circles.

Are we to say, then, that all early Greek literature was like this, a mass of συγγράμματα, utterly without artistic unity, based on some attempt to write down as much as could be remembered of the work of poets or bards before they should be quite forgotten? Not at all. Every ode of Pindar is a definite artistic unity. So is every tragedy and comedy. So, to pass a little later in time, is every complete speech of Antiphon or Lysias. What is the difference? The difference is that in these last we have a definite artistic composition made for a particular public occasion. In the Odes of Pindar we have the text of the Odes as sung by a chorus; not merely the note-book of a bard, with useful lists, formulae, transitions, &c., as in the Hymns and Hesiod; not a mere collection of such lyrics by Pindar and others like him as could be remembered. The first definite artistic unities that we meet with in Greek literature are occasional poems, that is, poems composed for some specific occasion.

The exceptions to this rule serve to illustrate it. We find some confusions in the text of Aristophanes' *Clouds* and *Frogs*; naturally, because each of these plays was revived for another occasion, and the text made for the first occasion has got a little confused with that for the second. The *Rhesus* was known to the scholiast with three different prologues; the *Iphigenia in Aulis* has come down to us with two separate prologues—which in our manuscripts are clouted clumsily together like the doublets in Hesiod. Doubtless the play had some changes made in it when it was revived. In just the same way we find traces of revision in speeches. In the duels between Demosthenes and Aeschines, for example, each speech as published seems to contain answers to arguments used in the opposing speech, which must of course have been inserted afterwards.[1] A nearer parallel to the treatment of the Homeric *Prooimia* offers itself in the κοινοὶ τόποι,[2]—not 'commonplaces' but 'common passages'—which we sometimes find repeated in different speeches. He would be a bold man who professed to determine the author of each.

There are traces of a development in the writing of history almost exactly parallel to that which we have noticed in epic and elegiac poetry. No book, indeed, has been preserved in a form to correspond with the *Theogony*. Yet a large number of the fragments of Hecataeus as quoted by our authorities read rather like extracts from a sort of informal gazetteer. If it ever appeared we should perhaps find in it traces of the professional story-teller's private book, containing the facts and dates and details, but the original book would be expanded and overlaid by masses of new material accumulated in later times. The same probability is even more obvious in some of the other fragmentary *logographoi*, for Hecataeus had literary pretensions and perhaps actually did something equivalent to publishing a book. The case of Herodotus stands, I think, by itself.

It is important to realize at once that he is a professional story-teller. Aristotle calls him simply Ἡρόδοτος ὁ μυθολόγος,[3] not as an insult, but as a description. Others call him ὁ λογοποιός, which is not very different. We have records of his recitations at Olympia and other places. Practically all

---

[1] See Aesch. *In Ctes.* 13–31, 31–48, 215–242; Dem. *De Cor.* 155–6.

[2] On *Loci Communes* see Cic. *De Inventione*, ii. 15. 48. E.g. Antiphon on the value of evidence given by slaves under torture; for it, 'Against the Stepmother', 5–13—against it, 'Murder of Herodes', 31 ff.

[3] Aristotle, Περὶ ζώιων γενέσεως; 756 b 6.

critics are agreed that his great book is made up of various more or less independent *logoi* now combined into a somewhat loose but no less real unity. All are agreed, for instance, that the Egyptian *logoi*, now book ii, are a comparatively late insertion, and the author himself speaks of his Assyrian *logoi*,[1] which have not been embodied in our present *syngramma*. But the real character of Herodotus' work, at least in its origin, is simply and correctly defined by Thucydides. It was, and was meant to be, ἀγώνισμα ἐς τὸ παραχρῆμα[2]—a performance or entertainment for the time being—a work of art like a drama or an epic lay, though of course with the interest more focused on information. Thucydides himself, on the contrary, intended his work to be a κτῆμα ἐς ἀεί, a book to possess and keep. To translate it 'an eternal possession', in the sense in which a great work of art is eternal, is to miss the whole point. If it comes to a question of eternal life on the ground of artistic beauty the works of the two great historians are much on an equality; if anything Herodotus is more of a poet. But the plain fact is that Herodotus composed *logoi* for public entertainment by recitation or reading aloud, whereas Thucydides really wrote what we call a book. He wrote a highly compressed, exact, severe, and difficult history, suitable no doubt for reading in scholarly or sophistic circles but much too hard for the general public, and aiming not at ἡδονή (pleasure to the reader) but at τὸ ἀτρεκές, 'exact truth'.

It has been asked whether it was Herodotus himself who made the *syngramma* that we possess, selecting and rejecting and 'stitching together', like a ῥαψῳδός, and so composing his *logoi* into a whole. Of course it was not he who made the division into books, called after the nine Muses, and there is no proof that he did the composition. Still the thing is too

---

[1] i. 106, 'I will tell ἐν ἑτέροισι λόγοισι how Cyaxares and the Medes took Nineveh.' i. 184, 'τῆς δὲ Βαβυλῶνος ταύτης πολλοὶ μέν κου καὶ ἄλλοι ἐγένοντο βασιλέες, τῶν ἐν τοῖσι Ἀσσυρίοισι λόγοισι μνήμην ποιήσομαι.'

[2] Thuc. i. 22.

well done, and the undertaking implies too much labour and skill to be mere bookseller's work, and if another great artist had been at work we should expect to have had some mention of him. There is also one positive piece of evidence. The ninth book is almost certainly unfinished: it does not come to a really effective close, a fact of which the most obvious explanation is that the author died before he had quite finished his composition. This is pretty certainly what also happened with Thucydides. Up to the end of book vii his work is magnificently finished, and then book viii is added in quite a different style. The documents are left in their raw state instead of being worked into the texture of the narrative, and the different points of view or attitudes of mind are not put into the form of speeches.

The opening words of Herodotus, as is well known, are quoted by Aristotle[1] in a different form: the order of the words is changed and Herodotus is a Thurian instead of a Halicarnassian. Apparently different copies of the book varied. Another difference from the printed book is brought to light by the controversy about Herodotus' use of his sources. Whenever there are two varying versions of some story to be given, he takes pleasure in attributing each to its source, sometimes pronouncing his own judgement and sometimes not; that is natural enough. Yet it does rather look as if, like most story-tellers, he picked up his stories where he happened to find them and did not usually think it worth while to make acknowledgements. He is accused of taking various passages from Hecataeus, which seems likely enough. Hecataeus would be the natural source for him to use, and there is no ground whatever for speaking of plagiarism. But the more ardent friends of Herodotus have an alternative explanation of the supposed borrowings which, whether true or not, is equally possible and equally instructive. There was a book current in later antiquity called Hecataeus, and

---

[1] *Rhet.* iii. 9. 2. Ἡροδότου Θουρίου ἥδ' ἱστορίης ἀπόδειξις. Hdt. i. 1. Ἡροδότου Ἁλικαρνησσέος ἱστορίης ἀπόδεξις ἥδε.

apparently based on the genuine *syngramma* of that author, but expanded and reinforced by lots of new information; and it is quite possible that the passages[1] about the crocodile and the phoenix and the Chersonese and so on, which Herodotus is supposed to have taken verbally from Hecataeus, were really taken bodily from Herodotus by the later revisers of this so-called Hecataeus. Either theory serves to illustrate the difference between the ancient and modern conceptions of a book and of literary property.

How many misunderstandings would have been avoided, for instance, if an ancient roll had permitted of footnotes! As it is, all mentions of sources, of criticisms and answers to criticisms, of evidence for disputed statements, and the like, have either to go into the text, if they are interesting enough, or to be left out altogether if they are not. But even without footnotes, the growth of a reading public and a critical public had a great effect on Greek literature. Polybius quotes and criticizes his authorities quite freely, almost like a modern writer. Dio Cassius is particularly full and scrupulous in so doing, far more so, for example, than Livy. And Diodorus, though in compiling his *Bibliotheca* or 'Library' he naturally writes out in full the various authors on whom he draws, generally lets us know who they were. We have reached an age of real libraries and books.

The case of philosophy is again rather different. One of the most famous puzzles in classical Greek literature is to explain how the *Ecclesiazusae* of Aristophanes, performed not later than 391 B.C., manages to quote and ridicule certain passages in Plato's *Republic*, books iii, iv, and v, which cannot have been published much before 370, twenty years later. The correspondences are far too close and too numerous

---

[1] *Crocodile*: Hdt. ii. 70; *Hippopotamus*: Hdt. ii. 71; *Phoenix*: Hdt. ii. 73: cf. Hecataeus 324 (from Porph. ap. Euseb. *Praepar. evangel.* x. 3, p. 466 B); *Chersonese*: Hdt. ix. 118, cf. Hecataeus 163 (*F.H.G.*, Jacoby).

to be the result of coincidence. They cannot possibly be later additions to the play. The *Ecclesiazusae* does parody and quote what we now call book v of the *Republic*;[1] and we may note also that in the *Republic* Socrates has a good deal to say about the ridicule which his ideas are likely to incur; he was judging, no doubt, from the ridicule they had already received in the *Ecclesiazusae*. Now what do these facts mean? They mean that long before the *Republic* as we know it was published, a treatise or set of treatises which now forms part of it was known to Aristophanes and struck him as both new and funny. I should imagine that Plato occasionally gave readings to a select body of friends. Perhaps, however, he merely gave lectures in the school, in which some of the same ideas were expressed in the same words. Perhaps Aristophanes, being a friend of Plato's, attended the lectures; perhaps a disciple copied down the lecture and showed Aristophanes his notes. At any rate, I think we can see that the *Republic*, as known to us, has a long, long history behind it. It cannot well have been conceived as one book; it is a book in ten volumes and, even apart from the strong evidence of style and matter, books of philosophy at that time do not seem to have been usually longer than one volume. One of the most important recent advances in the study of Aristotle has been Jaeger's analysis of the big composite collections, like the *Ethics* and *Metaphysics*, into their separate component books. The final composition of the *Republic* as an artistic unity in ten books is the last stage of a long process. A set of earlier stages may well have been the separate publication, in some slightly different form, of the treatises which are now parts of the *Republic*. But before any publication occurred there must have been a stage in which Plato's views and arguments were a matter of oral teaching in the school. Jaeger believes, and the belief seems reasonable, that the first stage of publication consisted in the copies made by disciples of the master's lectures. In that

[1] See my *Aristophanes*, 186 ff.; Adam, *Republic*, vol. i, Appendix I, p. 345.

stage they were ἐσωτερικοὶ λόγοι, meant for inside consumption. The existing writings of Aristotle, allowing for some revision and correction, may represent this stage. Aristotle refers sometimes to other classes of works. He speaks of οἱ ἐκδεδομένοι λόγοι, which seem clearly to be the published works, or the works meant for the general public, like the *Republic* and Plato's other dialogues. He also speaks of οἱ ἐξωτερικοὶ λόγοι and οἱ ἐν κοινῶι λόγοι, the nature of which is not clear.[1] They may be the same as the published works; they may again be lectures given in the school on public occasions or on occasions when the whole school was gathered together. They may be merely the same as τὰ λεγόμενα— common opinion. We do not know enough, or anything like enough, about the working of the school to be able to settle these points. But we can see the many stages through which a philosopher's teachings might pass before they reached the stage that we find in Aristotle, or the much later stage that we find in Plato. And this enables us to understand how it comes to pass that Aristophanes could make the ideas of the *Republic* material for a comedy something like twenty years before the *Republic* was published.

Looking back over this argument, one seems to see that Herodotus made a new era in the writing of history and Plato in that of philosophy. Herodotus did not merely leave his material written down: he did not simply write out one after the other the *logoi* which he had used for recitations. He worked them up into a whole with a plot and a continuous story. Similarly Plato did not, as far as one can see, merely produce an esoteric treatise, or so many treatises, like Anaxagoras, whose 'book'[2] could be bought for a drachma. He produced such work in the school of course, like other philosophers, but his peculiar contribution was the artistic dialogue, a work of art or *Epideixis*, written with that apparatus for persuading, charming, or even dazzling the hearer (ἀκροατήν), of which Aristotle justly observes: 'No one would teach

---

[1] See note, p. 81. [2] Plato, *Apology*, 26 d.

geometry that way.'[1] I cannot help recurring to an old belief of mine. We know that Plato admired Epicharmus and 'slept with the mimes of Sophron under his pillow'. I cannot help thinking that the brilliant young aristocrat began by writing Mimes or Conversations, which were meant like other Mimes to amuse the hearer. But his conversations were not between fishwives or abstract qualities or the like. They represented the actual talk of philosophers whom he knew and was able delicately to parody—as a clever undergraduate might give an imitation of a discussion at the Aristotelian Society between two professors. As Professor Woodbridge puts it:

'They are probably much more naïve and true to life than the philosophical dialogues which a modern might write. . . . Stories of conversations they are, told, possibly, for the delight of the recipient rather than for the deliberate purpose of arriving at a result or propounding a doctrine. Their frequent inconclusiveness . . . and lack of definite result may indicate their faithfulness to fact. . . .'

Later, as Plato's philosophical genius developed, the mimetic element became less important, the speculative and argumentative element more important; the humour dwindled away and eventually most of the beauty, till by the end of his life Plato had almost cast out the devil of poetry from his own heart as he wished to cast it from his city. But the result of his earlier work was that, for the first time, a treatise on philosophy became recognized as a piece of what we should call *belles lettres*, a thing which might aim at literary charm quite as much as did a panegyric or a funeral oration.

We must not be over-impressed by the accident that Plato is only represented to us by his finished and published works, and Aristotle on the contrary by his unpublished lecture-notes or ἐσωτερικοὶ λόγοι. Still it is likely enough that the accident is not mere accident. Plato's style is some-

[1] *Rhet.* iii. 1. 6.

thing quite extraordinary; ancient judges as well as modern have considered it absolutely the finest prose style known to human literature. So it is only natural that a special effort was made to preserve his dialogues, on account of their form, while from most philosophers the world only wanted their doctrines and arguments, the plainer the better. Indeed, Plato's care for exact form has had, it would seem, another curious result.

It is well known that as a rule the quotations[1] made from the *Iliad* and *Odyssey* by writers of the fourth and third centuries differ widely from our text. It seems, on the face of it, pretty clear that Aristotle and Aeschines, for example, used a text of Homer surprisingly different from ours, and the earliest papyri yield just the same evidence. But the curious thing is that Plato's quotations, which are very numerous, are on the whole fairly close to our present vulgate, as it eventually emerged from the hands of Aristarchus and his contemporaries. Now we may assume that, as a rule, an Athenian man of letters in the fourth century normally had his own version of Homer:[2] the evidence is pretty conclusive. It would seem, therefore, that Plato constructed his Homer text so well, with so much attention to detail and such sense of poetic style, that when his books were sent over to the Alexandrian Library his text was used as a basis by the great Alexandrian scholars, or at least exercised, in conjunction with the immense respect in which Plato was otherwise held, a great influence upon them.

That consideration leads us to a final problem, that of the Homeric text itself. It may be taken as fairly certain that our vulgate text first emerges in manuscripts about the year 150 B.C. Why is it that Homer comes to us in a form so completely finished and made ready for publication and reading, whereas Hesiod is left in the chaos that belongs to a period which knew not of publication or reading public?

[1] See *Rise of the Greek Epic*[4], pp. 289 ff.
[2] See Sengebusch, *Dissertatio Prior*, pp. 185 ff.

The answer is given by our other examples. The *Iliad* and *Odyssey* were made into artistic wholes for a special occasion, just like a tragedy or an Epinikian Ode of Pindar. They were meant for the great four-yearly Recitation at the Panathenaea, whereas a bard who wanted to recite Hesiod was free to do so in his own way, with variations that suited him. His book was his private affair.

The law enacted that at the Panathenaea the poems should be recited ἐφεξῆς, 'in order', each rhapsode picking up the story where his predecessor left it; but unfortunately we do not know whether that rule implies the existence of a fixed verbal text or even an accepted order of incidents. If there was an official text it must have formed the earliest large published book in Greek literature. There is some reason for believing that there was such a text, and there is no great difficulty in supposing that when the Pisistratidae fell, the text which was associated with their memory lost its sanctity, so that during most of the fifth and fourth and third centuries the text had again become fluid and variations in it were again largely a matter of choice.[1] Aristarchus and his fellow scholars had clearly no absolutely authoritative text before them; certainly they had no traces whatever of a pre-Athenian text. It is hardly possible for us, and it may well have been difficult for them themselves, to say whether they were trying to restore the official text used at the Panathenaea in the sixth century, or were simply trying out of a number of widely varying manuscripts, with the aid of their own learning and ingenuity, to put together the best text they could. With plays, epinikian odes, famous speeches, and even Platonic dialogues, the correct text was published by the author himself, and then the book went out to the use of the reading public; in the case of Homer the order seems to have been reversed. During the fifth and fourth and third centuries the *Iliad* and *Odyssey*, in considerably varying forms, became the best-known books in Greece, both for

[1] See *Rise of the Greek Epic*[4], pp. 283 ff.

school teaching and for private reading. Consequently the need for a recognized and definitive text became irresistible, and the Alexandrians supplied it. It was much the same, *mutatis mutandis*, with the more popular plays of Shakespeare.[1] The confusion of texts between the various quartos and folios, and the far greater confusion still between the various acting versions current up to the end of the eighteenth century and, indeed, up to the first half of the nineteenth, created an imperative demand for a thoroughly accurate critical text. Of course in Shakespeare's case, thanks to the invention of printing, texts were still available which the author had seen, or at least might have seen. In that of Homer there was no approach to this. The tradition had simply to be revised and corrected out of itself.

There are many other points about ancient books which might be explored, notably the whole complicated problem of literary property and plagiarism. The considerations which I have been putting before you apply, of course, mainly to the earlier stages of classical Greek literature, though there are certain kinds of writing of which they hold good right down through Roman and Byzantine times: *Lexica*, like Hesychius and the *Etymologicum Magnum*; scholia and commentaries; collective works of learning like the histories of philosophy contained in the so-called *Doxographi*, or world histories like Diodorus' *Bibliotheca*, or mythological handbooks like that of Apollodorus. The compilers of these continue to a great extent the methods of early story-tellers or collectors of *syngrammata*. All is grist that comes to their mill. But, as far as poetry and *belles lettres* are concerned, one may roughly say that the great change takes place with the advent of the published book and the reading public, though even in the Alexandrian and Roman periods, with their large literary publics and high standards of scholarship —and still more so in the unlettered centuries of the Middle

[1] See Odell, *Shakespeare from Betterton to Irving*.

Ages—the written word still remains first and foremost a thing to be recited, and the practice of copying out whole passages from previous writers without acknowledgement continues to a degree which modern critics, trained on the printed book, with pages and footnotes, find bewildering, if not incredible.

1933.

III

PROLEGOMENA TO THE STUDY OF
GREEK HISTORY

THE Oxford School of Literae Humaniores, by common repute the hardest and the most central course of study in the University, bases its humane culture on the study of Greek philosophy and Greek and Roman history. This is strange, for the aim of the school is to train not antiquarians but cultivated men with an understanding of life and its purposes. Its eyes are on the present and future, yet it bases its study of life on subjects which the immense majority of the human race regard as dead and exhausted. Let us try to understand this paradoxical proceeding.

As to philosophy the question is not so difficult. A man with his intelligence awakened, and the University is mostly meant for persons in that dangerous condition, cannot live without some philosophy. And it is an intelligible view, if not more, that the best way, or one of the best ways, of facing the problems of philosophy is to study them historically; to see what questions have successively impressed the leading minds of the human race and what sort of progressive answers have been attained. Educationally speaking, that mode of approach seems better, though doubtless less exciting, than the direct dogmatic inculcation of some current system.

But the study of ancient history does seem a curious and narrow basis on which to found a general culture. History of any sort is difficult to defend against the philistine. 'Teach me how to work wireless,' he will say, 'or how to cure diseases, or even teach me the present legal enactments and economic facts of modern society, and the various suggestions for improving them, and I do not mind learning such facts. But why on earth should I learn about the *Lex Julia* or the Constitution of Cleisthenes or even the Bill of Rights or Mr.

Gladstone's budgets, if it comes to that? But, even granting that some knowledge of past history is of use, why not either concentrate on the history of the last hundred years, which has a direct bearing on our own time, or else take the whole sweep of human history from—let us say—Tutankhamen to Adam Smith, instead of concentrating on the minute doings of the ancient Greek cities or even of Rome?' Let us try to clear our minds on these points.

I remember Mr. Sydney Webb making an effective point against the intellectual standards of this University. 'What a stupid set of people', he said, 'to talk of such a subject as History, or Modern History. There is no such subject as History, any more than there is such a subject as Research. There is only the History of something; there is Research into something. The History of Trades Unionism, of Cookery, of the Art of War, of the policy of Henry VIII, may be sense: but History by itself is nothing.'

The objection is logically valid. The answer is historical. ʽΗροδότου Ἀλικαρνησσέος ἱστορίης ἀπόδεξις ἥδε, 'This is the setting forth of the *Historiê* of Herodotus of Halicarnassus.' The book was the setting forth of his *Historiê*, his *inquiry* into things. It told people what he had inquired into and found out. And naturally he had inquired into the things which to his mind were most important and interesting. They were chiefly and centrally τὰ Μηδικά, the Great Persian War with all that helped to make it intelligible and to show how it happened. And his motive in inquiring and recording was, as he tells us, 'that the past should not perish from among men, nor great and wonderful deeds be without honour, whether done by Greek or barbarian'. Perhaps a finer and truer motive than that of Thucydides, though it is hard to say.

The word 'History' might, perhaps, have retained a wider meaning than it has (it might, for example, have included geography and ethnology), but that the second of the great Greek historians narrowed down the scope of his own *Historiê*.

Thucydides wrote a chronicle of the war between the Peloponnesians and the Athenians; and though he included both the deeds they did and the words they spoke on each side, and added a wonderful sociological study of early Greece and some other relevant philosophical observations, in the main he omitted ruthlessly everything that was not in the first plane of political importance. History in his hands became what we call 'political history', and so it has generally remained ever since. The word 'History' by itself means political history: if a writer means his *Historiê* to be something else, he is expected to say so.

This concentration of history on the public actions of the great ones of the earth, including of course the secret springs of those actions, has maintained itself for obvious reasons. The innocent snobbery or uncritical hero-worship of the mass of men likes to hear about princes and conquerors; also the things that these important people do, however commonplace or silly, are apt to have far-reaching consequences and therefore to be worth knowing about; and thirdly the events of political history—deaths and marriages of kings, big battles, great acts of parliament, and the like—form definite and separable events, with intelligible names, out of which one can build a framework of history. For example, the Romantic Movement, or the Rise of the Sophists, is a far more interesting and important fact than the death of William IV or the battle of Oenophyta, but they are not nearly so intelligible, datable, or definite.

Political history gives us a framework of dates and names and definite events. But does it give us a texture of events to which we can attach real value? Is it in any sense a fine story? Does it make us proud of our kind? As most decent people are said to turn sick when they shoot their first bird, I think most students of political history at some time or another are oppressed by its futile horror. 'These were wicked people?' said an Italian peasant girl to someone who was trying to teach her about the Roman Empire. 'Yes.'

'And they are all dead?' 'Yes.' 'Then let us not speak of them any more.' It is not merely that political history, like the daily newspaper, mentions only that which stands out, and the thing that stands out is usually a crime or a disaster. It is also that the whole story is generally sordid, and the part played by selfish and material interests so incredibly vast, compared with our ordinary expectations of behaviour in ourselves and our friends. Such unselfishness or heroism as appears is generally a response called forth by great oppression, a spark of good struck out by a mass of evil. If man is such a cruel and worthless beast, one is disposed to say, what value is there in the struggles of nation against nation or class against class? Nay, considering the frightful daily expense in blood and pain throughout the sentient creation involved in keeping alive this insatiable carnivorous ape that we call Man, is even his belauded conquest over nature anything in which we can take much spiritual satisfaction? The standards of conventional history are so miserably poor. It is always expecting us to rejoice or swell with pride because one set of men, who were numerous or had good weapons or were well fed, killed or frightened away another set of men, who were less numerous or had less good weapons or were worse fed; or because the inhabitants of some place have increased in number, or because they are richer or can move faster or can eat and drink more or can kill each other quicker: ideals all compatible with Will Dyson's caricatures at the beginning of the Four Years War, representing gorillas in aeroplanes, with goggles and jewelled waistcoats, dropping high-explosive bombs about the landscape. Such ideals provoke and leave unanswered the sort of criticism that was levelled by Plato against the statesmen who filled Athens 'with docks and ships and armies and such rubbish instead of self-control and honesty', and repeated with less power by Carlyle and Ruskin against what they regarded as the dominant spirit of modern times. There must be some element of value in the process of history, if there is to be any in the study of that process. Ranke says that the business of the historian is merely to study how things happen: but unless the things that happen are of some value, what good is it to study them?

Let us leave aside the party or sectarian or patriotic answers. We need not consider the glory-value, say, to a Turkish Sunni of studying how the Sunni have humiliated the Shiahs, the Moslems confounded the dogs of Christians, or the Turks routed the wretched Bulgars and Serbs and Greeks; nor yet the revenge-value of the same facts to the opposite parties in each case. Such emotions may be good or bad, but they are not germane to scientific history. Perhaps the real element of value in the whole process is that given in Aristotle's famous words about the πόλις, γενομένη μὲν τοῦ ζῆν ἕνεκα, οὖσα δὲ τοῦ εὖ ζῆν.[1] 'Civilization', says Professor Toynbee, 'is a tragedy with a plot.' If so, the substance of the plot is suggested in those words of Aristotle. Man built his city-wall in order to secure life itself; and ever since he has been struggling and destroying and rebuilding, piling Ossa upon Olympus and Pelion on Ossa, in the hope not exactly of scaling heaven but of attaining a life that he can call good. The search for a good life is the plot of history, the great adventure of man. Seen thus, history is a tragedy; not in the modern degraded sense of a story that ends in sadness or failure, but in the Aristotelian sense, which regards the tragic as that which is above us, the life we look up to and not down upon.

The search may be, as most moderns see it, something to be attained in a distant future, when all conditions have been made right; it may be, as the Greeks mostly saw it, attainable here and now, or else never, by living κατ' ἀρετήν. Also, there are many different elements which seem pre-eminently to give indisputable value to life. Diodorus,[2] following no doubt Ephorus and Dicaearchus, sees value in the process of

[1] 'It *came into being* for the sake of Life, but *is* for the sake of Good Life.'

[2] Introduction and *passim*. See *Rise of the Greek Epic*, p. 2.

increasing knowledge, in the progressive discoveries which add to man's social strength and 'humanize life'. That was the common Hellenistic conception, much resembling what our newspapers call 'Progress'. It may lie in attaining to true ideas about life and the meaning of things, a view which has its highest point in Plato and the Stoics, its lowest in certain requirements, ancient or modern, of dogmatic orthodoxy. It may lie, as many Romans would say, in the power of governing men, the great architectonic art above all other arts, the mark of the master man. It may lie in the finding of right laws and right constitutions of society, which make the life κατ' ἀρετήν possible or even easy. It may lie in the creation of beauty, that inexplicable but perfectly attainable end which is 'a Joy for ever,' in the sense that the thing of beauty can and does make human hearts thrill with delight at a distance of many thousand years. All these elements, and others, contribute to making life good in some sense which one can honestly accept. The pursuit of the Good Life is an idea that gives meaning to the chaos of history.

Now if this is so, it is difficult to think of any period of human experience so full of value to us as the classical periods of Greece and Rome. The pursuit of the Good Life was never so intense and varied, and perhaps never so hopeful, as in fifth- and fourth-century Athens, whether we judge by beauty, by the pursuit of truth, or by richness of ideas and variety of social experiment. Roman history again derives its value, partly from its being a continuation of Greek history, partly from its extraordinary achievements in the master art of government and the application of Greek law. And the two together constitute the great civilization which ran its course before the rise of our modern western civilization, and from whose dissolution we are sprung.

The only ages which can really compete with Greco-Roman antiquity are, perhaps, those which rest their claims either on material and mechanical development, like our own, or on the possession of some religious revelation. As to these two classes one may say, first, that the great need for children of coal and electricity like ourselves, who live surrounded, fortified, and smothered by vastly expensive and efficient machinery, is to be able to disentangle Life from the apparatus of life; and this we achieve by studying an age in which the spirit of man counted for so very much and the apparatus for so singularly little. Greek life was almost destitute of apparatus. For the second class, it is fair to say that even supposing, for example, that to a strict Moslem no age can in value be like that of the Hegira, to a strict Jew none like that of the patriarchs, to everyone who thinks at all there must be high and special value in any age not his own in which thought is really free and alive. Indeed, I believe that it is an incalculable advantage to an imaginative student, however devoted to his own religion, to study an age which did not know that religion. If the Greeks had been Christians they would be far less useful to us.

Thus, considering merely the subject-matter of Greco-Roman history, we find the three greatest historians directly concerned with the effort to form a community which shall enable man, in the fullest sense of the words, to live well. Herodotus relates the rise of an Athens which seemed fit to realize the highest and most diverse hopes of poor man and rich man, of statesman, philosopher, and artist: Thucydides narrates the failure of this hope, showing how the ideal Athens of Pericles' speech in book ii became the tyrant city of the Melian dialogue in book v, and thereafter inevitably fell: 'Fleet and army perished from the face of the earth. Nothing was saved. And of many who went forth few returned home.' Polybius, coming after a 200 years' interval, narrates how, the ideal hope having failed, a new republican city succeeded in giving the world not the best thing but a magnificent second best: compulsory peace and competent administration. There is a great unity in the story.

Here another problem suggests itself, and suggests also a new and peculiar value in the study of Greco-Roman history.

Is there a fact lying behind the metaphors implied in such words as *floruit* and *Blütezeit*, maturity and decadence? Do societies really rise and grow and pass their maturity and decline? Is the great Year-Daemon, who lies at the heart of Greek religion, master not only of vegetable and animal life but even of the city and the nation? There seems to be clearly such a growth and decay in the history of Athens and Rome, particularly in their literature and art, just as there is, say, in the painting of the Italian Renaissance. In modern times societies are so large and confused, and every national literature is reinforced by such a great variety of foreign elements and influences, that no such process can be traced, at any rate not by us who live inside the organism and are bewildered by its mass of detail. It seems to be nothing like so clear in the great ancient oriental empires. It can be traced in their art, but in other respects they never made the gigantic effort towards *Aretê* that Greece and Rome made, and when they fell they fell from no very great height. But if there is such a thing as the typical development of a civilization, it is obviously an important thing to study; and our Greats course gives us perhaps the clearest and best model to work on. In Rome especially there is peculiar clarity in the development, from the rude promise of the archaic period up to the Golden Age, the turn to silver, and the long decadence. In Greece the same process occurs, but it occurs with more variety in the different branches of human effort, political, literary, and artistic.

For another peculiar advantage of Greek history is the amazing variety of forms and ideas to be found within one small area during the great creative period. Aristotle found 158 different political constitutions to record, seldom going far outside Greece to look for them. And as for ideas, if we set aside those that are dependent on some particular historical phenomenon, such as devotion to the British Empire or the Catholic Church or the feudal system, it has been maintained with some show of truth that there is no single modern idea in the realm of ethics or politics which was not first struck out in ancient Greece and cannot be translated straight into the ancient Greek language. Even dogmatic religion and religious persecution, which one thinks of as purely modern or post-Christian inventions, have their germs in Plato and his sources. The difference is that our ideas are wrapped round and round in associations and euphemisms and accoutrements; the Greek ideas are naked and unarmed. At first we do not recognize them; but when once we do our values have changed and we are never again entirely at the mercy of catchwords. I am disposed to think that the greatest difference between ancient and modern speculation in political and social matters is that we tend to see problems in terms of money and machinery because money and machinery make such vast and obvious differences in modern life. The Greeks, or at least the Greek writers who have come down to us, saw them in terms of human relations. We tend to say: 'This trouble will be remedied by more houses, the spread of cheap electricity, or the development of a new market.' They said: 'These citizens are not just', or 'These persons in power are not temperate.' To them men and human character mattered so undisguisedly. They could treat the material conditions as a constant. We are so struck by the tremendous effects produced by material conditions that we almost treat the human element of character as a constant.

But, after all, these qualities of the subject-matter are as a rule only realized after longish study. What strikes one first, and is most prominent during a man's Greats course, is the actual character of the books he reads. Now of course it is very difficult for an Englishman, even if he is a good scholar, to read either Herodotus or Thucydides in Greek for the first time with sufficient ease and freedom to feel fully the literary quality of the work. Inevitably he is over-impressed by small points of language and manner and consequently misses the larger qualities. The power comes later.

I confess that the first time I felt the tragic power of Thucydides was one night when I read the seventh book straight through in Jowett's translation. But some general qualities of the Greek historians are worth noting particularly.

First, there is the greatness of their conception. In the case of Herodotus it is really marvellous. He not only sees the significance of the Persian wars to the future of mankind, but he takes in the growth of the Persian power as an autocracy of all Asia—in the Greek sense of that word—and the long, diverse, and multiplex threads of causation which led up to the war. Similarly in Thucydides the conception is great and remarkable. At the beginning of the war he saw that it was going to be something unique in its significance, ἀξιολογώτατον τῶν προγεγενημένων; he began at once—has any other historian ever done the same?—to prepare to write its history, and he saw it not merely as the clash of great material forces, but as a great spiritual tragedy.

Next, the two great historians are extraordinarily free from rhetoric, exaggeration, and bias. They really are, in their different ways, devoted to truth. I know nothing in antiquity, and not much in modern times, like this interest in the real fact which we find in the classical Greek writers. The later Greeks were offended by it. Diodorus, following Ephorus, makes the Persian wars a story of marvellous and superhuman victories. Plutarch—if the writer of the *De Malignitate* is Plutarch—accuses Herodotus of 'malignity' because he does not glorify the story with rhetoric or hide the poor side of human nature when it comes out. Dionysius[1] is pleased with Herodotus but accuses Thucydides of malignity (φθόνος) because he chose as his subject a war which ended in his country's defeat and did not consecrate his powers of eloquence to concealing the defects and augmenting the achievements of Athens. He might at least have begun with the liberation of Ionia and ended with the return of the exiles from Phyle and the amnesty. Think of the first chapters

---

[1] *Letter to Pompeius*, iii.

of Livy, naïvely claiming that, if any nation has a right to adorn its history with fables, surely the Roman people should have that privilege! One can no more imagine Herodotus or Thucydides saying that than conceive Mme Curie proposing to make false statements about the properties of radium on the ground that, if any metal has a right to have its merits exaggerated, surely radium has the priority. Of course Herodotus makes mistakes: he follows a wrong method in his estimate of the Persian army. He also at times falls under the glamour of his own story and the normal beliefs of his age sufficiently to accept the providential and supernatural colouring from which at other times he carefully abstains. But his primary interest is to find out what really happened and then tell it. There are two passages, for example, which I can still hardly read with dry eyes: the story of the oracles given by Delphi to various cities and especially to Athens just before the invasion, and the actual story of the fighting at Thermopylae. Yet if you try to analyse the narrative, its immense effect is never produced by rhetoric or exaggeration; all of it by close detail and unbroken sobriety. This is Greek and characteristically Greek.

Thirdly, there is in the Greek historians, as in all Greek literature, an amazingly strong dramatic sense. I do not mean an instinct for what we call theatrical effect: that is markedly absent. I mean a power of realizing both sides of an argument, and entering into the minds of both combatants. The Greeks, owing to historical causes, suffered much from *stasis*. The city wall, which was supposed to contain a definite number of tribes and clans and families, all united by common blood and common worship, so often in fact enclosed a σύμμεικτον πλῆθος, or 'mixed multitude', of such different races and antecedents and traditions that it was hard for them to live in unity. But, for all their dissensions, Greek literature from the beginning showed a unique desire to understand and appreciate its enemies as well as its friends. The *Iliad* itself, the greatest national poem of Greece,

reaches its greatest heights of pathos in the parting of Hector
and Andromachê and the death of Hector; its spiritual
climax is the revulsion in the mind of Achilles against his own
revenge. In such Attic tragedies as deal with the Trojan
war, like the *Troades* or the *Hecuba*, sympathy is with the
Trojans rather than the Greeks because obviously they
need it more. There is never any attempt to blacken the
character of the national enemy. Similarly in Herodotus,
though he looks on the Persian invasion as a fearful calamity
and on the victory of Greece as a triumph for freedom and
humanity as a whole—which no doubt it was—there is no
tendency to blacken the Persians. On the contrary, though
he relates some bad Persian excesses as well as various Greek
excesses, he takes obvious interest in expounding the Persian
education, with its three duties 'to ride, to shoot, and to
tell the truth' (ἱππεύειν, τοξεύειν, ἀληθίζεσθαι).[1] He never
ridicules or exults over the defeated enemy. He tells at some
length the crushing rebuke of Pausanias to the Greek *mantis*
who wanted to treat the dead body of Mardonius with
outrage. True, he accepts the current division of mankind
into the Greek-speaking and the unintelligible, *Hellênes* and
Barbaroi, but his prejudices, if any, are not in the least
nationalist. He respects the Egyptians for their actual
superiority to the Greeks in culture and antiquity: he has a
romantic admiration for the Scythians and other *Natur-
völker*, as Tacitus has for the Germans.

With Thucydides the absence of prejudice is so marked as
to be almost enigmatic. Were his sympathies with his own
country or with Sparta? Really, at times one is in doubt.
Was he in favour of a Periclean democracy or an oligarchic
revolution? The answer to these questions can be made out
by careful reading, but never for an instant do we find any
suggestion that one side is mostly black and the other white.
His interest in truth for its own sake, and his potent intellectual sincerity, are really rather above our standards and

[1] i. 136.

check our more facile enthusiasms. We understand the patriotic historian, or the enthusiast for a cause, like Treitschke or Motley or Macaulay. We understand the historian who is impartial about controversies or contests in which he and his contemporaries are not concerned, like Ranke or Gardiner. We understand the man who suppresses his personality and aims at an objective record based on documents, not an artistic personal presentment. But there is something strange to ordinary men in the combination of intense feeling with complete absence of partisanship, of ruthless and almost pettifogging exactitude with a degree of artistic composition worthy of a great tragedy, which we find in Thucydides. Of course scholars have been found who accuse Thucydides of bias this way or that; but they seem to me to refute each other. The only point about which exception can fairly be made is in his treatment of Cleon and Hyperbolus. It is worth while reading Grote's statement of the case for the jingo radical democrat, and then reflecting whether Grote would have used similar language if he had lived through the Great War and seen something more like the type that Thucydides was describing, βιαιότατος τῶν πολιτῶν καὶ τότε πιθανώτατος τῶι δήμωι.[1] It did not exist in Grote's day, or in Jowett's. Thucydides certainly expresses his opinion without much reserve; the passage about the Pylos command in book iv does seem to have a note of irritation in it. But our other witnesses more than bear him out. They call Cleon corrupt, which Thucydides never does. He sees Cleon as typifying the spirit which not only ruined Athens but dishonoured her first, the spirit of 'violence' which suited the warmongering mob.

As to Hyperbolus, though Thucydides passes over the detailed causes of his ostracism and merely says he was ostracized διὰ μοχθηρίαν καὶ αἰσχύνην τῆς πόλεως,[2] there is

---

[1] 'The most violent of the citizens and at that time most influential with the Demos', iii. 36.

[2] 'His low type and the shame he brought upon the city', viii. 73.

nothing incredible in that. He was no doubt an important *Dêmagôgos*; and Grote was tempted to think of him as the leader of a violent but high-minded parliamentary radical party. But the more intimate history of the French and Russian revolutions or even of the late war in some parts of Europe show that it is quite possible for persons of vulgar and even criminal type to come to places of great power in times of extreme excitement. Other authorities mention that Hyperbolus died poor, but they also say that he was μοχθηρός and appeared drunk in the Assembly, which was less charitable towards such weaknesses than the House of Commons in the eighteenth century. So probably, though not corrupt, he really was μοχθηρός and an αἰσχύνη τῆς πόλεως, and probably the mass of citizens who could not make up their minds whether to vote for Nicias against Alcibiades or for Alcibiades against Nicias, did come to the conclusion that you could not go far wrong in ostracizing Hyperbolus. In any case I agree with Bury and Cornford that there is no need to invoke any motive of personal revenge: it is clear that Thucydides had a profound antipathy to ῥήτορες of the Cleon–Hyperbolus type.

That is a digression: the main point to realize is that Thucydides rose to the height of understanding and depicting one of the greatest tragedies of human history, and saw that the maximum of tragic power depended on the maximum of truth.

This leads us to the fourth characteristic of the Greek writers which marks them out from the other historians of antiquity, and from those of most later ages so far as we can judge them. For of course we cannot properly judge ourselves. I mean their free and philosophic outlook on life. Freedom is of course relative. Everyone is limited by some personal or national or religious preconceptions. One can see that the authors of the Book of Kings, fine writers as they are, see the world through the narrowest blinkers. St. Augustine's magnificent *City of God* has to be constructed to fit a prescribed model, not of his own making. Even Macaulay sees the world through a glass which, though extremely fine and wide-ranging, can be easily identified as belonging to a particular party in a particular nation at a particular time. When we say that a man is 'prejudiced' or 'limited', we mean that if we showed him various strange objects he would be violently shocked by things which are not really shocking or stupidly unappreciative of things that are really beautiful or great. Now it is hard to imagine either Herodotus or Thucydides being shocked through narrow-mindedness. One can imagine Herodotus interviewing the Kaiser and President Wilson or even Lenin with complete understanding, and Thucydides writing speeches to express their points of view. One can imagine Herodotus admiring Scott's Antarctic expedition and the invention of X-rays or wireless with equal catholicity. And Thucydides too: though he would probably not condescend to explain such subjects except in so far as they directly affected the War.

This freedom of outlook is extraordinary; so extraordinary that we are perhaps tempted to exaggerate it and conceive of a Greek like Thucydides or Plato as actually writing and thinking in a vacuum. Of course no one does that. The Greek was guided and limited by his own inherited armoury of thought, just as he was conditioned by his economic and geographical environment. He was accustomed to slavery as an institution: i.e. he had hardly attempted to solve the extremely difficult problem of making human beings co-operate vigorously for a purpose that does not appeal directly to each individual without the use of compulsion. (It is worth remembering that the New Testament four times over tells slaves to obey their masters; but that was at a time when slavery was far more harsh than in classical Athens, and the danger of a slave revolt really pressing.) He was accustomed to the city: i.e. he conceived of each community as bound together by *philia* within and surrounded by a frequently hostile world without. Fighting was a necessary element in life: every day you might be called upon to kill or die to save your city and its freedom. His thought was also, in my opinion, deeply penetrated by a form of thought which originated in the worship of the Year-Daemon in his various guises. He saw all life as having a certain pattern or orbit, a birth, a rise, a time of triumph and probably of *Hubris* or excess, followed inevitably by retributive *Dikê* and death. As an early philosopher phrases it, 'All things pay retribution to one another for their injustice according to the ordinance of Time.' Or, as Herodotus[1] puts it in a more personal and mythological way, '*φθονερὸν πᾶν τὸ θεῖον*', '*φιλέει γὰρ ὁ θεὸς τὰ ὑπερέχοντα πάντα κολούειν*', 'The Superhuman is by nature jealous and cuts down that which towers too high'; *οὐ γὰρ ἐᾷ φρονέειν μέγα ὁ θεὸς ἄλλον ἢ ἑωυτόν*, 'God allows none to be proud but himself.' The idea haunts the Greeks and sometimes overcomes them in lazy moments, just as the idea of evolution haunts and overcomes us. Ours is the richer conception; but it is worth observing that it is affected by our normal modern reluctance to look facts in the face. It is an explanation of growth but not of decay. It tries to explain life without mentioning death, morning without evening or night. The Greek was not much subject to this particular delusion.

Thus the Greek's freedom of thought was not absolute. He had his own limits and his own tradition. But the limits were wonderfully flexible. The burden of accoutrement was very light. A Greek could face the world in one article of clothing and seldom wore more than five—a *chiton*, a *himation*, and a belt and perhaps two sandals—none of which at all hampered the movement of his body. And it was much the same with his mind.

Something like this can be said in general of all ancient Greco-Roman historians, though of course each has his separate character and value. But there is one form of

[1] i. 32 and vii. 10.

classification which we should notice. Some tell their story
directly. These are the historians proper; Herodotus, Thucydides, Xenophon, Polybius, Sallust, Livy, Tacitus. They are
consciously trying to narrate and explain the history which
they have lived through themselves or heard of from witnesses, or, occasionally, as with Livy, read in older books or
learned from tradition. Some, again, do not speak to us
directly. We only have the privilege, the rare privilege, of
overhearing what they said to their intimate friends or their
contemporary public. We have to interpret their words,
judge when they are joking or exaggerating or perhaps sometimes even prevaricating, and form our own opinion about
the true history. This class consists chiefly of Aristophanes
and the other comedians, the Greek orators, and Cicero.
Cicero, through his wonderful collection of private letters,
is the first of the ancients whom we know intimately, with
the same wealth of detail as a self-revealing modern. We
know him, I think, as well as St. Augustine or Rousseau or
Horace Walpole, and he has quite as interesting matter to
write about.

Now we treat these authorities differently from the historians proper. We have to watch their moods and their
motives. We have at times to detect things which they are
trying to conceal, and to conjecture what has put them into
a particular state of mind. We have to treat them not quite
as historians, but as pieces of evidence. For example, when
Aristophanes attacks Cleon in the *Knights* we may notice
that he is always indirectly championing the cause of the
subject allies, the Ionian cities who were bled and terrorized
by Cleon's mob, but that he never mentions them by name
till the last line of the play.[1] That is a piece of evidence to
be interpreted; it is not a piece of historical narrative.

Of course even the greatest and most explicit historian is
himself a piece of evidence as well as a narrator. But the
method of sifting and combining evidence, and thus finding

[1] ἵν' ἴδωσιν αὐτὸν οἷς ἐλωβᾶθ', οἱ ξένοι.

out more than our authorities intended to tell us, and sometimes even more than they knew, is one that becomes far more prominent in certain forms of historical research. We may, for example, go over the actual ground on which Marathon or Plataea was fought, or look for the passes through which invaders from the north must have come on their march southward. That will explain to us many things: we can see why a trade route followed one line rather than another; why two particular cities are always mixed up in one another's doings, while another just as near seems isolated. Again, we can read the vast mass of ancient Greek or Roman inscriptions on stone which have been recovered and edited. They will sometimes tell us in pompous official language some apparently uninteresting fact. For example, they will describe how some unknown person has received municipal honours from some city because of his industry in overseeing the corn-supply. And then, by comparison with other bits of information, we shall find that results can be deduced. We shall be able to reconstruct the municipal life and laws of some city of which we knew nothing, or supply some new fact that makes our old information intelligible. And of course no one is likely to forget the vast field of ancient history opened up to us by excavations, all of which require, besides the skill in scientific digging, a great enterprise of imaginative interpretation. Then there is history in papyri: not merely historical narrative like that of the historian, name unknown, whose *Hellenica* have appeared at Oxyrhynchus, but the history that lies hidden in quantities of contracts and receipts and demands for taxes and private letters which, added together and compared, have turned one of the darkest periods of ancient history into one of the most sharply illuminated.[1]

Again, if we are steady in our conception of history as the record of Man's Great Adventure on this planet, what rich history there is, for those who can read it, in the works of art

[1] Cf. Rostovtzeff, *A Large Estate in Egypt in the Third Century* B.C.

that have come down from antiquity! When some sixth- or
fifth- or fourth-century Greek got a piece of clay in his hands
and set to work moulding it into a figure or a cup, and then
painting upon it what devices his mind suggested, he was
writing down line by line an expression of himself and his
age. A greater stage in Man's Adventure is marked by the
priestesses of the Acropolis or by the Zeus Temple at Olympia
than by most great wars. The fact that so many hundred
thousand people fought and that one set beat the other set
does not tell you much about the quality of human life lived
at that time; the fact that a man at a certain time and place
conceived and carved those figures tells us the very essence of
what we want to know.

Then there is the language. A language is a record,
intensely and perhaps unanalysably subtle, of the experience
of the race which has created it. How came it that the Greeks
kept an aorist tense and a rich system of participles? Or,
again, how came it that Greeks built up a language so
amazingly capable of expressing the various requirements of
the human mind: the precision of prose, the magic and
passion of poetry, the combination of exactitude and far-
flung questioning that constitutes philosophy, the jests refined
or ribald that make men laugh two thousand years after?
Can one see by what efforts or what accidents this came
about; or what actual phenomena of language have led to
this strange power? One point seems to be clear, that it
depends on a richness of inflexions which enables a speaker
to vary greatly the order of his words in the sentence and
thus to capture whole territories of emphasis and suggestion
that are barred out from the uninflected languages.

And lastly, like the Art, but even more rich in meaning
and perhaps more easily deciphered, is the literature itself.
I mean not the statement consciously made by the writer,
but the form in which he unconsciously makes it, or the
degree of beauty to which he lifts it. For example, Aeschylus
says in the *Agamemnon* that he differs from others and 'thinks

his thought alone', inasmuch as he does not believe that divine vengeance overtakes great prosperity, as such. It is *Hubris*, not mere prosperity, that God smites. It is not really φθόνος at work, it is δίκη. That is a point of some minor historical interest, but it is not the kind of point I mean. Again, you may prove from certain passages that in the *Agamemnon* there were three actors or that there were twelve *choreutae*. There is an historical fact in that, but again it is not the important fact. The thing of infinitely the greatest historical importance is the sheer beauty and grandeur of the *Agamemnon* itself. Man, having been then on this planet, let us say, fifty thousand years, more or less, spent mostly in eating and being eaten, hurting and being hurt, at last produced the *Agamemnon*, or the *Iliad* or the *Aeneid* or what you will. So there was some meaning in the process after all! It led somewhere. It may even have been worth while! That, properly understood, is an historical fact of the very first importance. The fact is the beauty of the poem or statue itself, and you cannot understand the fact at all unless you can feel and appreciate the beauty. Otherwise the fact does not exist for you. This seems at first sight to cut off the facts of literature and art from what we usually call the facts of history—plain, solid facts, like 'Battle of Hastings 1066', which need no imagination to understand them. But such a distinction is an illusion. It really calls for any amount of imagination to understand the meaning of 'Battle of Hastings 1066'. It is only that the futile attempt to understand things without the use of the imagination is more instantly convicted of futility when the thing to be understood is a work of art. It is always convicted sooner or later. History, like art and poetry and philosophy, is after all a thing of the spirit, though doubtless, from some innate timidity or laziness, we are always trying to do without the spirit and to obtain the same result by some mechanical substitute. Which in the last resort cannot be done.

This lecture, and perhaps this whole course, will not give

you much information about your actual period of history. That must come by hard and methodical reading of the great texts. The course is meant rather to suggest ideas about the meaning and methods of history, and enable you at the beginning of your Greats course to get some help from the experience of us older students who have been there before and know the ground.

1932.

IV

PROLEGOMENA TO THE STUDY OF ANCIENT PHILOSOPHY

IN *The Golden Journey to Samarkand* the pilgrims explain that they mean to go 'always a little further' because it may be that somewhere beyond the next range of hills or the next stretch of sea,

> White on a throne or guarded in a cave
> There lives a prophet who can understand
> Why men were born.

That is very much the position of the philosopher. He gropes and explores this way and that, in the hope of getting farther into the heart of things and understanding the ultimate problems that now puzzle us.

But almost every student who feels the philosophic οἶστρος[1] in him, driving him on and on into strange country, must wonder why at Oxford he is not set straight face to face with the great problems themselves, instead of having to learn what various people in the distant past have thought about them. If it is necessary to study the theories and thoughts of other people, why cannot he begin straight to study Einstein, Russell, Bergson, Alexander, and the leading contemporary thinkers? Why above all go back 2,500 years to study the Greeks? As Mr. Wells has put it, surely all that is true in Plato must by this time be common knowledge, which later philosophers have used and built upon?

The answer to this question is twofold. In the first place, the main questions of philosophy are not for the most part meant to be settled, they are meant to be understood. Science is different. Science can ask a definite question and answer it: it can inquire into the chemical constitution of

---

[1] The sting of a gad-fly, such as drove Io wandering.

4988   K

the blood and produce a precise and correct formula. It can ask how to state the ever-increasing speed of a falling object and find a mathematical answer in the calculus. But there is no such complete answer to the questions 'Why men were born', or 'How we know things', or 'What is the difference between right and wrong?' just as there is no precise answer to the question 'What is the value of the *Ode to the Nightingale* or the tragedy of *Hamlet*?' You can get more and more light on such questions; you can see deeper and deeper into them; and of course—the point on which Kant laid stress— you can definitely reject various false and disastrous answers. But your real hope is to understand more, not to settle the question. Consequently it is not much good simply looking up the last text-book and copying the answers there given. The only method is to go through the process of thinking the questions over, more and more closely, with the help of the greatest minds who have thought about them before.

The second reason is quite different. It is that, in order to see the problems clearly, we must, as far as we can, try to get outside the thick atmosphere of tradition and convention in which all our thought, like the thought of practically every human society known to us, is stifled and imprisoned. One of the great lessons which anthropology has taught us is the overpowering influence on mankind of tradition and tribal custom, of inherited taboos and superstitions. The shell is practically unbreakable, except by the impact of invasion or penetration by another society. In Europe men's thoughts were largely set free by the great world-movements of the nineteenth century, but we see the reaction now. They are creeping back into their shells—at least into some shell or other; in Italy, in Germany, in Russia, new shells have been pieced together and, in each country, any expression of thought which breaks the shell is or has till lately been called to order and punished. It might be thought that after the overthrow of Fascism this rigidity of convention in the separate countries had disappeared, but it seems more

likely that new and equally rigid orthodoxies have been
spreading over many countries and, of course, rousing rigid
opposition in others. The shell may be hardening rather
than growing soft. All through the Middle Ages again there
was plenty of very acute philosophy, but it had to conform to
the inherited conglomerate of taboos and dogmas which was
for historical reasons dominant. Anthropology administers
its depressing cordial to the extreme conservative and the
extreme radical in about equal proportions. It seems to show
that these inherited conglomerates have practically no chance
of being true or even sensible; and, on the other hand, that
no society can exist without them or even submit to any
drastic correction of them without social danger.

Now if we want to think, we want to think freely and get,
for the time being, outside our shell, a shell largely made by
our inherited religion, by the Industrial Revolution, by the
popular newspaper, by the mechanization of life, and by the
enormous development of scientific discovery and material
invention on which our social life depends. If we content
ourselves with looking at the great permanent problems of
philosophy through the glasses of our present-day western
civilization we are simply hugging our prison walls.

How are we to get beyond them? What we want is to be
able, for a time, to look at the world through the eyes of
some people who are, first, intellectually great; secondly, as
free as possible from our own prejudices and conventions;
and thirdly, if possible, not very much hampered by their
own. The Greeks satisfy these three conditions. Their intellectual eminence is beyond question. I will say no more
of that. Secondly, they lived, broadly speaking, before any
of the main conditions that limit us had come into existence,
though of course at a later stage of our studies we shall have
to consider carefully what elements of their tradition are
still working unchallenged among us. Thirdly, of all peoples
known to us in history, the Greeks were far and away the
freest thinkers. It is hardly too much to say that—leaving

India and China out of account for the moment—there is
no philosophy except in Greece or derived from Greece.

This line of thought suggests a difficulty. 'If these people
were so different from us in social conditions and outlook,
are they any good to us? Did they ask the same questions
as we? Did they try to understand what we want to understand?' Yes, our civilization is descended from theirs and
the plain fact is that they did. It is commonly said that the
great dividing gulf between ancient and modern philosophy
is the Kantian *Kritik*. The idea that the laws of mathematics
and logic may be merely the laws according to which our
human minds happen to work, and give us no information
about the external world, is a modern discovery or theory,
and does not seem to have occurred to any of the ancients.
This is probably true, though some phrases of Democritus
asserting the entire impossibility of our knowing the external
world come rather close to it.[1] But in the main, the ancient
philosopher is just like Mr. Flecker's pilgrim, just like the
modern man in doubt, faced with a world and a self which
he cannot understand and about which he knows that he is
often going astray. Let us take two or three typical sets of
problems.

First, to what degree did the Greek philosopher try to
escape from his tradition? He was brought up on the λόγοι
τῶν Ἑλλήνων which Hecataeus characterized as πολλοὶ καὶ
γελοῖοι;[2] on Homer and Hesiod and other poets, on the
local ritual of the temples, with its fables and idolatries and
uncritical anthropomorphic polytheism. Could he really get
free from this nonsense? Just look at the fragments of
Xenophanes:[3] 'The gods do not lie and steal and commit
adultery. It is Homer and Hesiod who lie. There is only
one God': so far the thought is not so specially striking, but
note what follows. This one God is 'not like man in any way,

---

[1] Cf. Dem. Φυσικά in Diels, *Vorsokratiker* ii; Ritter and Preller, pp.
166, 167.   [2] 'The *Logoi* of the Greeks are varied and laughable.'
[3] Cf. Xenoph. Σίλλοι and Φυσικά in Diels; Ritter and Preller, pp. 78 ff.

neither in shape nor in mind. . . . If cattle and lions had
hands and could make works of art, they would have made
gods like themselves—horses gods like horses, cattle gods like
cattle, and so on.' This is really free thinking, thought that
we have to make an effort to follow. 'God has no parts;
οὖλος ὁρᾶι, οὖλος δὲ νοεῖ, οὖλος δέ τ' ἀκούει—the whole of him
sees, thinks, hears. He is not like man in any way, in shape
or in mind.' That 'or in mind' gives food for thought. It
reminds one of the medieval Arab mystic who said that to
call God 'just' was as foolishly anthropomorphic as to say
that he had a beard. And it is curious to what lengths the
early philosophers carried their denial of anthropomorphism.
This mind, this non-human mind, which they call God, in so
far as it has shape, is for Melissus and Parmenides a sphere!
It is also the One, the only existence.

There is a passion about Xenophanes and Parmenides
which makes it natural for them to write in verse, but, as in
Lucretius, it is in part a passionate scepticism, a rejection of
the blinkers and a longing for free vision, in part a belief in
the attainment of a new revelation. You can see that tendency
carried farther in the cases of Diagoras, who denied the gods,
and Anaxagoras, who went so far as to say that the sun was
not a god but a mass of white-hot matter. This determination to get free provides the clue to one of the most famous
controversies of the fifth century—the attempt to distinguish
between φύσις and νόμος—between the real law of nature
and the law of mere convention, accepted so long and
practised so instinctively that it seems like nature.

So far I have been showing how the Greeks, as soon as
philosophy began, rose above their own traditions and conventions, and thought freely. You will not find anything to
approach that freedom in, for instance, medieval thought.

Next, let us take some of the particular questions which
troubled them. First came the question, What is real in this
world we see about us? What is the world itself? What is
its ἀρχή or original stuff? What is it made of? Among the

early Ionian wise men the ruling desire seems to have been for some simplification or unification of this confused whole, which we all know to be a *Cosmos* or order. Thales, so far as we can understand his scanty fragments, said the secret was water. Without water there was no life; he saw the dead soil springing to life under the rain; he saw organisms germinating in the mud of the river. Water was the secret of life; and besides, water changed both 'up' and 'down', into vapour one way and into solid matter the other way. All matter was really water. His pupil Anaximenes took the same view, but he preferred to call this uniform substance by its highest, or rarest, term—vapour, Ἀήρ; vapour which condensed into water, solidified into mud, solidified farther into earth, rock, iron. All the differences in things were due to changes in condensation. Anaximander, a rather older pupil, taking the same fundamental conception, spoke of the original matter as the Indefinite or Indeterminate (τὸ ἄπειρον). The three Ionians had really the same view, but it was rather difficult to believe in this complete unity of matter; and other wise men, especially Democritus, one of the greatest figures in early philosophy, started a better explanation in a theory which has had a most illustrious history in the advance of science. Matter could be broken up by division or τομή into smaller and smaller bits, till at last you reached something Ἄτομον, *Individuum*, 'Indivisible'. These indivisibles were, apparently, of different shapes or qualities, and combined in infinitely different ways. From this, and not from mere differences of condensation, came the infinite variety of things. We could never know ἄτομα, but they were the only reality; they and the void between them. All else was a matter of our senses or our fancies.

But here we strike upon a rather curious contradiction. The Ionian philosophers chiefly impressed later generations as what we call 'men of science', not troubled by religion. Thales discovered that the light of the moon was only a

reflection from the sun; he found by a sort of trigonometry
a method of measuring altitudes; he is even said to have
foretold an eclipse. Anaximander invented the sundial, and
so on. They studied physical phenomena and particularly
what the Greeks call *ta meteôra*, 'the things in the sky', such
as astronomy, the solstices, thunder and lightning, &c. They
paid no regard whatever to the Olympian gods or in general
to what the Greeks called *theologia*, the stories or legends of
the gods. Yet, as Professor Cornford has pointed out, they
accepted without proof or question a number of primitive
religious ideas and principles; for instance, the conceptions
of *Moira* and *Dikê*, of purity and impurity, the principle
that 'Like alone acts on like', that 'Like alone knows like';
that the universe is a *Cosmos* or order, and is therefore One.
Thales even insists that the *Cosmos* is 'alive' (ἔμψυχος) and
'full of gods' (δαιμόνων πλήρης).[1]

Aristotle sometimes refers to beliefs of this sort as 'extremely ancient', and one cannot but recall the statements of
Herodotus[2] about the religion of the Pelasgians, who performed agricultural fertility rites and prayed to gods who
had no names or shapes. It was 'Homer and Hesiod' who
invented a theogony for the Greeks and 'gave the gods titles
and separate honours and arts'. The philosophers threw off
the artificial creations of 'Homer and Hesiod', but could not
get rid of the more primitive and instinctive religion.

The Ionians, then, dealt mainly with physical science.
But after all, thought others, is this the right way to ask the
question? Can we find out what is real by asking what the
material world is made of? The material world is always
changing, for one thing; man's body, the grass, the river,
are not the same to-day as they were yesterday; for another,

---

[1] Cf. Anaximander (fr. 9 Diels): all things perish into that from which they
came; 'for they pay reparation and atonement (δίκην καὶ τίσιν) to one another
for their injustice by the law of time.' Empedocles (of a different school):
'by earth we see earth, by air air', &c. Cf. also his fr. 115 on Impurity.

[2] ii. 51 ff.

we know the material world only through our senses, which are always deceiving us. For a third, it never exactly is what it professes to be or what we call it. The line we call straight is never straight, the table we call square is never square, the man we call wise makes foolish mistakes. Yet all the time there is one thing, or one world of things, which remains unchanging, certainly known and always absolutely exact: that is, Number or Arithmetic. Two and two are always four, the square on the hypotenuse of a right-angled triangle is and always will be equal to the squares of the other two sides, though all the material world should be dissolved into chaos. Hence starts the great school of Pythagoras, and later a large part of Platonism. Why cannot this world of certainty, of true knowledge as opposed to mere approximation and guess-work, be extended beyond the range of arithmetic? We know exactly the meaning of two plus two; or the square of the hypotenuse. Suppose we knew as exactly the meaning of justice, virtue, beauty—τὸ δίκαιον, ἀρετή, τὸ καλόν—could we not gain the same certainty about all the problems of our moral life? After all, they are real things, not words. They exist, though we cannot see them with our physical eyes. Let us define them and make sure of them, and thereby obtain the knowledge that solves the riddle.

'That is mere dreaming', said Heraclitus. And why after all should we seek for this unchanging reality? Why not face the plain fact that there is no such thing? All things are always changing, says Heraclitus. That is the essential truth. That eternal flux is reality. Πάντα χωρεῖ καὶ οὐδὲν μένει, πάντα ῥεῖ.[1] You can never step into the same river twice— 'nor even once', added a disciple, for while you are in it it ceases to be the same. All is γένεσις, not οὐσία, Becoming, not Being. Πόλεμος πάντων πατήρ; that is, all things come from a clash of opposites. . . . Heraclitus is the most exciting of ancient philosophers, and makes most the impression of a towering and intolerant genius. His magnificent paradoxes

---

[1] 'All things move and nothing stays: all things flow.'

endeared him to the Stoics, who read into him much of their own system and have often made it difficult to find his true doctrine. But the fragments are fairly numerous and enormously repay study.

So far we have been considering forms of the question 'What is real?' or 'What is the world made of?' It was the problem from which Greek philosophy started, and the start was brilliant. We can see how one form of answer led to another. But disappointment soon set in, and the main current of philosophy turned in a different direction. By the later fifth century people were saying, with Socrates and most of the Sophists, that these inquiries into nature and the world and the stars were fruitless. Such things were unknowable; better turn to more practical and manageable problems, such for instance as ethics and politics and the nature of the soul. This is just the opposite of what a modern man would say. To us it is ethics and politics and the nature of the soul that provide the unanswerable problems, whereas physical science and astronomy have already attained an immense body of concrete and practically certain results. The explanation of the paradox is fairly obvious. The Greeks could not progress far in physical science, or at any rate in the vast problems which they chose to take up, without a whole apparatus of scientific instruments for exact observation and measurement and experiment, which of course they did not possess. Consequently, after the first great outburst of curiosity and speculation about the world, the philosophers of the fifth century were thrown back on the studies which depended chiefly on introspection and reasoning power and imagination; the balance was somewhat redressed by Aristotle.

Socrates, we are told, began by studying physical science, as we should call it, and τὰ μετέωρα—things of the sky, such as astronomy; then, realizing that he knew nothing and could find out nothing certain, he turned to a new form of philosophy which may roughly be termed an analysis of introspection. People were always using terms like 'right'

and 'wrong', 'just' and 'unjust', 'beautiful' and 'ugly', 'know'
and 'think'; what did they really mean by these words, and
what reality lay behind them? It is a turn from judgements
of fact, which seem unattainable, to judgements of value in
human terms, which can perhaps be attained. The fundamental question is no longer 'What is the world?' but 'How
ought man to live?' (In Plato indeed this question is largely
made dependent on a theory of knowledge and of reality; it
is hard to make out how far the Platonic theories were already
held by Socrates, but not hard to see the connecting bridge.)
However that may be, the study of ethics developed with
amazing success in the four or five generations following
Socrates; indeed it may almost be said that no important
idea in the sphere of ethics has occurred to mankind since
the fourth century B.C. The question 'What is Righteousness?' or 'What is the good life for man?' has of course
presented itself to every community of men, however primitive, and generally speaking the answer has come in the form
of a system of *Themis* and taboo, things which 'are done'
and things which 'are not done'. If you observed all the
taboos you did nothing contrary to *Themis*: you did not
transgress and therefore did not incur punishment. Every
transgression of *Themis* must be atoned for. *Dikê* smote the
transgressor and restored the balance. *Themis*, when analysed,
proves to be the tribal custom; the thing that is always
done, always, that is to say, by the people who know. Hence
Themis is the special subject of oracles: in situations where
no ordinary person can say what you ought to do, the god
or the ancestral hero in his grave knows, and tells you what
is really *Themis*.[1]

It is noteworthy that Plato, perhaps under the influence
of Pythagoras, is greatly inspired by these primitive ideas of
Themis, though he develops them almost beyond recognition. In his splendid discussion of justice or righteousness,
the *Republic*, he finds that, both in the macrocosm of the

[1] See *Five Stages of Greek Religion*, end of chap. i on *Themis*.

city and the microcosm of the individual soul, righteousness
is a kind of division of labour. This seems puzzling until we
see that it is really the old primitive conception of tribal
organization in a new form. In the primitive tribe every
class has its appointed *Moira* or portion, its *Ergon* or function,
and things go right if each class and each individual fulfils
his *Moira* and performs his *Ergon*, and does not transgress or
trespass on those of others. In modern language each has his
social service to perform and his consequent rights. It is the
old *Themis*; but a *Themis* vastly extended by the imagination
and made more positive. A *Themis* in which you may be
called upon not merely to die for your country—the oldest
tribal laws involved that—but to die for the truth, or, as he
explains in a wonderful passage in the second book, to defy
the whole conventional law of your society for the sake of
the true law which it has forsaken or forgotten. No one who
has read it can easily forget the account of the righteous man
in the evil or mistaken society, how he is to be scourged and
blinded and at last impaled or crucified by the society that
misunderstands him, because he is righteous and seems the
reverse, and how after all it is better for him so to suffer than
to follow the multitude in doing wrong.

This conception of the good life as the performance of a
function or duty by a member in an organism or—to use the
later language of the Stoic school—a free will working with
God for the achievement of his unknown purpose—shows
an incalculable advance over the taboo conceptions, prevalent
in antiquity and on the whole usual among most people at
the present day. It is a great advance for example on the
conceptions of the Old Testament, or of medieval Christianity,
both of which, in different degrees, are based on sins and
punishments.

One feels the same reasonable and humane atmosphere in
Aristotle's *Ethics*, where instead of a system of sins and
punishments he operates with a system of psychological
tendencies or ways of behaviour, each of which may be too

weak or too strong for the general good. It is a question of proportion; the right thing is to attain some καιρός, or exact point, observe some μέτρον, or measure.

Both these conceptions are, in the main, social. The individual's chief business is to serve his community. Later on, when Greek civilization failed and sank after the strain of the Peloponnesian War, when the city no longer counted for much and the individual soul stood out in its own ultimate and infinite importance, there rose two great schools, the Stoics and Epicureans. They gave to the problem of ethics the two different answers which have divided thinkers ever since. How ought man to live? The Epicureans, following Democritus, said that he should so live as to produce a happy or satisfactory life. The good to attain was what they called ἡδονή, 'sweetness' or pleasure, while Democritus had called it εὐθυμία and others εὐδαιμονία. We, with a still feebler word, call it 'happiness'. The good was a state of well-being, and virtues such as courage, wisdom, temperance, righteousness, and the like were of value only because they produced well-being.

The Stoics took just the other line, that nothing was good except the actual quality of goodness, ἀρετή, which is generally translated 'virtue'. According to them it is the action itself that matters, or rather the will to act, without thought of the consequences. Nay, the consequences do not matter at all: pain or pleasure, riches or poverty, sickness or health, success or failure, they are not of the soul: who will care a fig for such dross when the soul stands naked before God? Also they are things not in our power, mere results of accident; the one thing that does matter is our will for the right, and that is absolutely in our power, sick or well, free or in chains.

Put briefly, either there is something that ought to be done for some absolute reason, irrespective of its consequences, because it is right; or else there is no such transcendent reality, and our business is to find out and follow the line of conduct that will on the whole produce the best results. Most people, I think, hold sometimes one view and sometimes the other.

Thus, in rough and bald outline, we see how the Greeks up to the time of Plato and Aristotle faced three main problems: (1) How can we think freely, unblinkered by tradition? (2) What, in this bewildering mass that surrounds us, is real? or what is the world really made of? and (3) What ought man to do or what is the Good?

As a matter of fact our study of Greek philosophy in the Greats School is almost confined to the writings of two philosophers, Plato and Aristotle, and indeed chiefly to one work of each, the *Republic* and the *Ethics*. The choice of these two is on the whole a happy one, and has come about through certain historical conditions. Plato in Neoplatonic form was a force in the early Christian Church, partly through the influence of St. Augustine, who knew him by means of Boethius and a Latin translation of Plotinus, partly through mere forgeries like the book of Dionysius the Areopagite, the supposed Platonist convert of St. Paul. Aristotle was only known through parts of his *Logic*, till the mass of his writings with all their splendid coherence and common sense were translated from the Arabic in the thirteenth century, and were accepted as a basis for Christian philosophy by Thomas Aquinas. His 'scholastic' system dominated Christian thought for two centuries, when it began to be rivalled by a revival of Platonism or Neoplatonism in the Renaissance. Aristotle, however, retained a firm hold in the universities, and the position of Plato in Greats is said to have been a bold innovation of Dr. Jowett's.

We have chosen, then, Plato and Aristotle; whom else could we have chosen? In the eighteenth century, when Greek was not widely known and Latin was, ancient philosophy was chiefly represented by Cicero and Seneca. Cicero *De Officiis* or 'Tully's Offices' became almost a popular book of devotion among the cultivated. A very fine book it is, but by now we have dug beneath its foundations and prefer something more original and less derivative. That inevitably takes us to Greece. If we look among the Greek philosophers, Plato and Aristotle are by far the best preserved. We have a very large mass of authentic writing from both. The only competitors conceivable would be the two Stoics, Epictetus and Marcus Aurelius—who are still read for their own message but are already imprisoned in a severe orthodoxy; Sextus Empiricus the great Sceptic, an interesting critic but not an original or inspiring philosopher; and possibly Epicurus. But neither in genius and originality, nor in bulk, nor in influence on the world of thought, could any of these stand beside the chosen two.

Also, the two present curious contrasts with one another. In the first place, while the tradition has preserved a large mass of the writings of both of them, it has awarded them a difference of treatment that is almost impish. It has preserved the whole of Plato's published work and none of his unpublished, unless we count the thirteen letters; while of Aristotle it has preserved masses of unpublished lecture-notes and no finished and published work at all, unless we count the *Politeia Athenaiôn*, which occupies an ambiguous position. Cicero, who knew Aristotle's *Dialogues*, speaks with admiration of his flowing style; but as the two writers have come down to us their styles form a contrast of the most extreme kind: philosophy written in the most exquisite language so that it charms and sometimes bewilders you like a poem, and philosophy written in jottings, rather like telegrams, containing sometimes the bare bones of thought, sometimes epigrams and brilliant phrases, sometimes apparently mere confusions and repetitions. It is extraordinarily interesting to study the two methods at the same time.

If we try to penetrate beneath the style to the thought of these two philosophers, certain other great contrasts present themselves. First of all, as we noticed before, Plato being much influenced by the school of Pythagoras not only put mathematics at the centre of knowledge, but showed also some of that inclination towards primitive mysticism which was found in Pythagoras, and which was further strengthened by Plato's deep resentment against the Athenian democracy. As against the *Demos* he was ready to champion the *Urdummheit* from which it had so proudly escaped, to idealize things Spartan because Sparta was the antithesis to Athens, and to praise the retired life of contemplation because there you escaped from the storms and dust of public life. Yet all the time he is a child of fifth-century Athens to whom political action and public service are the very breath of life, and both in his writings and in his practical life he is always groping after the ideal *polis*.

Aristotle lived a little later, when the separation between the philosophers and public life was an accepted fact. He lived in his school with no sense of grievance. He had made certain excursions into politics with his friend Hermeias the Dynast of Atarneus, but in the main he looks at the city from outside, yet with simple acceptance and admiration. He had lived much at the court of Macedon and seems to recognize how vastly more civilized a Greek city-state was than a semi-barbaric tribal monarchy.

Their respective attitudes to the *polis* are like their attitudes to poetry. Plato was always a πολιτικὸς ἀνήρ, chafing at the *polis* because it would not give him scope. He loved it and hated it. Aristotle was contentedly outside the *polis*, analysed it, and thought it a fine institution. Similarly Plato was too much of a poet; poetry intoxicated him and led him away from the truth; so he turned and rent it as an impostor and a source of evil, and went on writing it. Aristotle had a reasonable appreciation of poetry, and wrote it well himself, but was not dangerously intoxicated and misled by it. On the contrary, he put together a very successful scientific hand-book about it.

Next, as we have said, Plato was a mathematician, Aristotle was a biologist. Mathematicians, such as Professor

Whitehead, tell us—what most of us would not have suspected —that he was really a great mathematical thinker, and certainly mathematics profoundly affected his philosophic thought. He felt deeply that, however clumsy and inexact the material objects may be with which you are dealing, the eternal truths of arithmetic remain unchanged. They make a great transcendental *Cosmos*, a permanent reality of which the material world is a transitory image. And one great element, perhaps the greatest, in Plato's philosophy is the effort to find some system of truths which will apply to the whole of experience as the rules of arithmetic apply to questions of number.

Aristotle was trained under Plato. He spent twenty years in the Academy and took his mathematics in due course, but his main work seems to have lain in the observation, collection, and classification of scientific facts. His range is enormous; his conception of the realm of knowledge unsurpassed in comprehensiveness. He collects not only plants, animals, and concrete objects, he collects political constitutions, forms of reasoning, styles of poetry, records of dramatic productions. He analyses them and classifies them. He sees that history should not be only the history of states and wars; he invents the history of literature, of philosophy, and of culture. He is the first and greatest encyclopaedist. But he is also, we must not forget, a very great speculative thinker. His ideas of form and matter, of φύσις and τέλος, of ἐνέργεια and δύναμις, have been immensely fruitful in the history of thought, and he is the inventor of logic and metaphysics.

There is another point of similarity, and also of difference, between the two philosophers. The similarity is that in the writings of both there is variety, development, and change of opinion. It is not safe with either of them to isolate a particular text and say definitely, 'This is Aristotle's opinion', or 'Plato's opinion'. You must always consider other passages where the same subject is treated and see what opinion is expressed there. In Plato the line of development can be made out with some approach to certainty by means of the so-called 'stylistic tests'. Even so there remain difficult problems. About Aristotle there has been a quite recent change of opinion. His philosophy used to be taken as a static orthodox whole; fragments of the *Protrepticus* or treatises like the *Eudemian Ethics*, which expressed heterodox opinions, were either neglected or regarded as spurious. Professor Jaeger, however, who succeeded Wilamowitz at Berlin and is now at Harvard, has shown in a series of masterly studies that Aristotle went through a clearly marked development of thought from a time when he first ventured to criticize Plato, to a time when he tried to combine his own views with the main lines of Platonism, and a third in which he definitely refuted the main doctrines of Plato's system and constructed his own independently. His books and lectures can only be understood as 'stages in the living whole of his unresting intellectual development'. In ethics the three stages are marked by the *Protrepticus*, the *Eudemian Ethics*, and the *Nicomachean Ethics*.[1]

[1] As to the ἐξωτερικοὶ λόγοι, Jaeger considers that 'the ancient problem has been settled once for all'. Aristotle used his published works in his lectures and sometimes corrected them. Bernays thought much the same, but see Ross, vol. ii, pp. 408 ff. on Ar. *Met.* 1076ᵃ 28: 'Bernays accepts the distinction, which had certainly become current by the time of Cicero, between the exoteric and the acroamatic works of Aristotle. It may be admitted that all the subjects in question were probably treated of in Aristotle's dialogues, or in other lost works of his which were published, in the full sense. Thus it is certain that Aristotle criticized the Ideas in the dialogue *De Philosophia* and in the works *De Ideis* and *De Bono*; he may also have dealt with them as Bernays suggests, in the dialogues *De Iustitia, Sophistes*, and *Politicus*. But the meaning of λόγοι in the *Physics* passage, as the preposition διά shows, is not "books" but "arguments", and ὑπό in the present passage suggests the same, in view of the frequent tendency in Greek to treat the argument as if it were a person, as in Δίκαιος Λόγος and Ἄδικος Λόγος, ὁ λόγος αἱρέει, and many other examples quoted by Diels. By a comparison of *Pol.* 1323ᵃ 21–35 with *E.N.* 1098ᵇ 9–18 (dealing with the same subject) Diels shows beyond a doubt that by τὰ ἐν τοῖς ἐξωτερικοῖς λόγοις in 1323ᵃ 22 Aristotle

But the main difference in the development of the two philosophers is this. Aristotle from the beginning is a professional philosopher. We find him a student in the Academy, an independent teacher and researcher at Assos, and eventually at Athens at the head of a school of his own. Plato began —to put it bluntly—not as a conscious philosopher but as a brilliant young Athenian gentleman who followed Socrates and took a keen and not entirely unmalicious pleasure in listening to the confutations and humiliations of celebrated or pretentious people in which that philosopher or *scurra Atticus*[1] specialized.[2] Plato reported actual conversations, or invented imaginary conversations; the reports were always witty and lifelike, and at first—as in the *Hippias* and even the first book of the *Republic*—largely satirical. Then come other dialogues which are still lifelike and dramatic reports of conversations, but with the centre of interest altered. Such dialogues as the *Phaedrus*, the *Theaetetus*, the *Gorgias*, the *Phaedo*, are not strictly speaking philosophical treatises; they do not state a consecutive argument and lead to a dogmatic conclusion. As Professor Woodbridge of Columbia puts it, they give a picture of some of the ablest and keenest thinkers in Athenian society, as they talked together about some of the most interesting and difficult subjects in the world: about the theory of politics, and love, and the possible immortality of the soul, and the search for righteousness. As dialogue succeeds dialogue, the interest centres more and more on the philosophical problem itself, less and less on the dramatic or mimetic element, though still through all the work of Plato's maturity there is always a drama and prac-

means the same as he does by τὰ λεγόμενα in 1098 ᵇ 10, i.e. that in that passage at least ἐξ. λόγοι means "discussions not peculiar to the Peripatetic School". This is probably its meaning in the other passages also. The precise shade of meaning may differ in the different passages; in some the reference is to Academic doctrines, in others to discussions or distinctions which were familiar to cultivated Athenians of no particular philosophic school.'

[1] Zeno's phrase for him, Cic. *N.D.* i. xxxiv.   [2] Cf. above, p. 21.

tically never a demonstration. There is a problem discussed, an exchange of views and suggestions, a deeper understanding of the difficulties, but almost never a dogmatic answer. At most there is a myth, a deliberately invented fable, not professing really to state the truth, but only to suggest something like it, δι᾽ εἰκόνων, by images. Only in the master's latest and weariest work, the *Laws* and the *Timaeus*, does the element of drama or mime drop out altogether and leave us with a straightforward philosophic treatise, definitely argumentative and dogmatic. I always feel in the *Laws* that Plato in his disappointed old age is labouring under a cloud of fear and increased hatred of the *Demos*. The hope of his prime has left him. He dare not state the pros and cons, dig deeper, help his reader to think, and trust to the future for some good result. He dare not in his new city trust to the workings of reason and the spirit of the guardians. He lays down, in detail after detail, exactly what his citizens are to do and think; otherwise they are sure to go wrong. He is prepared with punishments for heretics. He has no hope of spreading his political gospel—all politics are too obviously going to the bad—but only hopes for a very small city, in some remote and isolated spot, keeping itself safe from degeneracy by rigid conservatism and the absolute exclusion of foreign influences. It is a curious commentary upon human history that the later Platonic schools based themselves so largely on the *Laws* and still more on the *Timaeus*. They longed for dogma; they wanted to be told what was true; and they had not the intellectual life and faith to follow the undying thought of Plato in his prime, and be left thinking, seeking, knowing their ignorance, and trying to understand δι᾽ εἰκόνων.

That, I believe, is in the main what a student of philosophy ought to do. In some respects, of course, we can attain definite advances and be fairly sure of results. In practical life we have to make up our minds and be clear. But for the most part philosophy, as Plato says, is born of wonder and really becomes false to itself when the element of wonder leaves it. In philosophy, as in poetry and art, it is the process that matters more than the result. To think more clearly, to see deeper, to bring a wider range of subjects into the grasp of reason, these are the true aims of philosophical study, and these can, so we think in the Greats School, be well attained by studying the great problems, not in the dogmas of a new handbook summarizing the latest results, but in close companionship with these two ancient men of towering genius, the great artist and the great man of science, who stand necessarily quite outside of our conventions and are victims to none of our catchwords.

Where should we end the history of Greek philosophy? There were great Greek philosophers, whose works are still extant, right on to the fifth century A.D. But in the third and second centuries B.C., not long after the death of Aristotle, there came over the Greek world a great change. The centre of Hellenic civilization, Athens and Greece itself, had broken down, chiefly perhaps owing to the economic consequences of persistent war; the circumference, however, spread farther and farther out. The Greek language, badly spoken, and Greek ideas, imperfectly understood, spread all over the Near East. Free constitutions ceased to exist; the world fell under the rule of so many conflicting military despotisms.

The change of social conditions brought about a corresponding change in thought. The Athenian philosophers had thought of the good life as being the service of society or of the city; the good man was the man who lived for his city-state. The later Greek philosophers seem mostly to think of the State as probably a bad thing; a great 'killing machine', an organization of might without right, in which unscrupulous adventurers and tyrants scrambled for rich prizes, though from time to time some fairly good and strong government rose out of the confusion.

Philosophy split into three main tendencies. The Stoics, with their minds fixed upon duty and devoting will and energy to fulfilling the purpose of God, threw themselves into the work of government much as the best type of Indian civilian devoted himself to the task of bringing good government to India. One of the most interesting books that have come down to us is the *Meditations* of Marcus Aurelius, who was personally a Stoic saint but officially a Roman emperor, and a very efficient one, though overwhelmed with work and anxiety. But it is worth remembering that the other book of devotion or meditation that has come to us from the Stoics was the work of a lame slave, Epictetus. Stoicism did touch both extremes.

As contrasted with Stoicism, the Epicurean school mostly abstained from office and public life. Ambition makes men cruel; the State, they held, is largely an organization for punishing, imprisoning, killing, and making war. It makes men unhappy, and the stronger it is the more people it makes unhappy. Therefore avoid it. Moderate your desires, cast out fear, live simply, love your friends and companions, and, if possible, when you die let it be written over your grave *Neminem tristem fecit*, 'He made no one miserable'. The Epicureans were in a sense the Tolstoyans of antiquity.

But the main current of the Hellenistic age was away from philosophy and towards superstition. The average man could not be bothered with questions of ethics or science. In a social chaos, in which all material and moral currencies were unstable and all governments falling, he wanted to save his property, or if not his property, at least his life, or, failing that, at least his soul. Together with the decline of civilization came an immense increase of superstition. New religions poured in from the barbarians. Plato had taught that the soul was immortal, but people now could only understand that as an ἀνάστασις τῶν νεκρῶν, a 'rising-up of the dead bodies'. Heraclitus had taught men to seek the λόγος of God. Philo metaphorically personified the Λόγος, and so people took it for a man, and went about looking for him. People professing to be divine or to have received divine revelations walked the earth as freely as they do in India to-day. It is in many ways an extremely interesting social phenomenon, this half-blind, half-educated stirring of popular aspirations in the Hellenistic age. It is full of analogies to the present day, and of social difficulties like those which are puzzling us. It is the society out of which one of the greatest Greek writers, St. Paul, arose and from which he received much of his education. It sought passionately for escape, for salvation, for some heavenly light, for goodness; sometimes for magic powers, or for some catastrophic regeneration of society in which the poor would come out on top and the rich lie howling. It is well worth sympathetic study, but it did little for science or philosophy because it had ceased to put its confidence in research and reason; it sought always for spiritual comfort or profit and cared but little for the bare truth.

1934.

V

THE 'TRADITION', OR HANDING DOWN, OF GREEK LITERATURE

THE object of us Greek scholars is to find out all we can about ancient Greece and—still more important—to understand what we find. For the first part of this work we have various instruments. The inscribed stones, immense in numbers, which happen to have weathered the ages and come down to us in a legible condition. The surface of the earth and sea in Greek regions, which naturally has changed far less than the human institutions. The excavations of ancient sites which have at times revolutionized our picture of pre-Homeric and pre-Hellenic history. The inscribed coins which, by all kinds of strange fates, have been neither decomposed nor melted, but have turned up still more or less decipherable and charged with message. The fragments of papyri, pre-served by the accident of the Egyptian climate and other chances. These give us bits of letters and of books which may have been handled, if not by Plato, at least by Calli-machus or Didymus or Mark Antony, and have added enor-mously to our knowledge of the more intimate aspects of history, administrative, social, and economic. Lastly, the customs and rites and ways of life of various races of mankind still existing in a savage or primitive state, which throw light on the condition from which the Greeks emerged as they became Greeks, and which enable us to understand vast masses of ancient myth and custom which seemed meaningless before. One could enumerate other instruments too. But the fact remains that by far the greatest part of our knowledge of the ancient Greeks comes from the books which they wrote, and which have come down to us by a long process of handing-on from generation to generation: *traditio* is the Latin word, *paradosis* the Greek. That is to say: The books which we now possess are those which, for one reason or another, have been constantly copied and re-copied, and never allowed quietly to pass on to the natural end of books and men. It is not only that they were always considered worth reading by somebody; it is that somebody was always willing to take the great trouble of writing them out again. That process is the literary 'tradition', and it is that that I propose to discuss in the present paper.

I will first make some general comments on the characteristics of the literary tradition, as compared with our other sources of knowledge. I will then consider the main defects in the tradition as a process: I mean, the question how far the things that are preserved are preserved accurately; and lastly, the defects in the content of the tradition, that is, what important classes of books are not preserved at all, and for what reason.

First, then, the general characteristics. Obviously the literary tradition, where it exists, is much fuller, more intelligible, more explanatory, than our other sources of knowledge. This is almost too obvious to dwell upon. At the very beginning of Hicks's *Inscriptions* you find the bases of the pillars of the temple at Ephesus inscribed βα . . . Κρ . . . ἀνέθηκεν: and how interesting it is! But, without Herodotus, not only could the inscription never have been read; without Herodotus, it would not have been interesting if it had been read. Βα[σιλεὺς] Κρ[οῖσος] would have been nothing to us. Think again of the condition of our Cretan remains unaccompanied by literature. How rich they are, and how enigmatical! A story is there waiting to be told, but there is—so far at least—no literature to tell it. Think how all our knowledge would be trebled if Sir Arthur Evans had unearthed for us some fragment of a Minoan historian.

It is as a rule literature that explains; consequently it is to a large extent literature that gives interest. This, however, is not a question of literature as against archaeology; it is merely a question of art against that which is not art. The Hermes of Praxiteles does not wait for a literary text to explain or illuminate him. It is he who explains and illuminates an otherwise quite uninteresting text in Pausanias. But, in the main, as compared with the great mass of archaeological evidence, the literary remains are what we call art—that indescribable thing which aims at stirring our interest and sense of beauty. And this brings me to the second characteristic of literary tradition.

It is what we, in our rather stupid phraseology, call 'ideal' in character; that is, it is occupied with the καλόν more than the ἀναγκαῖον, with what you aspire to do rather than what you have got to do. Of course there are degrees. In the higher poetry, as in the higher art, τὸ καλόν has things all its own way. And the same in most philosophy. Whatever historical conclusions can be drawn from the *Agamemnon* or the *Symposium*, it is quite clear that Aeschylus and Plato were not chiefly concerned in depicting contemporary facts. They were chiefly concerned with thinking and expressing the highest thoughts in their power, whereas the man who inscribed the Erechtheum accounts held it ἀναγκαῖον to get the figures right—and did not bother about τὸ καλόν except for cutting his letters clearly.

What of history? According to some conceptions of history, τὸ ἀναγκαῖον would be absolutely paramount. 'The task of history is to investigate how things happened', according to Ranke's dictum. But, as a matter of fact, I do not see how there can be any doubt that the works of all ancient historians —Thucydides as much as any—are works of art. τὸ καλόν has an enormous sway over their minds. I do not wish to raise the question whether the search for beauty and the search for truth are irreconcilable, either ultimately or in ordinary practice. Thucydides, the most accurate and scientific of ancient historians, probably possesses also the most terrible emotional and artistic power. But I do suggest strongly that in all ancient literary history there is a great deal of selection and idealization, a striving for τὸ καλόν, which removes it from the sphere of mere recorded fact. Do you want an

example—a gross example? Take the fact that almost all
ancient historians, in their finished work, refuse to give documents and speeches in the authentic words, but rewrite
them deliberately in a way that will harmonize with the
style and tenor of their own work. Mr. Barber has con-
vincingly explained why the prose literature of the Hellenistic
age has almost entirely perished. It had not, or did not
seem to have, enough beauty to keep it alive.

Our ancient literature, then, gives on the whole far more
of the καλόν than the ἀναγκαῖον. That makes the record a
little one-sided, and explains the extraordinary interest which
we tend to take in those few books that belong to the other
tendency, which are not lofty, not idealized, and have the
touch of common life in them. That is why we are interested
in the tract of the Old Oligarch on 'The Constitution of
Athens' and his remarks about the lodginghouse-keeper's
vote and the cabman's vote. It is why we revel in the fragments of familiar history that can be extracted from Aristophanes (though, of course, Aristophanes pursued τὸ καλόν
like any other artist, only his καλόν took the comic form).
It is why we accept with gratitude the non-literary papyri
and even such a 'child of the mud' as Herondas. These
things help to complete our historical knowledge, and to
make it alive. On the other hand, the fact always remains
that they are valuable not for themselves, but only ἄλλου
ἕνεκα, 'for the sake of something else'; for the sake, ultimately,
of that very selected and idealized literature against which
they are in conscious revolt.

These two qualities, the full and explanatory character of
the literary tradition and its pursuit of τὸ καλόν, must be set
against one clear inferiority which belongs to it as compared
with archaeological evidence. It is richer, but it is less trustworthy. Coins and even inscriptions can be forged; but
where you do get a contemporary inscription or coin, the
information which it gives you is final. Even in points of
language it is the same. Most of our knowledge of Attic

forms comes from the manuscripts and the grammarians; but they are not final authorities. If they tell us to write *Troizên* and all the contemporary stones write *Trozên*, we know that the matter is settled. *Trozên* must be right.

So much for the general characteristics of the literature as against the other evidence. Let us now consider how far the *paradosis*, or *traditio*, of the literature has been an accurate process. We can consider first the comparative soundness or corruptness of our manuscript texts in the matter of mere wording, and secondly the larger changes of form which belong to what is called the higher criticism.

As to the corruption of manuscripts, one important fact has come out clearly during the last twenty years. It is that on the whole the handing-on of our classical texts from Alexandrian times to the present has been astonishingly exact. I am referring here to verbal accuracy, to accuracy in transmitting the actual *grammata* or written signs from manuscript to manuscript down to the twelfth or thirteenth century. The evidence is in the papyri and ostraka and a few fragments of very ancient manuscripts or palimpsests. Let us take instances. Our oldest regular manuscript of Plato was written in the year A.D. 895, say 1,250 years after Plato's death. In 1891 Flinders Petrie discovered a large papyrus fragment of the *Phaedo*, which was written in the third century B.C.—more than 1,000 years earlier, very likely in the lifetime of people who had seen Plato. Here was a test case for the accuracy of the *paradosis*. The papyrus might well have shown that our text of the *Phaedo* was a mass of mistakes or interpolations. As a matter of fact, the differences between the traditional text and the papyrus were almost negligible—in that particular case they affected chiefly the order of the words—and where they occurred, the papyrus seemed most often to be in the wrong.

Again, there are many fragments of Euripides preserved on papyri or ostraka. In the preface to the first volume of

my text of Euripides I mentioned fourteen, to which more
must now be added. Of course the passages so preserved are
mostly short. But the total of lines covered is very considerable. Now, how many places are there where the papyri
or ostraka give an absolutely new right reading? I mean, one
which is preserved in no manuscript and has not been reached
by conjecture? It seems extraordinary, but I believe there
are only two places—*Phoenissae* 1036 and 1101. And even
those two cases of failure are almost a testimony to the
general accuracy of the tradition. In the latter a papyrus
gives us ξυνῆψαν, 'they joined', instead of ξυνῆψεν, 'he joined';
and no one happened to have made that conjecture, although
they easily might, if they had studied the scholia, which
evidently imply a plural. In the former, 1036, there are two
short lines, ἰήιον βοάν, ἰήιον μέλος, where for metrical reasons
we need an iambus more in each line. They are ordinary
iambic dimeters. They mean, you see, 'the cry of Iê, the
music of Iê'—Iê being one of the regular cries of wailing.
People emended by doubling the words βοάν and μέλος. The
scholiast observed that 'It is found in the poets that way,
Iê Iê, just like Iô Iô.' Yet by some accident we never thought
of emending the line to ἰηιήιον βοάν, ἰηιήιον μέλος—'the cry
of iê-iê, the music of iê-iê'. Clearly that is what the scholiast
meant. And it so happens that one of the Oxyrhynchus
papyri gives it so. Of course that is right.

Let me take two more instances to show how steady the
tradition has been. From the study of our fourteenth-
century manuscript L, Wilamowitz came to the conclusion
that L's group of manuscripts was descended from an archetype which contained all the plays of Euripides, not merely
those selected for educational purposes, without any notes,
but with variant readings written above the line. When
Grenfell and Hunt discovered the *Hypsipylê* papyrus, it
proved to be a manuscript without notes but with variant
readings written above the line, and of course the *Hypsipylê*
is one of the unselected plays.

A last instance of the same steadiness. In *Phoenissae* 131—

τὸν δ' ἐξαμείβοντ' οὐχ ὁρᾷς Δίρκης ὕδωρ;

See you not him crossing Dirce's water?—

a Byzantine group of manuscripts add at the end of the line a gloss λοχαγόν—'see you not that captain?' A late Byzantine gloss, critics used to say. But on a certain very ill-written ostrakon in the British Museum, dating from the second century, you have the word λοχαγόν already there. It is a mistake; a mere gloss. But it was in the text by about A.D. 150, and has been religiously copied by a whole chain of scribes.

Of course *humanum est errare*. All manuscripts have lots of mistakes in them. What I am here comparing with the papyri is not the text of any particular manuscript but the text that results from the critical examination of all the manuscripts by a good scholar using his knowledge as best he can. When by criticism you succeed in finding out what the 'tradition' really is, that tradition proves to be surprisingly accurate.

But here comes an important qualification. This evidence of the papyri only takes us back, at earliest, to the Alexandrian age. From the second century B.C. onwards the tradition has been careful; but before those thousand years of care there had been some two hundred of carelessness. The great Alexandrian scholars were probably almost the first people in the world to understand the meaning of accuracy in preserving an ordinary secular text. Some of the papyri themselves show us how careless a pre-Alexandrian text could be. Our scholia to the tragedians show that the greatest of our difficulties and corruptions were as a rule already there when the commentaries were made. Again and again the critical editor has to make his footnote *corruptela iam Didymo antiquior*. And if it comes to that, general considerations of the history of Greek literature would have led us to the same conclusion. It is late in the day that a man turns from the

natural conception that his book ought to be as good and
full as possible, to the scholarly and self-denying conception
that it ought to be exactly as the writer left it.

By the time of the Alexandrians, when our tradition began,
manuscripts were often already badly corrupted. An instance
of what I mean can be found in some of the latest plays of
Euripides. Our text of the *Phoenissae* is probably nearly as
good as the text that was edited by Aristophanes of Byzantium. Yet the play that we have is, in the opinion of most
critics, a mass of interpolation. It was acted, no doubt,
again and again, in Athens and in less cultured places, during
the fourth and third centuries, and the only copy the
Alexandrians could get was one that had been exposed—like
most plays that have life in them—to the improvements and
additions of the stage-manager. The same is hardly less true
of the *Orestes*. The *Iphigenia in Aulis* happens to have some
of its history recorded, so we can speak of it with more
certainty. True, the archetype of our two manuscripts was
defective at the end. In that respect the Alexandrians were
better off. But for the rest of the play how does it stand?
We know that the *Iphigenia in Aulis* was produced and prepared for the stage by Euripides the younger after his father's
death. An inscription tells us that 'The *Iphigenia* of Euripides'
—very probably this play—was acted again in 341 B.C., and
that the actor Neoptolemus received a prize for it. Doubtless it was acted often. And the version that has come down
to us bears the natural traces of this history. It has two
distinct and scarcely compatible prologues. It has passages
written in a metrical convention differing from that of
classical tragedy and approaching that of the New Comedy.
Unfortunately we have no scholia to the *Iphigenia in Aulis*.
But we may be fairly sure that, when the Alexandrian
scholars set to work to collect the works of Euripides, the
only copy they could get of this famous play was one already
badly knocked about by the actors. As a matter of fact,
both the extant prologues are quoted by writers of the

generation after Aristotle. The mischief had begun as early as that. In the case of the *Rhesus*, there were actually three prologues going in Alexandrian times. The *Rhesus* question is too complicated to discuss at length. But it is clear that the Alexandrians could not get hold of an uncontaminated copy of either of these plays.

Again, what are we to make of such a fact as the comparative condition of the several Homeric hymns? The 'Hymn to Aphrodite' is excellently preserved; the 'Hymn to Apollo' is in a state of confusion. But the confusion is not such as comes from faulty manuscript tradition. It does not yield to criticism and emendation. It goes back to the time when the old epic literature was but newly extinct and its fragments were collected and formed into such wholes or attempts at wholes as circumstances allowed, probably by people who had as yet no particular sense of scholarship.

To sum up: In the cases where ancient books or parts of books have been preserved to us entire, and where our manuscripts are of good average quality, we find that the tradition, from Alexandrian times on, has been to a surprising degree careful and trustworthy. I leave aside, of course, special cases, such as bad or mutilated manuscripts; anthologies in which the quotations were modified in order to stand without their context; and the handbooks which have been systematically interpolated and improved by their owners.

Let us next consider the content of the tradition. That is, how much of what it tried to preserve has it actually preserved? Here we have a very different story.

Take first the kinds of literature of which we seem to have a large stock: *epos*, drama, oratory, and history. Epic perhaps belonged to very early times, so that it is not surprising that we have only two poems remaining out of a whole wide literature, and those—as far as I can judge—in a very late recension. Of lyric poetry, too, we may say that it flourished chiefly in non-Attic regions, whereas our tradition has its roots in Athens. So we ought not to complain if out of a large number of lyric poets the tradition has preserved complete poems by only one, and of him only about a fifth part of his whole writings. The papyri give us a few complete poems by another. As for tragedy, there must have been, as far as we can calculate, well over 900 tragedies produced in Athens; we feel ourselves rich with thirty-three out of that number. But that is a vague way of considering the question. Let us take two periods to compare with our own, and to make out how the great losses took place.

We have a fair amount of evidence about the books in the Alexandrian library: that should be one point. For another we may take the interesting *Bibliotheca* or *Μυριόβιβλον* of Photius. Photius was Patriarch of Constantinople from A.D. 857 to 879, and the *Bibliotheca* is a list, with notes and epitomes, of 280 books which he had had read to him. It is dedicated to 'his beloved brother Tarasius'. Apparently Photius was in the habit of having books read aloud in his learned circle, where Tarasius was usually present. This is a list of books which Tarasius missed during the absence of Photius himself on an embassy to the Assyrians—that is, as Gibbon says, to the Caliph of Bagdad.

To take some definite figures, comparing first merely the Alexandrians and ourselves and omitting Photius for the moment: Aeschylus wrote ninety plays; the Alexandrians possessed seventy-two of them; we have seven. Sophocles wrote 123; we do not know the Alexandrian number, but it must have been very large; we have seven. Euripides wrote ninety-two; Alexandria possessed seventy-eight; we have nineteen. Of Pindar, the Alexandrians possessed seventeen books; we have four, not complete, plus some fragmentary poems on papyri. Of Simonides they had a considerably larger number of books, though we cannot be sure of the figure; we have none. Of Alcman they had six, of Alcaeus at least ten, of Sappho nine. They had twenty-six books of Stesichorus; we have nothing but fragments. They had the books of Heraclitus, Empedocles, Parmenides, Anaxagoras. They had the splendid mass of Hellenistic prose: Chrysippus, Epicurus. They had Dicaearchus' *Life of Hellas*; they had the great scientific and imaginative works of Eratosthenes; they had the thirty books of Ephorus' universal history, the twelve books of Theopompus' *Hellenica* and the fifty-six of his *Philippica*. They had great shelvesful of Old and New Comedy, of elegy and romance. Of all this the tradition has brought us only fragments.

I have been considering only authors of the first rank of genius or importance. Even in that region our loss is overwhelming.

Now let us turn to Photius. It so happens that Photius, in the 280 books of the *Bibliotheca*, describes no poetry. It was not that he disapproved of it. He speaks with respect of various poets, and he epitomizes novels and romances with a fullness that suggests enthusiasm. Of course we must remember that the pronunciation of Greek had completely changed, and that the Byzantines, having lost the sense of quantity, and scanning only by accent, had lost all that gives melody and meaning to the forms of ancient verse. But I think we shall see later the real reason for Photius' neglect of poetry.

Of the writers we have just mentioned, the only one that comes in Photius' list is Theopompus. It is 176th in the list:

'Read, the historical books of Theopompus. Those preserved amount to fifty-three. Even some of the ancients said that the sixth and seventh and twenty-ninth and thirtieth had perished. And these I have not seen either. But a certain Mênophanes—an ancient and not contemptible person—in giving an account of Theopompus says that the twelfth had perished also. Yet we read it together with the others. The contents of the twelfth are as follows. . . .'

That is one big loss that has come to us since the time of Photius.

And there are others. We must remember that Photius

mostly read Christian Fathers, and that the writers of the
Roman period were for him among the ancients. He had
several of them in a more complete state than we have,
Diodorus for instance; but those do not affect our present
question. Of classical Greek writers he had read Herodotus
—without much appreciation. Also Ctesias, in twenty-four
books, twenty-three of *Persica* and one of *Indica*. These are
known to us only by Photius' epitome. His Ctesias seems to
have been a rare book, since he took special pains with it,
just as he did with that twelfth book of Theopompus. He
had also the *History of the Diadochi* and the celebrated
account of the Red Sea by the geographer Agatharchides:
he devotes forty columns to it. He had apparently the history
of the Alexandrian Kephalion. But much the greater bulk
of his ancient literature consists of Attic orators. He had the
sixty speeches of Antipho, twenty-five of them considered
spurious, where we have fifteen. Of Andocides, like us, he
had only four. Of Lysias, where we are perhaps almost
content with an imperfect thirty-four, he had apparently
425, of which 233 were considered spurious. (If that corpus
were ever rediscovered what opportunities it would give to
our historians!) Of Isaeus he had sixty-four, fifty of them
genuine; we have ten and a half. Of Isocrates he had sixty,
twenty-eight of them genuine; of Hypereides he had seventy-
seven, fifty-two of them genuine. And so on. We have
twenty-one speeches of Isocrates, and know Hypereides only
from the papyri.

Masses of prose oratory! A great part of it not specially
eloquent in its form, most of it—to Photius at least—unintelligible as to its matter. That is the chief treasure that
he finds in classical literature. If you count the columns that
he devotes to his abstracts of the various writers, they tell
the same tale. Herodotus is dismissed in about half a column.
Himerius' *Meletai*, or studies in the art of rhetoric, are
epitomized in sixty-eight columns. It is the usual phenomenon of late Greek literature, the absorption of all other

literary subjects in the all-engrossing study of rhetoric. It is the same tendency that has enriched us with the vast unreadable mass of the *Rhetores Graeci*.

What is the meaning and the historical cause of that tendency? For what reason did sane human beings preserve sixty-four speeches of Isaeus, and let Sappho and Alcaeus and nearly all Aeschylus, and even the easy and famous Menander, perish? People talk about certain alleged peculiarities and abnormal sensitivenesses of these late Greeks. But it is a pity to assume that human beings were very unlike ourselves merely because they did strange things. So often the strange things they did are just what we should have done under the same circumstances.

Greek antiquity from Alexander onward had before it a great duty, and a duty which it consciously realized. It had first to spread, and then to conserve, the highest civilization that mankind had reached. The task, as we all know, was too hard for it. From about the second century A.D. ancient learning and civilization are conducting not a triumphant progress but a stubbornly defended retreat. The very feeling of defeat perhaps sharpened men's devotion to the cause.

Hellenism was based on culture; and the great emblem and instrument of that culture was the Attic Greek language. We often sneer at the late Atticists for writing in an idiom which they did not speak. But they were doing the right thing. The spoken idiom of a Spartan peasant still differed from that of an Athenian; both would have difficulty in making themselves understood in Macedonia. But the language of Plato was studied and understood by cultured men from Gades to Cappadocia; and those who could write it had a common ideal and a common birthright. In Plutarch's dialogues men from the remotest places meet together at Delphi, a professor from Britain, a sophist from Sardes, a Roman official, a Boeotian country gentleman; all can speak the same language and respond to the same ideas.

You will say that such an artificial state of things could not last? But it did last. It provided the world with that extraordinary chain of historians writing all in practically the same language and each with a consciousness of his predecessors, down to Photius himself, down even to Eustathius and to people well on this side of the Norman Conquest.

On the other hand, to keep this instrument going, a slow and constant sacrifice had to be made. Part of the cargo was constantly thrown overboard in order to save the rest. Plutarch in the second century knew his ancient poets well. He knew Pindar in his full condition, before the selection that we possess came into existence. But a century or so after Plutarch nobody read these difficult poets. Julian, enthusiast for Hellas as he was, had read hardly any more ancient poetry than we ourselves. The men who were practically fighting for Hellenism during those centuries of tough decline had enough to do to keep alive the bare necessaries of culture. Knowledge of course was still spread chiefly by lectures and speeches and by reading aloud. Civilization itself depended on the art of speech—not on what we call rhetoric, but on what the ancients called *rhêtorikê*: the art of speaking clearly, persuasively, intelligibly, and of course correctly, so that you should in the first place expound your culture well to such auditors as would listen, and in the second place let them draw in from your lips the best possible imitation of the pure Attic spirit.

The thing that a man can use in his own life is, as a rule, the thing that attracts and interests him. That is why the late Greeks read Hypereides and Isaeus and the private speeches of Demosthenes in preference to Aeschylus and Alcman. It is why, when they did read tragedy, they vastly preferred Euripides to Aeschylus, though as a matter of fact, having no sense of drama left, they preferred to read him in extracts in an anthology. That is why our tradition has so ruthlessly left most of the old poets to perish.

But the retreat took another form also. Let me quote as

typical some sentences from the preface of the physician Oribasius to his *Epitome of Galen*:

'Your command, Most Divine Emperor, that I should reduce to a smaller compass the medical works of the admirable Galen, has found in me the readiest obedience. For people undertake this profession, as Galen himself says, who have neither the proper talents nor the proper age; often they have not even begun the simplest education (τὰ πρῶτα μαθήματα) and consequently cannot understand properly a systematic treatise (τοὺς κατὰ διέξοδον λόγους). What I am now about to write will suffice for them; it will take a shorter time to learn, and it will be easier to understand, for I undertake that my reduction of the style to conciseness will never result in obscurity.'

Oribasius addressed his book to Julian (A.D. 362). That is a typical date, though many literary subjects had been epitomized long before. The seven plays of Aeschylus were apparently selected about then; with the result that afterwards few read anything beyond the seven. The same with the seven of Sophocles, and the ten (or nine) of Euripides, though in the last case a large fragment of an old uncommented and unselected *Euripidis Opera Omnia* happens to have survived also. Afterwards these selections were reduced to three plays out of each tragedian. Four books out of the seventeen books of Pindar had been selected and fitted with a commentary rather earlier. The old elegiac poets seem to have been treated in a different and less satisfactory way at a much earlier date. A miscellaneous expurgated collection seems to have been made and passed current under the name of Theognis. There is no need to multiply instances. The principle is always the same. The text is selected from one of the old complete text editions; the commentary is abridged from the συγγράμματα and ὑπομνήματα of scholars of the great Roman period, from Didymus to Herodian.

The clue to the matter is education. The task of keeping up the culture of the world has become a hard burden. Few men are reading the classics freely, for the joy of the thing. The classics are for youths to learn in the schools and

universities, not because they like it, but because it is good
for them. What the cultured world really cares for—apart
from the maintenance of orthodoxy—is the maintenance of
Attic.

The predominance of education explains another fact
about late Greek literature. The educational profession is
one possessed of extraordinary virtues, compared with most
other professions; but it has its weaknesses too. And one
of them is an occasional tendency to pretend to knowledge
which it does not possess. Late Greek literature is full of
books which—though no doubt written innocently enough
—obtained long life and popularity because they enabled
teachers to make a great show of erudition. First of all, the
anthologies. Many excellent fourth-century writers throw
about with a free hand their quotations from ancient literature; but we find on examination that nearly all their quotations occur also in the anthologies of Stobaeus and Orion.
Again, think what a display could be made by anyone with
a good memory who had read Athenaeus! He would be
equipped with anecdotes and quotations from all the most
abstruse and curious parts of ancient literature. One strange
book which Photius read with much interest seems almost
to have been specially written for this particular fraudulent
purpose. It is the *Kainê Historiê* of a certain Ptolemaios,
Πτολεμαίου τοῦ Ἡφαιστίωνος—whatever exactly that geni-
tive means. For some people think he was the father, not the
son, of Hephaestion; and Tzetzes thinks he was Hephaestion
himself. Ptolemaios was a writer belonging to a very good
period, the second half of the first century A.D. The book,
known to us only from Photius, consisted of anecdotes from
extraordinarily abstruse sources—among them Helen's personal narrative of the course of the Trojan War—generally
professing either to give information about things no one
could know or else to contradict the ordinary received tradition. He may really have been an eccentric man of amazing
but uncritical erudition, but Hercher, who has studied him

critically, prefers the alternative of regarding him as an *unverschämter Schwindler*. The important point for us is that such a book should have lived on and been popular.

Education and the needs of education in a world where intellect is decaying and knowledge gradually growing less —these are the guiding conditions of the *paradosis*. And if we reflect for a few minutes on that fact, we shall reach a rather important and interesting conclusion.

Of what sort are the books that education specially produces and selects? We ought to know, though we must remember that we live in, or just after, an age when education has been enlightened and progressive and daring; in the centuries we are now considering, from the second to the ninth, education was in a state of slow decay; it was frightened, conservative, and unhopeful.

First, education selects the undoubted classics; not specially because anybody likes them but because everybody approves of them. They read Shakespeare at Amelia Sedley's school because it was right, though they doubtless left out a great part of him and did not much like what remained. Our Greek *paradosis* has duly preserved Homer and Plato, Demosthenes and a good deal of the canonical Attic writers. Doubtless it was actuated more by a sense of duty than by genuine taste; but in any case it clearly did right, and we ought to be thankful that it had a sense of duty. Secondly, education selects and produces handbooks and aids to knowledge. I need not dwell on the extent to which these bulk in our tradition. Thirdly, if it goes farther, if it goes beyond the indubitable classic and the mere text-book, it tends to choose what is correct, obvious, and sober. It avoids the kind of writing about which there tend to be very different opinions, which seems to one man inspired, and to another utterly silly. It avoids literature that has a special personal quality, it avoids the intensely imaginative, the enthusiastic, the rebellious. It is guided by the respectable educated man: it shuns the saint and the bohemian.

Suppose it had been a little otherwise. Suppose that as well as Aristotle's defence of slavery we had the writings of his opponents, the philosophers who maintained that slavery was contrary to nature. Suppose that, to compare with Plato's contemptuous references to the Orphics, we had some of that 'crowd of books' which he speaks of. Suppose instead of Philodemus we had all Heraclitus and Empedocles and the early Pythagoreans. Suppose we had Antisthenes and the first Cynics, the barefooted denouncers of sin and rejectors of civilization. Suppose we had that great monument of bitter eloquence and scorn of human greatness applied to history, the *Philippica* of Theopompus. Suppose we had the great democracy of the fifth century represented not by its opponents but by the philosophers who believed in it—by Protagoras, say, and Thrasymachus. Suppose that we had more of the women writers, Sappho above all and Corinna and Nossis and Leontion. Suppose we even had more literature like that startling lyric, Grenfell's Alexandrian Erotic fragment, in which the tragedy is, that between a man and a woman *Cypris* has taken the place of *philia*. 'It has been free choice in both. Friendship came before passion. Anguish seizes me when I remember.' (It is explained by Wilamowitz in the *Göttinger Nachrichten* for 1896.)

Had the conditions of the *paradosis* been different, all that might easily have happened, and our conception of Greek literature would have been fuller and more varied. The Byzantines had grave limitations for the work of *traditio*. But they had the wisdom and the humility to see what their duty was, and the constancy of mind to do it. They did preserve the old literature, though they could not understand its value. They believed it was beautiful even if they could not see the beauty. They believed it was full of wisdom and virtue and the search for truth and for some forgotten thing called freedom. And though they understood neither the drama, nor the poetry, nor the philosophy, nor even the history, they did at least copy letter by letter the great books which were destined, when they met with readers capable of comprehending them, to bring about the rebirth of civilization.

We understand these books not perfectly by any means, but better than the men of the Renaissance and far better than the Byzantines. We can begin to see the meaning of the philosophers, to reconstruct the setting of the historians, to appreciate the technique and the spirit of the great poets.

The incessant and loving labour of many centuries has at last handed on to us a seed of life, and a seed that has not yet borne its full fruit.

1913.

VI

HERACLES, 'THE BEST OF MEN'

WHEN Diogenes the Cynic, being then a rather unpleasant boy, wished to attend the lectures of Antisthenes and was asked his ultimate purpose in life, he replied Παραχαράττειν τὸ νόμισμα, 'To deface or restamp the coinage'. It was a criminal offence, and it happened to be the particular one for which Diogenes' disreputable father was at that moment in prison. Most sons would have avoided such a delicate subject, but not so Diogenes. He meant to deface all the images and superscriptions upon all the *nomismata*—the word of course means 'conventions' as well as 'coins'—because all the labels of the world are wrong. Above all, that which is called good, ἀγαθόν, is not good. In other forms of the story Diogenes is told by the Delphic Oracle to παραχαράττειν τὸ νόμισμα, and in Suidas the phrase is definitely attributed to the Oracle, not to Diogenes. At any rate Diogenes practised it, and left it as a heritage to the Cynics and some of the Stoics.

But long before the doctrine took this sharp and paradoxical form we can find the germ of it half-realized and struggling into existence. Greek is a language fond of antitheses, and there is no antithesis more common in all forms of writing than that between *logos* and *ergon*, the thing said and the thing done. It does not mostly denote intentional deceit, in which a man professes one thing and does another. It refers much more to a 'lie in the soul', or to the bewildering deceitfulness of the world itself, the habitual disappointment of human expectations and the way things have of, so to speak, not being themselves. Every *ergon* has its *logos*, every coin has its stamp and superscription, but so often the two do not fit. One can see this well in the celebrated passage of Thucydides[1] about the psychological effects of the prolonged war:

[1] iii. 82.

'The meaning of words had no longer the same relation to things but was changed in people's estimation. Unthinking recklessness (τόλμα ἀλόγιστος) was considered trusty courage (ἀνδρεία φιλέταιρος), prudent delay was specious cowardice, moderation was the pretence of a weakling, to be intelligent all round was to do nothing at each point. Frantic excitement was counted as part of man's duty. Sureness in planning was a plausible pretext for shirking. A man in a rage was always believed and anyone who opposed him suspected.'

After that the form of expression changes. Thucydides, as Mr. Cornford has pointed out, labours under the difficulty of having no properly formed technical language in which to express his philosophical ideas, though in this particular case it would perhaps not have helped him much. I suppose if we tried to express in modern language what Thucydides meant we should have to say that a kind of behaviour which used to be called τόλμα ἀλόγιστος and thereby stigmatized as bad was now called ἀνδρεία φιλέταιρος and thereby encouraged as good. With some of the other qualities the analysis would be different. With 'sureness in planning', for instance, it was not so much that the pains taken to make sure of something were in themselves objected to; it was that a man who acted carefully was suspected of having motives which he dared not avow, as in the French Revolution a man who did not get drunk was suspected of having something to conceal. Again, in saying that 'a man in a rage was always believed' Thucydides is not describing a change of nomenclature, but a change in the public state of mind—a change of the sort that has been observed since in times of revolution or war.[1]

[1] His meaning is also slightly obscured by the well-known confusion in Greek language, and consequently no doubt in Greek thought, between a quality and a reputation for a quality. If a man ὀφλισκάνει ζημίαν he simply 'incurs a penalty', but if he ὀφλισκάνει δειλίαν, he does not 'incur' or 'acquire' cowardice, he 'incurs the reputation of cowardice'. So when the educated women in *Medea* 218 δύσκλειαν ἐκτήσαντο καὶ ῥαθυμίαν, literally they 'acquired a bad name and laziness'; what they really did was to acquire a bad name and a reputation for laziness.

But one sees at the back of this chapter, not merely the writer's profound horror at the moral collapse of his world, but also a bewilderment at the difference between things and their names. Professor Werner Jaeger has made the very interesting suggestion that it was this sort of change in the meaning of words, and the moral bewilderment which was associated with it, that made Socrates insist so much on definition. If one could only make sure what τόλμα ἀλόγιστος really is, there would be no danger of confusing it with ἀνδρεία φιλέταιρος, which is evidently something quite different. The name would suit the thing, the superscription would really denote the coin, *logos* and *ergon* would correspond.

I wish to take some instances of this restamping, this laying bare of the difference between the superscription and the metal beneath, not from its conscious stage in post-Platonic Greek philosophy, but from its tentative and pre-conscious stage in fifth-century literature. I will begin with the conception of ἄριστος ἀνδρῶν, literally 'the best of men'. This proud position belonged traditionally to Heracles. 'Whom of all the sons of God would you call the Best Man?', asks a character in the *Clouds*.[1] 'I suppose there was never anyone better than Heracles', is the answer. So in the *Heracles* of Euripides:[2] 'Ask all Hellas who is the Best of Men; will they not answer Heracles?' So in the *Trachiniae*[3] we hear that Deianîra has slain πάντων ἄριστον ἄνδρα, 'the best man in all the world'. As a ground for this reputation the saga supplies a most abundant list of adventures and particularly of labours. I will not dwell upon them. The Heracles saga is one of the crudest of all Greek myths, the most savage in its conception of ἀρετή, goodness; and perhaps for that very reason it cried aloud for allegorizing interpretations and ended by being the most ideal and edifying of all. Without dogmatizing on a very large and obscure subject, we may notice that Heracles shares many of the attributes

[1] 1049.   [2] 183.   [3] 811.

of what Dr. Jane Harrison called 'the Eniautos daimon' or
Year Spirit, and some French scholars 'Le Renouveau', or
renewal of life, which comes with the new sun and the new
year. He is, as usual, the son of a god and a mortal woman.
He was worshipped by the Pythagoreans as ἡ δύναμις τῆς
φύσεως (the power of nature or growth); he carries a horn of
plenty and a club which was once a green bough. He is
burned each year, but reborn. He is both Ἥρως and Θεός,
a dead man and a living god.[1] His *Eidôlon* is seen in Hades,[2]
though he himself is among the immortals and wedded to
Hêbê, eternal youth. (An *Eidôlon* of him was burned each
year on Mt. Oeta; so the thing that was destroyed and went
to Hades was evidently that *Eidôlon*, not Heracles himself.)
He has other marks of year-gods; his death is due after
twelve months, or after 'the twelfth harvest', he is apt to
have children in sets of fifty, like the cattle of the sun, and
so on. But these marks are common to a very large set of
divine beings; what is more specially characteristic of Heracles
is, I think, that he seems to have been the hero of a subject
peasant population in a low state of culture. His weapons
are either bare arms, or the primitive club, or—also primitive
—poisoned arrows. His feats are like the feats of a very
strong peasant. He always works for a master. He fights a
bull, a boar, a deer, a lion, a water-snake, he drains a marsh
and cleans some impossibly dirty stables. There is often a
humorous touch about the stories. He is set to plough and
does the work well, but getting hungry at midday he eats
the ox. His master is frightened of him. From time to time
he smashes things or kills persons unintentionally by his
unmanageable strength; he performs prodigies of eating,
prodigies of drinking, prodigies still wilder in the exercise of
other appetites. The most varied contests are set before
him, and he is always the conqueror, Καλλίνικος. It is
because he is always καλλίνικος that he is ἄριστος ἀνδρῶν; he

[1] Hdt. ii. 44; Pind. *Nem.* 3. 23; Paus. ii. 10. 1 on the cult in Sicyon.
[2] *Odyssey*, xi. 602.

has proved himself best by beating all competitors in fighting, shooting, wrestling, eating, drinking, and other primitive rustic contests. We should observe also that because he is καλλίνικος he is essentially κωμικός—not comic; that would be γελοῖος; but a natural addict to the κῶμος or revel which distinguished a victor in the games. Observe, he is not a warrior. The armies attached to him in Apollodorus do not fit the picture; they are as incongruous as the masses of inconsistent armour which are piled on to the lonely wanderer in Hesiod's *Aspis*; greaves, breastplate, helmet, spears, chariot, and Mycenean shield as well as the bow and club. The only possible rival to Heracles as ἄριστος ἀνδρῶν in the poetic tradition was really a warrior; I mean Achilles. Achilles was ἄριστος Ἀχαιῶν, he was the best in war, the most fierce and formidable in character, the fleetest of foot, and the most beautiful. But Achilles as a type of ἀρετή did not have much success. Even in Homer, the author of our text has to correct him. The poet expressly condemns his treatment of Hector as κακόν and ἀεικές, and often puts the main sympathy of the audience on the side of Hector. In fact it is only by his passionate repentance that Achilles is made to earn our forgiveness. In the fifth and fourth centuries, when ἀρετή was becoming identified with δικαιοσύνη, εὐσέβεια, σωφροσύνη,[1] or the other qualities needed in a citizen, Achilles drops out of the running. Plato in the third book of the *Republic* has a sweeping condemnation of his dragging Hector round the tomb of Patroclus, his sacrifice of the captives, his 'qualities of meanness and avarice combined with an overweening contempt for gods and men'. Not till the fall of Greek civic life did Achilles re-emerge as the ideal of Alexander the young *Kallinikos*.

Heracles utterly outlasted him. It is the very fact that he was not a warrior that opened the way for his ultimate idealization in post-classical times, helped out by the fact

---

[1] Justice, Piety, Temperance. Cf. Aesch. *Theb.* 610, σώφρων δίκαιος ἀγαθὸς εὐσεβὴς ἀνήρ.

that he is not a citizen either. He did not merely slay enemies or sack towns: he did not get mixed up in the worldly and narrow issues of political life. He remained unspotted by the world and just performed great deeds, daring and suffering in the service of his village, of Hellas, of humanity; he 'made the earth gentle'—ἐξημέρωσε γαῖαν; he became ultimately the great saviour, the hero-philan-thropist, which Achilles never thought of doing. Yet, naturally enough, one of the first steps in raising him in the social scale was to give him hoplite armour and make him a Dorian warrior, the ancestor of the Spartan kings.

The obvious hypothesis, which I see no special reason to reject, is that when the invading Dorians claimed to be sons of Heracles returning to the Peloponnese, they were justify-ing their usurpation by a pretence of the usual sort. Heracles was the great aboriginal hero, doubtless resembling in various ways some Dorian object of worship. So the invaders said they were his exiled children returning to claim their own. Hence, Heracles becomes typically the ancestor of the Dorians, and in his first promotion upward is made, awkwardly enough, a sort of ideal Spartan—*der echte dorische Mann*, as Wilamo-witz puts it. This seems to have been the role he is made to assume in the various *Heracleae*, or epics about Heracles, but I doubt if the character ever suited him. He was at first much too boisterous and plebeian and jolly; afterwards too much the votary of moral virtue labouring for the deliverance of the world; always too personal and too unmilitary. In Athens he seems to have been frequently a hero of comedy, a roistering strong man, much at home in the *kômos* or revel. The satyr-play—where of course he was a favourite figure—suited him perhaps even better. There was just a touch of the truly heroic in this hero of the revel who was not only κωμικός but also ἀθλητής, also καλλίνικος. We see it clearly enough in the *Alcestis*.

Let us spend a few moments on the *Heracles* of Euripides before entering on our main subject. Euripides brought

Heracles first into the pro-satyric tragedy *Alcestis*, and later, encouraged by that success, raised him into tragedy itself and tragedy at its loftiest. I do not mean that I consider the *Heracles* of Euripides to be a very great work of art. I do not. It is broken-backed; it has too much conventional rhetoric; but for sheer loftiness of tragic tone the last act, after Heracles awakes from the trance in which he has murdered his children, will stand beside anything in ancient drama. Thus we have in Euripides' play definitely an idealized Heracles, an ἄριστος ἀνδρῶν whom even civilized fifth-century Athenians can accept. The lust, the greediness, the drunkenness, the undirected violence, have all disappeared. There is not a hint that Heracles was other than a thoroughly good husband and father. His murder of his children is made definitely the result of an external and supernatural agency, the malice of an evil goddess against an innocent man. Heracles is an ideal figure.

The most one can say against his character in Euripides' play is this. When a writer of fiction wishes to make a character go mad or change his nature he has obviously a choice before him, a choice between contrast and preparation. Suppose, as here, it is a case of violent homicidal rage, produced by some external accident, he can get an effect by making the victim in his normal state a particularly gentle and reasonable person who is utterly transformed. (There is a good story by Mr. Wells on those lines, about a quiet hen-pecked husband who is transformed by accidentally eating a highly stimulating fungus.) Or he can equally get an effect by showing certain slight tendencies in the normal man which blaze out into excess in the new conditions. It is clear that Euripides in his treatment of Heracles follows the second method and not the first. Heracles is a warm-hearted and passionate fighter who goes mad passionately and pugnaciously. The pretensions of Theseus are more modest, but he makes an excellent foil by showing equal generosity and courage, together with perfect *Sôphrosynê*. Both are, in their different ways, ideal heroes: Theseus a citizen-king and Heracles pre-civic.

Thus Euripides took the Heracles of tradition, purified him of his grosser qualities, idealized him as a type of ἀρετή, a hero labouring under the yoke of a bad master and the frown of malignant gods to do great deeds and make the earth habitable for man. I am not sure whether this can be called παραχάραξις, but there is a change of moral estimates behind it. It is rather a heightening of the existing χαρακτήρ with some vigorous expurgation of the saga material.

Wilamowitz used to think it probable, though of course not certain, that Sophocles had seen the *Heracles* of Euripides and wrote the *Trachiniae* afterwards. Mr. Earp's researches tend to reverse the chronology. But whatever the dates, the relation of the two poets to one another is almost exactly the reverse here of what it is in the two *Electras*, and indeed to what it usually is in their other writings. There Sophocles gives a heroic or Homeric treatment to the Orestes story; Euripides reduces it to false gods and morbid psychology. Here Euripides has taken a traditional heroic figure, expurgated its grosser side and idealized its higher; he has also—curiously enough—made the hero kill his wife without telling us a word about the wife's point of view. Sophocles has taken the same heroic figure, accepted by certain traditional standards as ἄριστος ἀνδρῶν, but has emphasized the utter savagery and brutality of those standards, and—most surprising of all—has shown us the whole miserable story through the eyes of one woman, and presumably the one who suffered most. He has indeed defaced and restamped the accepted coin.

Let us take first the relevant parts of the Heracles saga in as canonical a form as we can find, and then consider Sophocles' attempt to alter the stamp upon it. It would be best of course to find the *logos* as it was in Sophocles' own time, before he had dealt with it; but since that would involve much uncertain speculation about 'suspected passages' in Homer and fragments of Hesiod, Archilochus, Panyassis, and Bacchylides, we must content ourselves with the story in Apollodorus, which is deeply affected by Sophocles' own work, but still keeps in the main its traditional character, modified by a steady conventional whitewashing.

'After the Labours and after killing his children, Heracles returned to Thebes, gave Megara to Iolaüs, and wishing for a wife himself heard that Eurytus, prince of Oechalia, had proclaimed the hand of his daughter Iolê as a prize for any who could beat him and his sons in archery. He went to Oechalia and did beat them in archery, but did not receive his bride. Iphitus, the elder of the sons, urged that Iolê should be given him, but Eurytus and the others refused. Soon afterwards cattle were stolen from Euboea by Autolycus, and Eurytus suspected that Heracles was the robber. Iphitus did not think so, and came to Heracles . . . asking him to help search for the cattle. Heracles agreed, and gave Iphitus hospitality, but, in a second fit of madness, threw him over the walls of Tiryns.'[1]

Later on we are told:

'Coming to Calydon Heracles wooed the daughter of Oineus, Deianîra, and wrestled for her hand with the River Acheloüs who wore the shape of a bull. . . . So he won Deianîra.'

Later on he has to go to Trachis to be purified of a man-slaying.

'Taking Deianîra he came to the river Euênos, where Nessus the Centaur regularly carried travellers across the ferry for hire. . . . Heracles crossed the river by himself, and entrusted Deianîra to Nessus, who attempted to do violence to her in the midst of the passage. Heracles heard her cry, and shot Nessus to the heart as he reached land. He, feeling death approach, called Deianîra to him and bade her, if she wished to have a charm to make sure of Heracles' love, to make a certain mixture out of the blood which flowed from the wound made by the arrow. Which she did, and kept the charm by her.[2]

Later: 'When he came to Trachis he collected an army

---

[1] ii. 127–9.   [2] ii. 152.

against Oechalia in order to punish Eurytus.' He took the city, plundered it, and led off Iolê as a captive. He determined to set up an altar to Zeus, at Cape Kênaion, and 'sent Lichas the herald to Trachis to fetch festive apparel. From him Deianîra heard about Iolê, and believing that the blood from the wound of Nessos was really a love-charm, smeared the robe with it.' The rest is directly abbreviated from the play. The robe proved to be charged with a burning poison. Heracles hurled Lichas into the sea. Deianîra committed suicide. Heracles ordered his son Hyllus to take Iolê to wife. Then, with a slight difference,

'He climbed Mt. Oitê, built a pyre, mounted it, and ordered that fire be set to it. No one was willing to do this till Poias, father of Philoctêtês, passing by in quest of some lost sheep, consented to do it. To him Heracles bequeathed his bow and arrows. It is said that, as the pyre burned, a solid cloud formed, together with thunder, and carried him to heaven. There he received the gift of immortality, was reconciled to Hêra, and wedded her daughter Hêbê (Youth).'

So much for the bare story. The clue to Sophocles' treatment of it in the *Trachiniae* is best given in the lyrical passage 505–25, describing the wooing of Deianîra by Achelôüs and Heracles, the gentle and bewildered prize fought for by monstrous creatures mad with lust.

'When this bride was to be won, what far-reaching arms spread out to possess her, what beings went forth to that ordeal of battle, blows everywhere and everwhere blinding dust? Here the strength of a river, towering horns, crashing hooves, and a vision of a bull, 'tis Achelôüs from Oiniadae; and there the Zeus-begotten from Bacchic Thebes, bent bow and spear and club sweeping the air; crashing they met together, mad for a bride, and none save the couchèd Cyprian was near, holding her wand above them.
'Thud of fists and rush of arrows and crash of wild-bull horns in confusion; close-wound grapples and deadly shocks of brow on brow and groaning from both: while a girl tender and sweet-faced sate on the side of a wide-looking hill, awaiting the master that should be hers. (I speak as one that hath borne a child.) The bride's face for which

they rage waits piteous-eyed for the end; and suddenly she is gone
from her mother, like a lamb left alone.'

I need add nothing to make that picture clearer, but we
may notice Deianîra's own story of the wooing as told in
the Prologue: 'I had of marriage such an agony of fear as no
maid in Aetolia besides. My wooer was a river, Achelôüs.'
She describes the strange forms in which he seemed to come,
bull, snake, mixed monster, with water streaming from his
shadowy beard.

'With the fear of such a suitor before my eyes I was always praying
that I might die ere I was drawn into a bed like that. At last, in
answer to my longing, came the great son of Zeus and Alcmena, who
closed with him in battle and delivered me. The manner of that
struggle I cannot tell; for I know it not; if there be any who dared to
look without terror on what he saw, such an one might speak; I sate
there stunned with fear, that my beauty would in the end bring me
misery. At last the God of Battles ordained well—if indeed it was
well—and I was the chosen bride of Heracles.'

I will call attention briefly to four points, all perhaps
sufficiently obvious. First, river-lovers are not always like
this, monstrous and terrible. Think of Enipeus and Tyro in
the eleventh book of the *Odyssey*: how Tyro went to meet
her lover, and the beautiful great wave 'stood up around
them like a mountain, and hid the god and the mortal
woman'. Think of the wooing of Strymon and the Muse in
the *Rhesus*, when

> Her arms went wide to the wild sweet water
> And the love of the river around her rang.

Second: observe how misty and dreamlike the battle is; the
half-seen monster, the φάσμα ταύρου, the blinding dust, and
the one watcher unable for very terror to see clearly. There
is the same dream-like effect of horror unseen, or not quite
seen, elsewhere in the play; e.g. where Heracles in his
torment rages ἐκ προσέδρου λιγνύος, dimly seen 'through the
smoke that clung about him'. Thirdly, Heracles brought

deliverance from the more obvious horror, but was it really deliverance? Or was it only monster against monster, both raging in lust, ἱέμενοι λεχέων, for a prize too gentle and innocent for either? She has married her hero, and has had since then, as she explains to the Chorus, no day or night free from fear.[1]

That refers to her happy days, before the tragedy begins. For the later time we must follow the outline of the story, and see where Sophocles has laid his emphasis.

Heracles has been lost for a year and three months. A messenger brings news of his safety and his great victory. The household breaks into a paean of triumph, in the middle of which the herald, Lichas, arrives, leading a procession of broken-hearted women. Heracles has sacked the city of Eurytus and brought these captives. 'These . . .', says Deianîra, 'in God's name who are they? They are pitiful!' And there they stand, in all their misery, before our eyes, while Lichas tells his story. It seems that Heracles had gone more than a year ago to stay with Eurytus; had had angry words with him; and at last, being drunk, had been thrown out of the house. In revenge for this he waited for a chance and treacherously murdered Eurytus' son, Iphitus. Since this was not a fair fight but a 'slaying by craft', Zeus was wroth with Heracles and condemned him to a year of servitude to a barbarian queen. Heracles, unable to avenge himself on Zeus, swore to do so on Eurytus (whose only fault was that Heracles had murdered his son), and when his year was over destroyed him and all his city.

Is it merely the barbaric story of a rude age—or is this something rather different? In other words, is Sophocles emphasizing the horror of it, or merely accepting it as natural? The answer is not difficult. First, he has kept the miserable train of women captives before our eyes through the whole scene, which no dramatist would ever do unless he intended us to feel their misery. And, lest we should

[1] 29 ff.

possibly fail to appreciate it even so, he makes Deianîra
speak:[1]

'An awful pity hath come into my heart, friends, seeing these
unhappy beings, homeless and fatherless, wanderers on a strange land.
Once the daughters of free men, belike, and now they have the life
of slaves! O God of Battles, never may I see thee move thus against
any child of mine: or, if it must be, be it not while I live! Such dread
I have when I look at them. (*Speaking to one*) Poor child, and who art
thou among women? Unmated or a mother? By thine aspect thou
art innocent of all such things, a maiden of noble race.—Lichas,
whose daughter is this stranger?'

Lichas professes not to know. He never thought of asking.
It only comes out that she has never spoken, and never
ceased weeping, 'since she left her home swept through by
the wind—ἐξ ὅτου πάτραν διήνεμον λέλοιπεν'.

It is clear where Sophocles has laid his emphasis. It is
not so much, in Sir Richard Jebb's words, that he 'has missed
a chance of winning our full sympathy for his hero'; he is
deliberately making us feel pity for his victims and something
like horror at him. Was this monstrous being, this τέρας,
much improvement on Achelôüs after all?

But there is more coming. It turns out that Lichas has
been lying. The extremely discreditable story we have heard
so far has been garbled in the interests of Heracles. The
truth was that Heracles fell in love with this daughter of
Eurytus—the one to whom Deianîra had spoken—demanded
to have her as a secret concubine (κρύφιον λέχος), and, when
her father would not consent to this dishonour, killed him,
ravished the princess, and sacked all his city. Deianîra in
a beautiful speech gets the whole truth from Lichas:[2]

'She to whom you speak is not a coward, nor ignorant of the human
heart, how it takes not always pleasure in the same thing. . . . It is
folly to stand up to fight, front to front, against Love. He does what
he will even with the gods. He has done it with me, and why not
with another woman like me? I should be utterly mad if I blamed

[1] 298.   [2] 438.

my husband, caught by this affliction, or this woman either. Hath not Heracles possessed other women ere now, aye, more than any living man, and not one of them hath had harsh word or taunt from me; nor shall this girl, though her whole being be melted in her love. I pitied her as soon as I saw her because her beauty hath wrecked her life, and all innocent she hath brought her fatherland to wreck and slavery.'

The story confirmed, she is true to her promise to seek no harm to Iolê, but she thinks of the *philtron* or love-charm left to her by the dying centaur. It is worth noticing that she dislikes the thought of using a *philtron* at all: such things are not for clean women like her, but under extreme stress she agrees to try it . . . unless indeed her women think it wrong. If they do she will not use it. They approve, and she proceeds with her plan. It is characteristic of her innocent nature that she never thought of doubting the word of the dying centaur. He had professed to love her, and she took the gift of the charm to be a sign of his love and his wish to atone for his violence. She prepares the *philtron*, anoints the robe with it, and sends it to Heracles. But, Lichas asks, is there no message that she would like to send? Yes, one message.[1] 'Thou hast seen my greeting to the strange damsel, that I welcomed her kindly?' 'Yes,' answers Lichas, 'my heart was filled with joy and wonder at the sight.' 'Then what is there more to say? I am afraid to send word how much I want him. He may not want me.'

We have not quite finished with Deianîra, but must turn for the moment to him to whom this timid and tender greeting has been sent, the ἄριστος ἀνδρῶν, the man or τέρας. Deianîra has already discovered that the *philtron* was not what it seemed, before the time that her son Hyllus comes from Heracles to tell his mother that she is a murderess. He tells of the sacrifice offered by Heracles in his new shining robe—such a sacrifice! Twelve bulls in the first place, but a hundred beasts killed in all, and all slaughtered handsomely

[1] 627-32.

by his own hand! Presently the poison begins to bite his flesh. He roars for the herald Lichas. 'Where did he bring that robe from? What is it?' As he stammers his answer, Heracles has a spasm of pain, and immediately seizes Lichas by the foot, swings him round his head, and dashes his brains out on the rocks below. A cry arose from the people, but no one dared to come near Heracles. He was leaping and flinging himself to the ground, shrieking and cursing till the rocks rang. ἀμφὶ δ' ἐκτύπουν πέτραι | Λοκρῶν τ' ὄρειοι πρῶνες Εὐβοίας τ' ἄκραι.

Above all he was cursing his wife. At last he bade Hyllus lay him on a bier and bring him home to Trachis. So far Hyllus. Deianîra has listened; she knows it all. There is nothing to be said and nothing now matters. Without a word she creeps into the house, with her son's curse echoing after her. We hear presently how she has died, as a hero's wife should, with a sword driven unshrinkingly into her heart.

Then we see approaching a strange, wild-looking escort— ξένων γὰρ ἐξόμιλος ἥδε τις βάσις—suitable for a τέρας rather than a real man, and Heracles, whom we have heard so much talked about but never seen, is borne in sleeping. Shall we now know him better? Is there really some greatness, some generosity, behind the ravenous lust and fury which is all that others have seen in him? Is there something in the Son of Zeus, the ἄριστος ἀνδρῶν, which when we come near it we can recognize as divine? Quite the reverse. He is more horrible when seen close. As soon as he wakes he is all rage and cursing, against his pain, against his frightened bearers, above all against Deianîra. He cannot move, but calls to Hyllus: 'Bring forth your mother and give her into my hands. Let me see which sight grieves you most, this pain of mine or her mangled beauty, torn limb from limb as she deserves.'[1] He curses himself for weeping: he has never wept before. He goes through all the labours and triumphs that

[1] 1069.

he wrought when he was strong; now he is as nothing: he
has only just enough strength to deal with that woman. Let
them only give her into his hands! It is interesting to notice
that Cicero, who translates this speech in the *Tusculans*,
discreetly expurgates these outbursts of cruelty.[1]

Hyllus, with great difficulty, gets the furious creature to
listen, and tells him the facts, Deianîra's knowledge about
Iolê, her mistake about the love-charm, and her death. Will
the man even now show some touch of sympathy, of com-
punction? Not a touch. It is almost incredible, but he does
not say a single word about Deianîra, nor apparently give
her a single thought. As soon as he hears that the poison
comes from the dead Nessus, he recognizes, through remembrance of an oracle which said that 'no living man'
should slay him, that his death is at hand. He is now slain
through the act of one long dead. He turns upon Hyllus
with two monstrous commands: 'First, set me on a pyre and
burn me to death; next, make Iolê your wife.' Hyllus' whole
nature rebels against both; but instantly Heracles is ready
with his everlasting curse, and Hyllus yields, though he will
not touch the pyre with his own hand. So be it. 'Lift him,
ye followers', says Hyllus in the final speech of the play,
'Grant me a great forgiveness, and mark in the gods a great
cruelty, in all these deeds that are being done. They beget
us, they are called our fathers; and they look down on agonies
such as this. None has knowledge of That Which Shall Be,
but That Which Is is fraught with pity for man and shame
upon the gods; and pain beyond compare to him who still
lives to bear the burden of this blind wrong' (I think he
means himself). The Chorus follow him with a last word to
the still silent Iolê: 'Thou too, damsel, come and stay not at
the house. Thou hast seen death in shapes great and strange;
thou hast seen wounds manifold and of strange anguish. And
behold, in all this there is nothing that is not Zeus!'

What does it mean? one asks: is this Sophocles the εὔκολος,

---

[1] *Tusc.* ii. 8. 9.

R

who is generally contrasted with the other tragedians as
being the gentle and contented artist untroubled by the
riddles of the rebellious intellect? Has there often been a
more extreme and poignant statement of the oldest and
most piteous side of the woman's cause—the cause not of
the woman who is superior, or intellectual, or advanced, or
anything but womanly in the last degree, tender, chaste,
devoted, living for others, and therefore the more battered
and broken amid the lusts of a brutish world? Has there
often been a more horrible representation of the type that
throughout all ages has been by a large number of people
held to be ἄριστος ἀνδρῶν—the all-admired grabber, smiter,
and conqueror, who is stronger, harder, greedier than other
men? And it is Sophocles the pious, not Euripides the
blasphemer, who finishes his play with this direct arraign-
ment of the gods and of Zeus himself.

My general answer would be that Euripides gets to his
results by an intellectual process. Sophocles, when he gets
there at all, gets there by feeling; Euripides' thought is
conscious and explicit; it often takes the form of argument.
Sophocles' feeling is subconscious and overflows. Consequently it has a sort of dumbness and unexpectedness
which makes it the more terrible.

The meaning of the last speech of Hyllus seems fairly clear.
It has many parallels in Euripides. If we watch seriously the
doings and farings of the world we do see the tender things
of life trampled down by the brutal; we see infinite mistakes,
and we cannot but feel a large pity for mankind in all the
evil that man suffers and inflicts and regrets. And further—
if we regard the non-human part of the universe as definitely
the work of conscious, reasoning, anthropomorphic beings,
such as the Greek gods—we must, if we give them human
qualities at all, attribute to them an appalling cruelty.

Similarly in the last line, κοὐδὲν τούτων ὅτι μὴ Ζεύς, the
meaning is, I suppose, that if among the many inadequate
interpretations of the physical non-human world which man

has at various times suggested, we accept the conception, common both now and all through antiquity, that it all represents the workings of an anthropomorphic will or purpose like our own and actuated by the same kinds of motive, then the evil is the work of that will as well as the good. It is a problem that often recurs in Greek philosophy.

But it was not my purpose to try to analyse either Sophocles' view of life as a whole or the particular state of mind which he tried to express in this remarkable play. I took the *Trachiniae* as a rather unexpected example in early Greek literature of this change in the conception of ἀρετή and this process which I have called—I hope not too pedantically—*paracharaxis*, a defacing or restamping of the coinage. The badness of the metal is brought to light, and after that the image and superscription must be changed.

In later Greece Heracles was particularly subject to *paracharaxis*: he was the typical hero, the most famous, the most popular. He was labelled ἄριστος ἀνδρῶν, the Best of Men, and he changed as the idea of goodness changed. We remember that when Horace spoke of the *Justum et tenacem propositi virum*, the man whom *Si fractus illabatur orbis impavidum ferient ruinae*, he thought at once of Hercules and Pollux, who by that form of virtue were raised to Heaven. Horace had learnt the doctrine, directly or indirectly, from Aristotle's *Hymn to Virtue*, in which we hear that Heracles and the Dioscuri were inspired to all their labours by the thirst for Aretê.[1] What kind of *Aretê* was most admired by the Stoics we can see from Seneca's description of the ἄριστος ἀνδρῶν: 'Hercules conquered nothing for himself. He traversed the world not desiring but judging what things to conquer; enemy of evil, champion of good, bringer of peace to land and sea.' He was the saviour, who toiled and suffered for mankind. The unedifying parts of the tradition are set aside. The philosopher Epictetus is much bolder. Without losing his hold on edification, he accepts freely a

---

[1] Hor. *Odes*, iii. 3; Aristot., Hymn in Ath. xv 695A; Seneca, *Ben.* i. 13. 3.

large dose of the real old unexpurgated myths. He first explains how Heracles 'traversed the world seeking out cases of Oppression and Good Citizenship (*Hubris* and *Eunomia*), casting out the one and establishing the other'; and then proceeds, 'He was at home everywhere. He had friends in Thebes, in Argos, in Athens, in all his wanderings; nay he had wives wherever it appeared opportune. He had children, and abandoned his children without a tear or a regret or a thought that they were left fatherless. For he knew that no man is fatherless; there is a Father who cares for every man unremittingly and always.'

Other allegorists wander away into physical explanations in which Heracles represents Time or the Sun; religious or philosophical explanations in which he possesses mystical revelations or wins all his victories by means of philosophy.[1] He destroyed the boar—that is, the swinish element in man; the lion—that is, the element of anger; he put to flight the Cerynean deer—that is, he drove the element of fear out of human life; and the Stymphalian birds—that is, the winged hopes which feed our folly.

Perhaps the passage that best illustrates the general prevalence of this kind of wholesale *paracharaxis* or restamping is the one brief entry in 'Suidas'. An encyclopaedia mostly represents orthodox views:

'Heracles. The son of Alcmena. History reveals him as a philosopher and depicts him wearing a lion-skin, carrying a club and holding three apples.' (He means the Apples of the Hesperides.) 'The myth relates that he got the three apples by slaying the dragon with his club: i.e. by conquering the serpent-like reasoning of evil desire by the club of philosophy, clothed in meditation as in a lion-skin. And thus, having slain with his club the serpent of desire, he took the three apples, i.e. the three virtues—Not to be angry, Not to love riches, Not to love pleasure. By means of the club of philosophy and the lion-skin of bold and temperate reason he conquered the poison of evil desire and practised philosophy until death.'

[1] Epict. iii. 24. 13–16; cf. Pauly–Wissowa, *Suppl.* iii. col. 1104.

It is marvellous what man will do to transform his tradition as long as he is not asked to give it up. The *paracharaxis* is obvious. The primitive strong man is simply turned into a Stoic saint. The label is kept and the content altered. But I think it is fairly clear that quite a different *paracharaxis* was at work on the Heracles of the *Trachiniae*: a change nearer to the original, more rebellious, more subtle, and forming a deeper criticism of life. The late allegorist made straight for edification as the crow flies; he did not as a rule attempt to study the saga in itself. Sophocles studies the saga, tests it, and finds it evil, and shows how the false ideal which it represents really works in human life. The hero himself is left, his exploits are left; all the content, so to speak, is left as it was; but the stamp or superscription is shown not to fit. The ἄριστος ἀνδρῶν of conventional tradition comes out as something monstrous, something which cannot be called 'good'; the son of Zeus is not above human standards, but below; a son, one might almost say, worthy of that inscrutable being who is responsible for all the misery and chaos of the world. The focus of our sympathy and admiration, the one thing stamped as true gold, is the hitherto unregarded Deianira.

We know a good deal about the fifth-century conceptions of Heracles. He was a butt of comedy, with peasant characteristics, and a half-hero in satyr-play, true; but he had long been a hero of *epos* also. Hesiod, Archilochus, Pîsander, Pîsinoüs, Panyassis, had all celebrated him: he had made his way into the Homeric poems: he was glorified by Pindar and Bacchylides. It seems possible that Euripides had already introduced him to the tragic stage as a hero of the higher type, a hero not perfect, but entirely sympathetic to the audience. Doubtless at the heart of every saga there lies the germ of one essential tragedy: Euripides saw one possible tragedy, not very true to experience or penetrating as a criticism of life, not really the essential gist of the saga itself, though a moving story told with much beautiful poetry.

But Sophocles saw, perhaps, that in the facts as stated there lay a greater tragedy, well known, eternal, perfectly true: triumphant ὕβρις and strength and violence, swollen by the general praise, made more selfish by the devotion of others; and standing against it the simplest and most typical example of devoted service and sacrifice, the love of a woman for a brutal master. Some of the great tragedies of the world are built, like *Hamlet* or the *Oresteia* or *Oedipus*, on some strange and rare combination of incidents; some, like the *Medea*, the *Alcestis*, perhaps the *Bacchae*, are seen happening all about us in every age. The *Trachiniae* belongs to the latter type. You can see Heracles and Deianîra most Monday mornings in some police court or other, as you can see in Broadwood asylum Medeas who have murdered their children. The strange thing is that in an age supposed to be somewhat inconsiderate of women, a poet who had no special taste for paradox or even for speculation should have studied with such sympathy this particular form of the variegated suffering inflicted by one sex on the other, and this particular type of idealized womanhood—a type so terribly out of fashion just now that I should apologize to my younger readers for even mentioning it, were it not that, as I am sure they will agree, things of real beauty lie deep below the changing tides of fashion and remain, to those who care to regard them, a joy for ever.

1928.

VII

EURIPIDES' TRAGEDIES OF 415 B.C.:
THE DECEITFULNESS OF LIFE

IT was persuasively suggested in Wilamowitz's *Introduction to Attic Tragedy* that the production of the *Troades* in 415 formed an epoch or turning-point in the life of its author. One of the most exquisitely written of Euripides' plays, it is perhaps also the most unspeakably tragic, not because of any startling catastrophes in the story, but owing to the profoundly tragic conception which it embodies of life as a whole. If I may quote what I have said about it before:

'The only movement of the drama is the gradual extinguishing of all the familiar lights of human life, with, perhaps, a suggestion at the end that in the utterness of night when all fears of a possible worse thing are passed, there is in some sense peace and even glory. The situation itself has at least this dramatic value, that it is different from what it seems. The consummation of a great conquest . . . the very summit of the day-dreams of unregenerate man, it seems to be a great joy and is in truth a great misery.'

One might call it typically *paracharaxis tragica*, showing how the things that are called good are those that should be called evil, the things pursued those that should be fled from, and all the superscriptions false.

The cause of this tragic disillusionment may doubtless be sought in the history of the time. During the summer and winter of 416 B.C. there occurred an event of very small military importance to which Thucydides nevertheless devotes twenty-six continuous chapters in a significant part of his work—the part just before the final catastrophe. I refer of course to the siege and capture by the Athenians of the little neutral island of Melos, the massacre of all its adult men, and the enslavement of its women and children. The island had no strategic importance. Its capture had no recorded effect on subsequent history. And the whole of the discussion in the twenty-six chapters of Melian dialogue is occupied, not with political or military problems, but purely with the statement of a moral or non-moral position, the assertion by the Athenian war-party of a gospel of pure *Hubris*, the sort of *Hubris* which in tragedy and other imaginative literature regularly leads to a fall, as it duly does in Thucydides' history.

Now we know from Aelian both the date of the production of the *Troades* and the names of the other plays of the tetralogy to which it belonged. 'Euripides was second in the competition with the *Alexandros*, *Palamêdes*, *Troades*, and the satyr-play *Sisyphus*.' We also know from quotations and references something of the subjects of these plays. The question arises whether there is any unity of plot or purpose running through the whole tetralogy or whether the *Troades* stands alone in its tragic message. The last is the accepted view: both the *Alexandros* and the *Palamêdes* seem at first sight to be romantic plays of a fairly common type, with no tragic doctrine at the heart of them. But let us look more closely.

The plot of the *Alexandros* can probably be deduced from Hyginus *fab.* 91. Hecuba, queen of Troy, being pregnant, dreamed that she gave birth to a firebrand, and from the firebrand came serpents. The prophets said that the child, when born, must be put to death. It was given to one of Priam's retainers to slay, but he in pity left it, wrapped in a leathern bag, πήρα, in a place where some mountain shepherds found it, and reared it as their own. They called it Paris from the πήρα. Paris grew up in slavery, became a herdsman, and was especially proud of a certain bull. Long years afterwards Hecuba, whose grief had never ceased, was allowed to hold a great funeral celebration for her lost child. A bull was needed to be the chief prize at the games; and Priam's servants proceeded to commandeer Paris' bull. Paris in anger followed them, entered for the games, and defeated all competitors, including his brothers, the princes. Hot words arose, and Deiphobus—generally an unsympathetic figure—drew his sword to kill the daring slave. Paris beat him off, fled to an altar, and was recognized by Cassandra as her brother. She cries that he must be put to death, but she is regarded as obviously mad. Paris is welcomed and accepted by Priam.

There are some twenty-three fragments of the *Alexandros* in Nauck's *Fragmenta Tragicorum*, 42–64; about 42 lines of Ennius' adaptation; while a papyrus published by Cronert in 1922 contains hardly any complete lines but a good many in a fragmentary or illegible condition. The evidence has been surveyed and the play conjecturally put together in outline by Professor Snell of Hamburg in a fine article published as *Heft* 5 of the *Einzelschriften* of *Hermes*, 1937. Snell's results complete and for the most part confirm those which I reached in a paper written about the year 1920.

The prologue as given by Ennius tells of Hecuba's dream, the comment of the prophets, Priam's decision, the exposure of the child, and Hecuba's grief: καὶ χρόνου προὔβαινε πούς, 'The foot of time moved on', but Hecuba was not comforted. Then apparently came a scene between Hecuba and someone who comforts her.[1]

> 'Fresh tears should fall not for afflictions old.'
>
> 'Oh surely griefs should bend with passing time.'
>
> 'I know it, but 'tis easier thus to speak
> Than to endure long evil patiently.'
>
> 'All men must die: 'tis wisdom temperately
> To endure an anguish that must come to all.'

Ennius gives us a scene between Hecuba and Cassandra: Why does Cassandra, so changed from her accustomed modesty, burst in with burning eyes? Cassandra's answer is very interesting: 'Mater, optimarum multo mulier melior mulierum.' Apollo is compelling her. 'Mater, tui me miseret, mei piget.' 'I pity you, I am grieved for myself. Your other children

---

[1] Nauck, 43–7.

are children to be proud of. They help, I only hinder; they obey, I stand in the way.' Then the paroxysm seizes her. 'Adest, adest fax.' 'It is here, it has come, the firebrand, wrapped in blood and flame; after lying hid for many years. Citizens, help, put it out!' Either now or in a later scene Cassandra has a vision of all that will come, the judgement of Paris, the death of Hector, the Trojan horse, and the rest. She is, it would seem, led away by Hecuba's handmaids. Presently there enters a messenger (not, I think, the Old Servant who had originally exposed Paris) telling the results of the Funeral Games which have just taken place. There were crowds of competitors, many are named, others not; in the end,

> Where victory should be thine thou hast defeat,
> And where it should not, victory, O King.
> Thy slaves have brought thee triumph, not thy sons.

A herdsman from the mountains, called Paris, has come, followed by a throng of other herdsmen; his bull had been lawlessly taken by the king's men and put up as a prize, and he has won it. A fine-looking man, people said:

> 'How like yon herdsman is to Priam's sons.'[1]

The words ἦ καὶ στέφουσιν αὐτόν; . . . 'Are they crowning him?' . . . καί φασιν εἶναί γ' ἄξιον . . . 'Yes, and say he is worthy' . . . can be made out in the papyrus. The shepherds are now calling him Alexandros, 'Repeller of Men', because no one can stand against him.[2]

The papyrus then gives fragments of a dialogue between Deiphobus, who is furious at the success of the slave and the dishonour done to the family, and Hector who has no jealousy.

> ἀλλ', ὦ κασίγνηθ' Ἕκτορ, οὐκ ἀλγεῖς φρένας
> Nay, brother Hector, is thy heart not sore?

Perhaps this is where the Supplementary Chorus of Shepherds following Alexandros comes in. We know from the scholia

---

[1] Nauck, *Adesp.* 286.   [2] Ennius, *Alex.* fr. vi.

to *Hipp*. 58 that there was such a second chorus in this play.
Then comes an *agôn* between Deiphobus and Alexandros, with
Priam as an arbiter, of which the papyrus has considerable
remains, very fragmentary and illegible. In Nauck we find:

> Thou art wise, O Priam, yet I warn thee clear,
> There is no burden heavier on a house,
> Nor no possession deadlier, nor in use
> More wasting, than a slave with heart too high.

> I have tried them. It is thus all slaves are vile,
> All belly, and no thinking of the morrow.

How can you make a friend of such people?

> A slave who loves his masters and their kind
> Takes on him a great war 'gainst all his fellows.

In short, says Deiphobus,

> 'Tis deep dishonour to possess a slave
> Who stands above his master.

From Alexander's defence we have apparently the opening
words:

> O King, a fearful evil among men
> Are slanderous words, and often the true man
> Who hath no tongue by tongues that run too well
> Is broken.

Then follow some phrases about the corrupting influence of
wealth and princely luxury.

> A sorry thing, it seems, for rearing men
> Is wealth and delicate living. Poverty
> Brings suffering, but the children that she breeds
> Are better both to labour and to dare.

He adds:

> Wealth maketh men
> Unrighteous, and doth many deeds of wrong.

Priam rejects the slanders of Deiphobus, and says to the
herdsman:

> Time will reveal thee; by his test alone
> I know thee for mine evil or my good.

There follows, it would seem, the best-preserved fragment of the play, a lyric of ten lines quoted by Stobaeus on *eugeneia*. All men have the same ultimate ancestry, the same appearance; τὸ φρόνιμον εὐγένεια, 'Nobility is a thing of the mind.' It is a gift of God, not of social position.

Then comes in the papyrus a scene in which apparently Deiphobus and Hecuba plan the death of Paris. Deiphobus we understand, but what is the motive of Hecuba? A serious wrong done to her children might make her murderous, but it is hardly likely that she would be roused to the murder point by a mere defeat in the games. I suspect that the reward offered by Priam to the victor in the games comprised something amounting to a share in the royal inheritance, the position of a prince of Troy, the hand of one of Priam's daughters, or the like. Priam expected one of his sons to win; if so the second reward would not apply, but there were various other princes competing, so there may have been alternative prizes: for example a special rank, second only to Hector, among the Priamidae, or else the hand of a Priamid princess, perhaps Cassandra. One fragment[1] has something about marriage (γάμωι νιν εἰκατ). One can imagine Hecuba made furious at the thought of the admission of a slave into the inheritance of her sons and the degradation of her daughter by his embraces. I doubt, however, whether she would insist, as Snell makes her insist, that the cowherd must die by her hand, especially while Deiphobus is there.[2] Cronert supposes an error in the papyrus, but the whole trouble seems to have been made by a false conjecture [τῆ]ιδε χειρὶ δεῖ θανεῖν, where τ and η are conjectural. It may have been [σῆ]ι δέ, [πιστῆ]ι δέ, or the like. Then

---

[1] 49 Snell. Cf. 59 N.

[2] Snell makes Hecuba try to kill Paris herself, reading τῆιδε χειρὶ δεῖ θανεῖν, and proposes to make the recognition by means of a *Gerôn* or *Senex* of the well-known type (cf. Soph. *Electra* and *O.T.*; Eur. *Electra*), who had been directed to kill the child but had not done so. There is no particular evidence for this, and I think the result would be less effective.

Deiphobus' answer 'He is not unwoundable', or 'It will not be for lack of wounds . . .'[1] becomes more natural. There follows a scene in which Hector again takes the generous line. He is ready to accept as a friend a man so valiant as the cowherd and blames Deiphobus for taking his defeat so ill. At the end come some half-lines of Hecuba which may be completed in different ways:

$$οὗτος \ μὲν \ ἀεὶ \ . \ . \ . \ . \ .$$
$$ῥέξεις \ δ' \ ἃ \ λυπούμεσθα$$
$$κτανόντες \ ἄνδρα \ δοῦλον$$

These lines may mean that Hecuba has been convinced by Hector. 'Hector is always wise; you, Deiphobus, are about to do a thing which is the cause of our grief, when we are shown to have murdered a slave.' Or else: 'Hector is always generous; but all the same you will do the deed, removing the cause of our grief. By killing a slave we shall . . .' This latter seems to me now on reflection to be the most natural.

Soon afterwards we have Alexandros entering and flying for refuge with sword drawn to the altar; the altar is that of Zeus Herkeios, the intimate Protector of the Family, where Priam afterwards was slain.

We have the words:

> O cowards and vile, the slavish heart within,
> Hid in your naming, showeth in your lives!

and

> Woe's me, 'tis death! and through my faithfulness
> Of heart, which hath saved other men from death.

Clearly at this point, while about to be slain at the altar, Alexandros is recognized and saved and welcomed by Priam as a son. How the recognition is brought about is not clear. Hyginus says, by Cassandra: Ovid, Servius, and others say by means of γνωρίσματα (tokens). Clearly both are compatible; but it seems dramatically necessary that Cassandra should be the chief agent, and this falls suitably in with the

[1] οὐ μὴν ἄτρωτός γ' ἐστὶν (εἰσιν? Cr.) εἰς Ἅιδου δόμους.

regular tradition; cf. Andr. 297 ὅτε νιν παρὰ θεσπεσίωι δά-
φναι βόασε Κασάνδρα κτανεῖν.[1] The θεσπέσιος δάφνα was by
the altar of Zeus Herkeios.[2] This being clear we have a
highly dramatic series of *Peripeteiai* or contrasts. Paris flies
to the altar; Deiphobus goes to murder him.

> *Chorus Leader*: 'You must not kill a suppliant!'
> (μὴ κτεῖνε, τὸν ἱκέτην γὰρ οὐ θέμις κτανεῖν.)[3]
> *Hecuba*: 'Suppliant or not, kill him!'
> *Cassandra* (entering in a state of possession): 'It is he; it is the ex-
> posed prince, the son of Priam and Hecuba!'
> *Hecuba* or *Chorus*: 'How do you know?'
> *Cassandra*: 'Look at those γνωρίσματα. He is the Firebrand; kill him.'
> *Hecuba*: He is my son, save him.'
> *Deiphobus*: 'My brother! I cannot kill him!'

The violent change of mind in Hecuba is exactly like that of
Meropê in the *Cresphontes*, when she recognizes her sleeping
son at the moment when her axe is lifted to strike.

Snell mentions that on certain Etruscan urns there is a
painting of Alexandros with Phrygian cap, palm-branch, and
sword, at an altar; against him come a young man with a
sword and a woman with an axe. He takes the woman to be
Hecuba; I should say Cassandra. The urns also have a figure
of Aphrodite, which suggests that Aphrodite spoke the
epilogue, ordaining reconciliation of the enemies and perhaps
foretelling Alexander's expedition to Greece. The references
to Aphrodite in the Helen scene of the *Troades* rather bear
this out.[4]

At first sight there does not seem to be much restamping
of conventions in this play, beyond the usual romantic
commonplaces. The slave is better than the free man: the
high-born princes are beaten by the cowherd, and by their
jealousy afterwards are branded as having the real slave-

---

[1] 'When beside the holy laurel Cassandra cried the command to slay him.'
[2] v. *Aen.* ii. 513 Ingens ara fuit iuxtaque veterrima laurus.
[3] Nauck, *Adesp.* 937.
[4] *Tro.* 929, 940, 983.

nature in their hearts. That is a common enough tone in
romance; and here even such value as one might attribute
to it is taken away by the fact that the so-called slave, the
cowherd, is really a prince. All that remains is the not very
startling argument that riches spoil their owner, and that
poverty trains the character. One could read the whole play,
as far as the evidence of the fragments goes, as an ordinary
romantic play of intrigue, were it not for one thing. We
must not forget that this brave and beautiful cowherd, who
has been saved from death on the mountain, who fights the
princes for his pet bull, who is slandered and wronged and
threatened with death, but just at the nick of time recognized
and restored to the mother who has always mourned for him,
is really the firebrand girt with snakes whose life means his
country's ruin. Cassandra knew that his death was the right
thing; the sparing of his life was the calamity. But of course
no one believed Cassandra. As she says of herself:

> πρὸς τῶν παθόντων κἂν κακοῖσι κειμένων
> σοφὴ κέκλημαι, πρὶν παθεῖν δὲ μαίνομαι.[1]

All through the play we are kept rejoicing over the things
that mean evil to come, and dreading and praying against
the only thing that can bring safety. And the apparent
happy ending consists in Hecuba taking to her heart the
firebrand and the serpent. The true comment on the happy
ending is made in the third play of the trilogy,[2] where
Andromachê says woe now lies heaped on woe: 'by the wrath
of God when thy son Paris escaped from death, who for the
sake of his loathed love wrecked the towers of Troy. For that
the bodies of dead men lie stretched in blood under the eyes
of Pallas, and the vultures tear them; he failed not to bring
upon Troy the yoke of her slavery.'

The thing that seemed victory was really defeat; what
seemed the averting of evil was the rejection of salvation;
the thing beloved was the thing to be loathed and the brave

---

[1] Nauck, *Adesp.* 414.   [2] *Tro.* 597 ff.

and young and beautiful prince was the embodied curse of the land.

This last conception had, I would venture to suggest, certain connotations for the Greek mind which we are apt to miss. Greek myths, and perhaps particularly the myths of Greek drama, make great use of foundlings who turn out to be princes. Generally they are the forbidden offspring of a maiden and a god; very often they are twins; sometimes they are the bearers of some antenatal curse or the like. We may leave aside the various pairs of twins; Amphion and Zethus, exposed by their mother Antiopê; Aeolus and Boeotus by Melanippê; Eunêos and Thoas taken from Hypsipylê; Romulus and Remus taken from Rhea Silvia, &c. Apart from twins we have Ion, the exposed son of Apollo and Creusa; Telephus, the exposed son of Heracles and Augê; Hippothoüs, the exposed son of Poseidon and Alopê; Perseus, exposed son of Zeus and Danaê, and various others. They all start as unknown foundlings with the world against them, and eventually are recognized as of princely birth. The motive has been extraordinarily persistent through the whole history of romantic literature. Amid the great inventiveness and variety of Menander's plots, this foundling baby holds its place with a tenacity, and involves its innocent elders in scandals with a matter-of-factness, explicable only by its ritual origin. It holds equal sway over the other poets of the New Comedy and the Roman stage; and does not relinquish its hold in medieval romance. Church influence seems to have been impotent to alter this motive, if it ever seriously tried. Almost every interesting knight in the Arthur and Tristram cycles, and, as far as I know, in the Provençal romances after them, begins life as a foundling or at least an illegitimate child. This applies to Merlin, Arthur, Isaye le Triste, Galahad, and partly to Lancelot and Tristram. The motive passes over into the Alexander romance. In whatever country a particular version of the romance is current, Alexander is generally the lost or concealed love-child of the king or queen of that country.

This outcast foundling who is really divine cannot well be separated from the wonder-child of the Year-ritual, of the *Hymn to Hermes*, of the *Ichneutae*, of the Heracles saga, and the like; the baby Vegetation-god or Year-god who is born and grows with such miraculous speed; fights, marries, fights again, dies, and generally revives, in the so-called Mummers' play, and in a hundred myths and rituals from one end of Europe to the other. Alexandros, outcast as a baby, nourished on the mountain, inseparable from his favourite bull, unjustly oppressed and triumphant over his oppressors, and finally recognized as the royal prince, seems to belong to this type.

But here comes the curious point. In the primitive Year-ritual there seems to have been a conception not only of the young Year Daimon as normally something free from the defilements of the old, something pure and therefore blessed, but also, on occasion, as something misbegotten and perverted which may carry a curse. At any rate, whether connected with the regular Year-baby ritual or no, there are clear traces in the myth of the baby who must not be allowed to live, either because he will kill his father or for some other reason. Oedipus ought to have been killed, because otherwise he would kill his father and dishonour his mother. Perseus was to have been killed, because otherwise he would kill the king, his grandfather. All the first three kings of the world, according to Hesiod, are involved in similar trouble with parricidal babies. Ouranos fears de-thronement and ruin at the hands of Kronos, Kronos at those of Zeus, Zeus at those of the son of Thetis. And it may be assumed that the thing they feared would be death were it not that *ex hypothesi* they were immortal.

Now most of these Curse-babies are more or less sympathetic; I mean our sympathies are with them as against the tyrant they destroy. We are on the whole with Kronos

against Ouranos, with Zeus against Kronos, with Oedipus
against Laius; we are certainly with Perseus against Acrisius,
and do not much mind when the latter is killed. In many
cases the babes do not bring a real curse. Oedipus is different.
He does bring a curse to all his people and himself. And the
curse atmosphere, the sense of darkness and horror, affects
the whole of his saga, at least in those treatments of it which
have come down to us. But Alexandros in this play seems to
have been treated in a peculiar way. He is the Curse-child,
doomed to bring ruin on the whole land, but he has all the
attributes of the Blessing-child, the young and pure and
victorious. The destroyer comes in all the guise and manner
of the Saviour. Thus in the *Alexandros* as in the *Troades*
there is a *paracharaxis* of the obvious values of the world:
what seems like the mercy of the gods is not mercy, what
seems like the deliverer is the destroyer, and after all the
unexpected turns of good fortune, and the generous efforts
of Priam, the apparent 'happy ending' results in leaving
Troy doomed to destruction.

The general idea of the second play of the tetralogy, the
Palamêdes, comes out clearly from the references and quotations. Palamêdes, the man of παλάμαι, or devices, has a
curious career in Greek legend. He is partly a sort of superfluous Prometheus, who invented the art of writing or at
least some parts of it, weights and measures, *pessoi* and other
games; on the whole he takes such minor inventions as
Prometheus does not claim. He is more conspicuous still as
a superfluous Odysseus. As such he has no place in the *Iliad*
and *Odyssey*, where Odysseus is sympathetic, but in the
Cypria he is the virtuous rival of the unscrupulous Odysseus
and is murdered by Odysseus and Diomede. He becomes a
favourite character in late romances, like those of Dares and
Dictys, where he is sometimes commander-in-chief of the
Greek armies in place of Agamemnon. Dares describes him
as 'gracilem longum sapientem animo magnum blandum'.

In classical times he is a type of the innocent man unjustly condemned. Socrates in the *Apology* speaks of meeting 'Ajax son of Telamon and Palamêdes and any other of the ancients who has died by unjust judgement': and this was his character in tragedy, where of course the character of his rival, Odysseus, became progressively darker. All three tragedians wrote plays called *Palamêdes*, and Sophocles a *Nauplius* as well. In the third play of our trilogy Odysseus is called definitely σοφὸς κακὸς δέ, and evidently that was his character in the second. Palamêdes, the true wise man, was destroyed by Odysseus, the 'clever and wicked'. So much is certain, and probably the particular way in which the destruction was compassed is that related by Hyginus,[1] and stated to come from tragedy. Odysseus persuades Agamemnon by means of an alleged dream to move the camp for one day; he thus gets access to the site of Palamêdes' tent and buries a sum of gold under it. Then he arranges that a letter shall be found on the dead body of a Trojan, purporting to be from Priam to Palamêdes, referring to the gold he has sent him as a price for betraying the camp. Palamêdes is accused before Agamemnon. He denies all knowledge of the letter. His tent is examined, the buried gold is found, agreeing in amount with the sum named in the letter. Palamêdes is condemned and slain, the innocent slandered to death by the wicked. He is chiefly defended by his brother Oiax, who seems at the end to have been imprisoned in the hope of preventing him from revealing the truth. We learn, however, from the *Thesmophoriazusae* that from his prison he manages to throw out to sea some blades of oars, inscribed with the true story. The winds and waves will bear them to somebody. As a matter of fact, we remember, they came to the father of Palamêdes, Nauplius, and he, when the Greeks were returning from Troy, rowed out alone in his boat[2] and lit the wrecking lights on Cape Caphêreus which destroyed the whole fleet of his son's

---

[1] *Fable* 105.

[2] μονόκωπος ἀνήρ, *Hel.* 1128.

murderers. In the *Troades* this wreck of the victorious fleet
cannot find a place in the actual plot, but it is arranged by
the agreement of Poseidon and Athena in the Prologue and
hinted at later more than once.[1]

The fragments for the most part fall into place.[2] Palamêdes
in the tradition was a great inventor. In the first fragment
he relates how he invented letters and the art of writing, so
that now a man in absence can learn about his home, when
dying can leave a tablet saying how he wants his property
divided; while all sorts of disputes and false statements are
brought to an end by the written record. Yes; and by this
same art of writing the inventor is done to death! The irony
is complete. The third fragment contains a διαβολή addressed
to Agamemnon—we may suppose by Odysseus.

> O King, men's fortunes have their varied forms;
> But all to one end move. All mortal men,
> Live they with wisdom or see naught of her,
> Labour for riches, and who gaineth most
> Is wisest.

Consequently, I presume, Agamemnon must not be surprised
at Palamêdes', for all his wisdom, turning traitor for a bribe.
There is a couplet for the defence by Oiax, explaining that
one man of genius is more important than many commanding officers:

> Ten thousand of us could be generals;
> But wise, scarce one or two in the long years.

From the same speaker apparently we have:

> The man whose words are well but ill the deeds
> Behind them, shall be never wise to me.

> One true man shall o'ercome a thousand false
> Since Right is with him and the hand of God.

> The memory of the righteous liveth still
> With God and man, immortal and alone.

The course of the play, it would seem, shows that these

---

[1] Especially 456, 1100 ff.   [2] Nauck, 578–90.

sentiments do not in fact hold good of the common world. There seems to be a quotation or semi-quotation from the *Palamêdes* in the passage of Aristophanes' *Frogs*[1] where Dionysus asks how Athens is still to be saved, and Euripides answers:

> To mistrust those whom now we trust
> And call to serve us those whom now we spurn
> May save us yet.

There is certainly one in the *Thesmophoriazusae*[2] where the imprisoned Mnesilochus determines to throw out wooden tablets, as Oiax threw the oar-blades: 'Ye tablets of planed wood, take the gravings of my chisel, heralds of my affliction.'

In the remaining fragments we find something about inscribed oar-blades, about the beaks of ships, about the bells of sentinels going their rounds at night, and of course there is the celebrated lyric phrase;

> Ye have slain, O men of Hellas, ye have slain,
> The all-wise voice, the Muses' nightingale,
> Which brought to no man pain,

words applied afterwards to the death of Socrates as well as to that of Protagoras.[3]

The *paracharaxis* is clear. The wicked man is he whom the world trusts and calls wise, the innocent he whom the world condemns and kills. Also the benefactor of mankind is slain by men because of his benefits and through his benefits. And lastly, with a view to the third play which is to come, the Greeks as well as the Trojans are now under a curse. The war is to go on: the end is to be what men call victory for one side and defeat for the other. On both sides men put forth their extreme effort; and the result is the fulfilment of the curse upon both.

It is worth while, before considering the definite message of the *Troades*, the only play of this tetralogy which has come down to us complete, to cast one brief glance at the

[1] 1443 ff.   [2] 770 ff.   [3] Nauck, 588.

satyr-play which closed the tetralogy. There is no necessary
jar in such a close, for disillusion can be ludicrous as well as
tragic. This play is called *Sisyphus*. And the name implies
the sort of theme that would suit the three tragedies. The
doings of the arch-deceiver will illustrate well the mocking
injustice of the world. The only surviving fragment is
addressed to Heracles:

> Son of Alcmena, noblest of mankind,
> 'Tis joy to me to see thee safe from death
> Returning, and the bloody murderer slain.

I think the indication is sufficient. I know of no part of the
Sisyphus saga which brings Heracles and Sisyphus together
after the death of a 'bloody murderer' except one. When
Eurystheus sent Heracles to take from the Thracian tyrant
Lycurgus the horses which Lycurgus fed upon human flesh,
Heracles slew Lycurgus, mastered the raging horses, and
was bringing them back in triumph to Argos when unfortunately he met Sisyphus, who stole them! That suits
the fragment, and suits the tone of our tetralogy.

I ought perhaps in order to show what that tone is to
say a little about the one extant play, the *Troades*. I do
not in the least pretend to reproduce the full inmost meaning
of the *Troades*; I have already tried to translate it; I want
only to isolate and call to your attention certain elements in
the strange and tragic conception of the world which is
expressed in that play. It would be ridiculous, of course, to
collect the statements made by various characters in the play
and attribute them to Euripides. I think, however, that
certain speeches in certain situations must generally be taken
as expressing the truth; that is, what the poet in that particular work intends to treat as the truth. For example,
what Cassandra says must be true. The one certain and
notorious fact about Cassandra is that she sees and speaks
the truth, but is not believed. Any dramatist putting Cassandra on the stage must so represent her. Again, though
gods in their private capacities are *capables de tout*, a god

pronouncing judgement *ex cathedra* must be meant to carry weight. Lastly, if a playwright allows a character to have a supernatural vision of things unseen by common men, he must intend us to pay serious attention to the content of the vision. When Poseidon in the prologue describes the condition of Troy one believes him; one believes that the avenging storm is waiting for the Greeks on the Aegean; one believes especially the final judgement:

> How are ye blind
> Ye treaders down of cities, ye that cast
> Temples to desolation, and lay waste
> Tombs, the untrodden sanctuaries where lie
> The ancient dead, yourselves so soon to die.

The largest judgement made by Cassandra about the world is on the same lines, with the edge of paradox sharpened. In the very depth of Troy's defeat she sees the beginning of her triumphant vengeance. She herself is enslaved and defiled; she sees in this not so much the end of her virgin holiness but the beginning of her life as one of the Powers of Hell, μίαν τριῶν Ἐρινύν. It is the first step on the path which will leave her and Agamemnon, an unholy pair, never to be parted, as dead, naked, and polluted bodies, to be torn by dogs in that storm-beaten chasm among the rocks. Her last debasement means Troy's ultimate victory.

This leads easily to Cassandra's long argument—one could imagine it all worked out as question and answer by Plato —to prove that the conquered righteous are happier than the unrighteous conquerors. Are the Greeks to be called happy? Were they not mad to make the war at all, causing the deaths of men in thousands, all to bring back one woman who did not want to come, and whom nobody valued? The Trojans only fought through necessity; they fought the best fight, and died the best death, to save their country. Then during the ten years, which is a large span of human life, who were the happier? The Greeks, exiled, away from their wives, homes, and children, lived lonely and surrounded by hatred, and had none to care for them when they died. The Trojans had those whom they loved always near them; when they were slain,

> dear women's hands about them wound
> White shrouds, and there they sleep in the old ground
> Beloved.

So far the argument has proceeded on what one may call ordinary rationalist lines. Then it takes a lift towards something like mysticism: what has been Hector's fate for good or ill?

$$\delta\acute{o}\xi as\ \acute{a}v\grave{\eta}\rho\ \ddot{a}\rho\iota\sigma\tau os\ o\ddot{\iota}\chi\epsilon\tau a\iota\ \theta av\acute{\omega}v.$$

The almost untranslatable line is the very definition of Greek happiness: he was ἀνὴρ ἄριστος, the perfect good man: δόξας, all the world knew he was so; and οἴχεται θανών, now it is over and achieved. And even Paris—is there any word for him? There is a word common enough in the poems of the sentimental moderns, but unexampled, I think, among the writers of classical Greece. Πάρις δ' ἔγημε τὴν Διός. 'He won the love of the Child of Heaven.' Which would you rather: win the love of a child of heaven and be destroyed, or vegetate successfully?[1]

The first lyrical speech of Cassandra[2] is a call to the dance. It is a marriage dance, a dance like that of the stars in their courses—for what? For the blessed state of her father who is lying dead, and for her own possession by Agamemnon. This equivalence of death and marriage, with its conception of death as a union with the world of darkness, and of Hades himself as a bridegroom, is, of course, fairly common in Greek poetry.

Another note struck is rather more curious. Ὁ χορὸς ὅσιος. 'The dance that she leads is holy.' Φλέγω λαμπάσι τόδ' ἱερόν. 'I purge with a brand this holy place.' The holy dance celebrates the dishonouring of the virgin priestess; the holy

---

[1] 365-99.   [2] 308 ff.

place is the battlefield after the battle, strewn with dead bodies, the ruin of broken shrines, and all manner of pollution. Has the holiness of Cassandra herself, now perhaps at its highest intensity just before she yields her sacred crown and fillets back to the God who gave them, so that they at least shall never be defiled, some power to annul the evil of the world and the foulness of the material things among which she moves? This would only carry a slight step farther the doctrine so magnificently stated by Theseus in the *Heracles*[1] that no pollution of the material world can stain the purity of the soul, of the divine sunlight, or of the love between friend and friend. This became, of course, one of the most radical doctrines of the early Stoics. Or again, is it the presence of death that brings purification? At the end of the play, in a passage to be noted later, Hecuba calls to Priam, but her call is unheeded. He cannot hear her:

μέλας γὰρ ὄσσε κατεκάλυψε
θάνατος ὅσιος ἀνοσίαις σφαγαῖσιν.

Darkness has covered his eyes. He has gone through all the foulness and impurity of carnage to the holiness of death. The carnage, the whole process of slaying and dying, is unclean; but behind the carnage, the noise and rage and suffering, is that world where there is no suffering nor rage nor noise any more, the world of eternal peace. I do not suppose that Euripides felt it necessary to think out definitely which of these alternatives he meant. They combine well enough together. The conception of death untouched by evil, the peace-bringer, the φάρμακον κακῶν, is common enough in Euripides from those beautiful lines of Macaria in the *Heraclidae* onward. There may be some reward for her beyond the grave, but better not:

εἴη γε μέντοι μηδέν· εἰ γὰρ ἕξομεν
κἀκεῖ μερίμνας οἱ θανούμενοι βροτῶν,
οὐκ οἶδ' ὅποι τις τρέψεται.

[1] 1231-4.

U

May there be nothing! For if even there
We who must die shall have no rest from care. . . .
I know not whither one can turn.

An even profounder revaluation of the things of this
world is expressed in the vision of Hecuba[1] and in all that
she says thereafter. It is not clearly or dogmatically out-
lined: it would be far less satisfying if it were, as well as less
poetical. Hecuba has been performing a funeral rite over
her dead grandchild, a pretended healing of his wounds one
after another, in order, it would seem, that he may have a
whole body in the next world. She feels the futility of it;
it is a name, not a real thing; and she breaks off:

Not I, but he,
Thy father far away, shall comfort thee.

It seems as if she was staying with head bowed over the dead
child, while the women of the Chorus chant a few lines of
low lamentation. Then she suddenly cries out:

O women, ye my beloved . . .

and stops. The leader bids her speak on. 'Yes, call us thine.
What is the meaning of that cry?' Her answer seems to be
the description of what she has seen in a moment of vision.
'So after all there was nothing in the hand of God, nothing
except affliction for me, and for Troy the doom to be hated
beyond all cities! . . . And in vain we made our sacrifice
of bulls.' The torrents of passionate prayer and sacrifice
were all wasted, for the purpose of Zeus all the time had
been fixed. Nothing else had ever been possible. The result
is, so to speak, that she knows the role for which she is cast
and can play it. The role of Troy and the queen of Troy is
to be hated of God, to go through the very extreme of
affliction till all that was high in Troy is made low: and
through that role they have achieved a splendour which will
be an inspiration to poets for all ages to come. Otherwise,

[1] 1237 ff.

ἀφανεῖς ἂν ὄντες οὐκ ἂν ὑμνήθημεν ἄν,
μούσαις ἀοιδὰς δόντες ὑστέρων βροτῶν.

We had not been this glory, nor our wrong
An everlasting music for the song
Of those hereafter.

The vision remains with her to the end. First, she recognizes that prayers are of no avail. At one moment indeed a cry of anguish, 'Ἰὼ θεοί, 'Ye Gods!' escapes her, but is immediately caught back:

Why call I on the Gods? They know, they know
My prayers, and would not hear them long ago.

She sees the fire rising and consuming Troy: she rushes forward to fling herself into the flames and die together with her city, but is caught and held back. She tries to realize the full situation in its almost incredible horror. 'Does Zeus see them, their own Zeus of Mount Ida, the very father of Troy?' Yes, he sees them, but he has no pity. Desperately in the growing darkness Hecuba kneels and beats upon the ground, crying to those who must have pity, her own dead, her loved ones, above all to Priam. But Priam cannot hear her, nor help. He has gone away from the foulness of war, he is with Death the Holy. There is no help anywhere, no turning to the right or left. The full role must be played out, to its last agony and its extreme splendour.

This conception, new, as far as I know, at the time when the play was produced, was afterwards developed and clarified as one of the central doctrines of the Stoics. God the great dramatist hands to each of us at birth the script of the part he has to play. The good actor takes the script, whatever it may be, and plays it well. Whether it be the part of king or slave, conqueror or conquered, matters nothing. What matters is that it be well played.

Thus the new superscription that is stamped upon the world's metal in the *Troades* is not merely *Vanitas vanitatum, omnia vanitas*. This is its first stage, an exhibition both of

the injustice of a world in which the innocent suffer and the
unworthy triumph, and the irony of a world in which those
who triumph and conquer and win their will are, if anything,
more profoundly discontented and miserable than those
whom they have defeated. So far, one might say, all is
vanity. But beyond that first stage there is a glimpse of
another scale of values, in which there is something—call it
a glory, or splendour, or, for lack of a better name, beauty—
something at any rate which is the material for eternal song,
in playing one's part to the last word and enduring what fate
sends. One might speak of this view as the doctrine of
Stoicism romanticized; but, of course, it is not really that. It
is the vague anticipatory vision of that great truth or half-
truth which the Stoics afterwards formulated, divined afar
off by a poet through his accustomed atmosphere of romance,
not through the dry light of exact reasoning. As in many
other points, Euripides anticipates the doctrines of later
philosophy.

Thus I think it is fairly clear from the extant evidence
that the whole Trojan tetralogy of Euripides in the year 415
was inspired by the same spirit as the *Troades* itself, and
found in that tragedy its climax of expression. The first
play gave us the curse upon Troy due to mistaking the
Curse-child Alexandros for the child of blessing, and cherish-
ing the destroyer in the belief that he is the Saviour. The
second gave us the curse upon the Greeks, due to their
preference of the false wisdom over the true, their belief in
the lie, their rejection of the truth, and ultimately their
murder of the innocent. The last shows the fulfilment of
both curses; the vanity of conquest and glory and all the
received values, a world merged in the blackness of utter
night, and then a suggestion of some new value, undefined
and difficult of surmise, stirring in the heart of the darkness.

VIII

THEOPOMPUS, OR THE CYNIC AS HISTORIAN

HISTORY is the most worldly of the Muses. She is such a respecter of *personae*; so imposed upon by success; so readily content to measure the values of life by conventional standards, such as territory, wealth, and population. And for that very reason history provokes various forms of *paracharaxis*, mostly shortlived. I do not merely mean partisan differences of opinion about policies or individuals, one historian liking the Reformation and another hating it, or the like. I mean a real difference in valuation. For example, Herodotus ascribes the writing of his history to the desire 'that great and wonderful deeds, performed both by Greeks and barbarians, be not left uncelebrated', while Gibbon says that 'history', his own included, 'is little more than a record of the crimes, follies and misfortunes of mankind'. Yet both are essentially describing the same things. It is the difference between Plutarch with his pious and sane admiration of great men, and, let us say, Teufelsdrökh's epitaph on his incredibly high-born and bemedalled German count who *plumbo confecit* so many thousands of partridges and *in stercus convertit* so many thousand hundredweight of the flesh of various quadrupeds more attractive than himself.

I do not wish to dwell on the changes in the focus of attention among the early Greek historians: how Herodotus, following Hecataeus, seems to start by being interested in strange countries and peoples and then in the deeds they did; Hellanîcus in the task of reducing to order the superabundant *logoi* and other records with which fifth-century Greece was flooded; Herodôrus in bringing to bear on these traditions, with somewhat grotesque results, the most up-to-date and enlightened scientific doctrines of his age; Thucydides in concentrating his study upon that which was of primary importance and could be certainly known; Xenophon, in a modern or at least a Hellenistic manner, in dividing or scattering his interests among many subjects and becoming a man of letters, perhaps mainly because he was not allowed to continue as a man of action.

I wish for our present purpose to pick up Greek history at a later epoch as it emerged from the school of Isocrates. He was, I suppose, though far from the greatest, probably the most influential man of letters of the fourth century. His style dominated the Greek language forthwith and lived to dominate, through Cicero, the Latin language as well. He taught his pupils to avoid hiatus in prose as they would in poetry; to avoid the repetition of the same word, to compose in correct periods. He also taught them to combine politics and philosophy.

He was a great publicist at a time when statesmanship in general showed more ingenuity than wisdom. On all the main public problems of Greece he was right, and apparently, at least that is the impression he makes, he alone. His political ideas were higher in tone than those current about him, but they were also more practical. He saw the only way to save Hellas from ruin was to put a stop to her internecine wars. He saw the safest and most beneficial line, at least to believers in Hellenism, into which the ambitions of Macedon could be diverted. He saw, more clearly than any of the practical statesmen, that Hellenism is a thing of the spirit, and should be welcomed in Boeotians as much as in Athenians, in barbarians as much as in either. Critics call him a rhetorician; but his *rhêtorikê* was almost the opposite of what we sneeringly denote as 'rhetoric' at the present time. He taught his numerous pupils—comprising among them a surprising number of the men who became famous throughout Greece —to compose smoothly, correctly, quietly, and above all with lucidity and balance. He helped to lay the foundations for that invaluable vehicle of civilization, the *Koinê Dialektos*, through which, at the price of becoming easy, flat, common, and a little soulless, the Greek language in the Hellenistic period evangelized the whole Mediterranean world.

He was always right, and he had a deservedly high opinion
of himself; which, of course, makes him an irritating writer.
He was a man of letters, a moralist, and a class-conscious
educator. Like all publicists, he is always telling other people
what they ought to do, and how to do it, not often doing
anything very good himself.

But I think it is quite misleading to say that he corrupted
history by rhetoric. On the contrary, it may well be maintained that he reformed the study of history, and that—as
usual—practically all his reforms were right. I deduce his
principles from the work of his pupils, especially Ephorus
and Theopompus.

1. He saw that history should be universal and not local.
To a philosopher, the great adventure of mankind is really
one; and besides, without insisting on that somewhat high
doctrine, you cannot practically understand the course of
policy in one nation without knowing the effect of its neighbours upon it. Ephorus entitled his great work ἱστορία κοινῶν
πράξεων, 'An Inquiry into the Common Fortunes'—into the
way in which we human beings have all fared. That is a
great idea, and one can see the effect of it in the fine introduction to the *History* of Diodorus Siculus.

2. He saw, as did Aristotle, that history should be the
record of man's whole *praxis*, or 'faring' in this world, not
merely a record of wars or even of great deeds. A special
history of human inventions was current in later times under
the name of Ephorus, and seems to have been not a separate
treatise but a series of extracts from his general history.

3. The records of Greece were rooted in an inextricable
and unverifiable mass of myths and legends, which earlier
writers had tried in vain to harmonize or reduce to reason.
The school of Isocrates cut them boldly out. Ephorus put
faith in no tradition earlier than the return of the Heraclidae. That was not rhetoric but courageous criticism.
Mere rhetoric would have expanded itself on the myths and
legends.

4. Greek history from its earliest days had laid stress on the importance of exact geography, but the Isocrateans emphasized it still more. Ephorus throughout all his thirty books had a geographical excursus whenever it was wanted and never failed to make the geography clear. Theopompus mentions that he travelled personally to every city and every important meeting-place in the Greek world. And both are quoted by later writers as authorities on geographical points. That, again, is scientific history, not 'rhetoric'.

5. His pupils are blamed for their use of fictitious speeches. But what were they to do? Thucydides, the greatest master of history, had devoted special pains to the speeches which he put in the mouths of his characters. He used them, not to make effects of eloquence, but to explain political situations or the objects of national movements. And he did so, admittedly, with great success. The pupils of Isocrates improved on his example. None of their speeches are preserved, so we cannot tell how good they were, or how inopportune; but to attain the same end in a more legitimate manner the Isocrateans seem to have started each book with a more or less philosophical comment on the history there narrated. Ephorus had a 'proem' to every book.

6. We cannot make out much about their methods of research; but Ephorus was famous for his wide reading and minute inquiries, while Theopompus spent his whole life in travelling for the sake of his great contemporary history, the *Philippica*.

7. Lastly, no doubt, Isocrates laid stress on *rhêtorikê*: history must be written in a clear, distinguished, and attractive way, so that the ordinary man can understand what you mean, and not at all like Thucydides. It should be in Attic, because Attic was becoming the common language, but it must be easy Attic intelligible throughout the Greek world. He did not insist on lively colours: modern critics find his whole style of writing dull. He did insist on euphony and symmetry, and probably also on purity of diction. If so

Theopompus, at any rate, disobeyed his master; he is constantly blamed by the Atticists for his improper vocabulary.

All these reforms, I venture to think, were, roughly speaking, on the right lines. I mean that, if we with our present knowledge had lived at that time, I think we should have agreed with Isocrates. And they were successful. Ephorus and Theopompus, more than any other writers, formed the average man's conception of Greek history for many centuries after their death. To a great extent they founded the *fable convenue*, as it lived in the mind of the common man.

It is curious that the result was not better. The reforms and methods were all very well, but they could not turn mediocre minds into great minds. The other conditions were wrong. I suspect also that Isocrates made the usual mistake of the zealous educator; he laid so much stress upon matters of secondary importance that those of primary importance were neglected. The pupil who got full marks from him was sure to be second-rate.

Not that Ephorus and Theopompus are like one another. The traditional criticism says—I quote from Suidas—'Ephorus was simple in character, and in the expression of what he had to say supine and sluggish, with no tension; Theopompus was in character astringent and satirical, in diction abundant, fluent, and impetuous, and very candid (φιλαλήθης) in his writing. Isocrates used to say that Theopompus needed the curb and Ephorus the spur.'

He needed the curb; the fragments as a whole, while they show no great liveliness or charm of style, do indulge in some unmeasured language. He is praised by Suidas (and blamed by Professor Bury) for his interest in the hidden motives which actuate soldiers and statesmen, and his constant stream of comment on their personal characters. The fragments thoroughly bear out this criticism. He was doubtless conceited; and critics speak severely of his lapses in this respect. But we must remember that a modern writer need never praise himself. He simply arranges with his publisher that such-and-such a sum is to be paid for advertisement, and thus having secured the blowing of a large and expensive bugle, can afford in his own preface to be modest as a violet. Theopompus had not these advantages. He mentions in his preface to the *Philippica*[1] that he was contemporary with Isocrates, Theodectes, and Naucrates of Erythrae, and these three shared with him the first place in literature among the Greeks. But Isocrates and Theodectes, through lack of means, wrote speeches for pay and practised as sophists, teaching the young and thus receiving rewards, while he and Naucrates, having independent means, spent their whole lives in the pursuit of wisdom and knowledge. As compared with Naucrates, he suggests that he might well claim the highest place, having produced no less than 20,000 lines of epideictic speeches and more than 150,000 lines of historical writing, in which a reader will find the doings of both Greeks and barbarians up to the present day; and further, because there is no place of common resort and no considerable city in which he has not made a stay and by his public addresses left a remembrance of his accomplishment in letters.

He proceeds to show that writers of earlier times were far inferior to those of his own age, and not worthy of even second place. The art of writing had made such great progress during his lifetime.

It does seem more convenient to leave that kind of statement to the publisher's circular.

We know Theopompus chiefly from some 383 quotations in later writers, most of them taken from his *Philippica*. There is also, of course, the important papyrus fragment, about 30 octavo pages in length, discovered at Oxyrhynchus in 1911 and attributed to Theopompus by many critics. The identification is too uncertain to form a good basis for any argument, and I shall refer to the papyrus little. Roughly speaking, the tone seems to me to recall Theopompus, but

[1] Jacoby, *Fragmenta Historicorum*, vol. ii *b*. 25.

the writing to be rather less lively. The question of author-ship must, of course, be decided on other grounds.[1]

The fragments leave on me a peculiar impression. The historian seems haunted by a sense of the unreality of the pageant which he describes. The story of human ambitions and achievements fascinates him, but it chiefly appeals to his taste for satire. He is always using his bludgeon upon the characters of his drama; there is more denunciation than subtle analysis, but there is at least a constant attempt to strip off the trappings of the general or statesman and exhibit the poor frail human creature beneath.

Now this tone was very common in the fourth century, that age of disillusion. It was doubtless particularly marked among the intellectuals of Athens, who were on the whole traditionally opposed to the ruling *Demos* and who had among them many aristocratic refugees from Ionia and elsewhere. The *Demos* itself seems to have been rather proud of its great writers and philosophers, but to have resolutely excluded them from public life, just as in certain British dominions it is said to be a disadvantage to a politician to have received more than an elementary education. The great public let the philosophers manage the affairs of God and the soul and mathematics *et tout ce galimatias-là*; but it did not encourage them to take part in politics or interfere with things that really mattered. One result of this divorce between intellect and public life is that the intellectuals are all rather captious towards democracies in general and that of Athens in par-ticular, all a little inclined to idealize the Spartans, and emphatically to treat as sour grapes the public rewards from which they were excluded. We may take as typical the fact that Aristotle in the *Rhetoric* never mentions Demosthenes.

Now Theopompus made his centre at Athens after his expulsion from his native Chios, where he and his father belonged to the oligarchic party. And I find that the common opinion about him is merely that, as a Chian oligarch, he

[1] See ibid., Commentary on fr. 66.

was naturally pro-Spartan and anti-Athenian, while towards Macedon he was inconsistent in his attitude, partly perhaps from interested motives and partly because of his addiction to 'rhetoric'. This explanation, I confess, does not seem to me to account for the facts. And I cannot help suggesting that we shall get a more consistent picture of the man by giving full weight to his words about Antisthenes, the founder of the Cynic school.

Most philosophers fare badly at his hands, almost as badly as statesmen. 'Antisthenes alone', says Diogenes Laertius, 'is praised by Theopompus. He says he had extraordinary power, and could convert ($\upsilon\pi\alpha\gamma\alpha\gamma\epsilon\sigma\theta\alpha\iota$) anyone in the world by his harmonious flow of argument.' Did he, then, convert Theopompus? Perhaps not in the full sense; but even when we allow that it was only natural for a defeated Ionian intellectual to feel that the world in general was going wrong —as, of course, it was—and thus to share the general pessimistic feelings of the disciples of Socrates, we shall find in Theopompus here and there a good many touches that seem personally characteristic of Antisthenes. About Plato, for instance, Theopompus says, 'His dialogues are in the lump useless and false, and most of them not his own. Some come from the diatribes of Aristippus; others from Antisthenes; many also from Bryson of Heraclea.'[1] Antisthenes had said it made him feel like a king to be abused by Plato for doing right. Again when he saw a horse snorting and prancing absurdly, he said that he understood Plato's love of horses; he was just like that horse. Hearing that Plato had been sick he wondered if he had evacuated his conceit. Evidently, it would seem, the two men shared a strong prejudice and a taste for Cynic plain language.

As for the Athenians in general, Antisthenes has some sharp comments. When they boasted that, unlike most Greeks, they were autochthonous, natives of the soil, 'much the same', he said, 'as the snails and locusts' ($\dot{\alpha}\tau\tau\dot{\epsilon}\lambda\epsilon\beta o\iota$). As

[1] Fr. 259.

for their democratic system, he advised them to vote their
asses to be horses; no difficulty, considering what creatures
they voted to be generals. He went beyond Lord Acton's
opinion on the difficulty or impossibility of a great man
being a good man. Such people are apt to have 'a poverty
in their souls' which makes them insatiable and ready for any
crime in their desire for power and riches.[1] One need hardly
comment on the Cynic's contempt for wealth and worldly
fame or on the brutality of language with which he expressed
it. All these qualities we shall recognize in Theopompus.

First, however, let us see whether the view that Theopompus is merely philo-Spartan and anti-Athenian will fit
the facts. Take fragment 13 (in *Hellenica Oxyrhynchia*,
Oxford, fr. 14).

'The treatment of the Helot nation has been utterly ferocious and
cruel. They have been reduced to slavery by the Spartans for many
generations, some of them being Messenians and the others Heleatae
from the marsh country of Laconia.'

A more lively phrase is attributed by Plutarch to Theopompus the Comedian:

'The Spartans, as governors, were like dishonest wine-sellers. They
first gave the cities a taste of the sweet wine of freedom, and then,
when they had accepted the sample, supplied a bitter and poisonous
tyranny.'[2]

Fragment 240 (233 H). 'Xenopeitheia, the mother of Lysandridas,
was the most beautiful woman in the Peloponnese. The Lacedaemo-
nians murdered her and her sister Chrysê, when Agesilaüs, in the course
of a political intrigue, had his colleague Lysandridas driven to exile.'

Thus even Agesilaüs, Xenophon's hero, the best of the
Spartan kings, is not spared. We may compare the statement in the papyrus,[3] that Agesilaüs gave protection to a
certain Persian deserter 'chiefly because his young son was
so good-looking'.

This is enough to show that Theopompus was not a

---

[1] Xen. *Symp.* iv. 34 ff.　　　[2] Plut. *Lysander*, 13.　　　[3] Chap. xvi.

partisan of Sparta. But the truth is, Sparta did not interest these Cynics much. They were out to attack Vanity Fair, the pride of life, and above all luxury. Sparta did not give them much scope. There was better sport in baiting Athens. For example:

Fragment 213 (205 H). 'Chares was a slow and heavy man, but lived for luxury. On his campaigns he carried about with him female flute-players and harp-players and other less pretentious prostitutes. And the funds contributed for the purposes of war were partly spent by him on this sort of licence and partly left behind in Athens for the speakers and movers of decrees and private informers. The Athenian public never resented these proceedings. On the contrary they were the cause of his exceptional popularity, and justly so. For this was the way in which the people of Athens generally lived.'

Fragment 143 (139 H). Again, there was a certain Charidemos of Oreus to whom the Athenians gave the special honour of citizenship; why?

'They say his daily life was indecent and so arranged that he could be always eating and drinking. He ravished free women, and reached such a pitch of intemperance that . . .'

I omit further details. So you see he had well earned his Athenian citizenship.

Fragment 90 (90-1 H). Part of the tenth book of the *Philippica* was 'On the Demagogues at Athens'. It was afterwards published separately. It condemns Eubulus and Callistratus for luxury, though the latter, he admits, discharged his public duties well. As for Eubulus,[1] he was not only luxurious himself, but he managed the Athenian finances so well that he raised the whole standard of living of that deplorable people and so destroyed their morale! It tells how[2] Cleon was the first to shout and use bad language on the *Bêma*, and how he once came into the *ekklesia* garlanded for a feast and bade them put off the meeting, as he happened to be making a sacrifice and was about to entertain foreigners at dinner.[3] And they did so! It tells how Hyperbolus, after his ostracism,

---

[1] Fr. 99, 100.   [2] Fr. 92 (94 H).   [3] Ibid.

lived in Samos, and how, when he died, they put his body
into a sack and flung it into the sea.[1]

Fragment 105 (103 H). Of another general he tells us:

'Chabrias the general was unable to live in the city, partly because
of the debauchery and prodigality of his life, partly because of the
Athenians, who are harsh to every public man. Consequently their
distinguished men have preferred to end their lives abroad, Iphicrates
in Thrace, Conon in Cyprus, Timotheos in Lesbos, Chares in Sigeum,
and Chabrias himself in Egypt.'

He resents the heroic part played by Athens in the time of
the Persian wars and the fifty years that followed. He speaks
of[2] certain alleged treaties and the story of Marathon, 'and
all the other impostures and deceptions practised by the
Athenians against Greece.' And we have a curious fragment
which looks like a petulant answer to someone who claimed
that Athens was full of philosophers and savants and poets:

Fragment 281 (267 H). 'Athens is full of Dionysus-flatterers and
sailors and footpads, as well as professional false-witnesses and informers
and prosecutors.'

I cannot feel sure who are meant by Διονυσοκόλακες. If it
were Διονυσιοκόλακες all would be simple. Many persons at
Athens, including Plato, were open to the charge of being
'flatterers of Dionysius' the tyrant of Syracuse. But the
flatterers of Dionysus would seem to be merely the actors in
the theatre, normally called 'craftsmen of Dionysus'.

On the other hand, there are one or two passages about
Athens which show that Theopompus could, on occasion,
show sympathy even to that misguided city. He notes
with indignation[3] that after Chaeronea, when the Athenian
ambassadors came in dignified grief to Philip's camp, he
burst in upon them revelling and tipsy. The author of the
papyrus, too, goes out of his way once or twice to praise or
defend Conon, the Athenian general.

Naturally enough, on the analogy of the great democracy,

[1] Fr. 96 (98b H).   [2] Fr. 153 (148 H).   [3] Fr. 236 (228 H).

Theopompus attacks all democracies. For example:

Fragment 62 (65 H). The Byzantines had been for a long time democratically governed and had a city situated at a great market, so that the natives were accustomed to spend their time about the market-place and harbour. Consequently they are dissolute, and the ordinary shops there are used as drinking-places and worse. The people of Chalcêdon, before the union with Byzantium, all regularly followed a better life and better pursuits. But when once they tasted the democracy of the Byzantines they were corrupted, and became luxurious . . . drunken and extravagant.

But then monarchs and oligarchs fare no better, not even the regular hereditary monarchs, so much praised by those Greeks who hated tyranny:

Fragment 134 (252 H). Of Dionysius the Second, 'The King had bad sight, his eyes having been destroyed by drink; he sat in the barbers' shops and amused the customers.'

Fragment 114 (111 H) describes how Straton king of Sidon and Nicocles king of Cyprus conducted a competition in debauchery and extravagance.

Oligarchies are less picturesque material, but are not much more sympathetically treated:

Fragment 121 (118 H). Hegesilochus, who set up an oligarchy in Rhodes, is described as guilty of all crimes. Among them, he played dice for the possession of free-born women.

Fragment 124 (121 H). Nicostratus of Argos, the chief man in the city, of great birth, wealth, and estate, surpassed the record in vile flattery and service to the Great King. He took his son to Susa and left him with the King! He set a separate table at dinner, piled with viands, for the King's *Daimon*, hearing that it was the practice of the courtiers. The explanation is that 'He was greedy and a slave of avarice without a rival.'

I need not dwell upon his tyrants. They have all the stock villainies associated with their unpopular profession. Apollocrates and Nysaios are conventionally abominable. Clearchos, tyrant of Heraclea Pontica, has a little more character.

He used to destroy people with aconite, a poison to which an antidote was discovered in the plant peganon. Consequently those who received an invitation to dine with Clearchos took a large dose of peganon before they started.[1]

It was sometimes a part of the literary tradition to idealize the unspoilt natural man, as Herodotus had done before this time and some of the Stoics and Tacitus did afterwards. Menedemus of Eretria had recently written a book *On the Morals of the Barbarian Peoples*. The noble savage was always imposing on the Greeks. But not on Theopompus. The description of the semi-savage Illyrians[2] and the utterly bestial Tyrrhenians[3] make one incline after all to prefer the over-civilized corruption of the Attic *Demos*. And one character who unites in his person two dangerous traits, by being both a barbarian and a tyrant, Cotys of Thrace, surpasses his rivals by committing sacrilege, cutting his wife into small pieces with a dagger, and going mad.[4]

But what of Philip, the conquering Macedonian, whose personality so dominates the age that Theopompus calls his whole history *Philippica*? Everything was full of Philip, infected by Philip. I condense the well-known chapter from Polybius together with two from Athenaeus.[5]

'Philip acquired immense possessions which he scattered and flung right and left. He and his companions were the worst of managers, since they did not understand decent or moderate living. They lived always plundering, always squandering. Philip himself was the cause of this; since in his life as a soldier he never had time to think of economy, but was accustomed to wild excesses of rapacity and expenditure. And his companions consisted of men specially selected from all Greece, not for good qualities, but the reverse. Anyone who was notorious for raging passions, for unscrupulousness, for impudence, fled to Macedon and became Philip's friend.'

Their dissolute way of living is described. There was a sort of competition in dishonesty and trickery among them.

---

[1] Fr. 181 (177a H).   [2] Fr. 39 (39 H).   [3] Fr. 204 (195 H).
[4] Fr. 31 (32 H).   [5] Frr. 224, 225 (217a–c H).

For they despised the old-fashioned rules of sobriety, order, truthfulness, and good faith, and liked to boast of their drinking feats, of the amounts they had stolen, or the lies and tricks they had practised. There were not more than 800 companions in all; yet they owned as much land as the 10,000 richest men in Greece, and were always seizing more. 'Never has history known of such wild beasts. Nature meant them for murderers, but their habits turned them to prostitutes.'

That, it would seem, is the road to success, fame, and wide-flung empire! Those are the kind of men who win the glittering prizes of the world. Indeed in what was called his Encomium of Philip, he said that if Philip continued as he had begun, he would end by being King of Europe.[1] Is there not a curious bitterness in calling the whole history of the age *Philippica*? It was all, in Theopompus' eyes, affected by the same poison.

This catalogue of villainies is becoming tedious, but after all there is a clue to it. To a good Cynic or Stoic only one thing mattered, Virtue, and the surest sign of Virtue was temperance, simplicity of life, and a contempt for all bodily pleasures and the vanities of the world. In considering any statesman or soldier the question that Theopompus puts first is about his private life. After all, he will say, that is the real man; it is by that that God will judge him; why should any but fools judge him by such trivialities as worldly success or failure?

It is a comfort—if we may consider such a low thing as comfort—to see that Theopompus can occasionally show some more real, and less dogmatic, appreciation of character. He has high praise for the unbroken temperance and moderation of one great Spartan conqueror, Lysander, and a rather charming account of another, Agesilaüs.[2]

When he arrived in Egypt, the chief generals and civil officers of the King immediately proceeded to the ship to pay court to him. . . .

[1] Fr. 256 (246 H).   [2] Fr. 107, cf. 22 (22a, b, d H).

There was great enthusiasm and expectation among all the Egyptians because of the name and fame of Agesilaüs, and they ran in crowds to the sight. They found no magnificence and no head-quarters; only a small and unimpressive old gentleman lying down on a patch of grass by the beach, wrapped in a rough cloak of cheap quality. A spirit of scoffing and mockery began to take possession of them. . . . They were still more surprised at his strange behaviour when the royal gifts were brought and offered to him. He accepted the grain and calves and geese; but the delicacies and cakes and perfumes he pushed aside. Then when the envoys pressed and forced him to accept them, he ordered them to be taken and given to the Helots. However, Theopompus says, he was pleased with the papyrus used for garlands, because of the smoothness and cleanness of the crowns it made, and on his departure he asked for some from the king, who gave them.

The story might come from a Cynic *diatribê*.

Again, there is an interesting picture of a great Athenian gentleman:[1]

Kimon of Athens used to put no watcher in his fields or gardens. Any of the citizens who liked might come in and pluck the fruit and take whatever they wanted from the fields. His house also was open to all. He had always a simple dinner prepared for a large number, and poor citizens used to come in and dine. He used to help those who made requests to him day by day; and it is said that he always took about with him two or three young men laden with small change, to give to those who came to beg of him. They say also that he used to subscribe to the funerals of the poor. And it often happened, when he saw one of the citizens badly clad, that he would tell one of his young men to change with him. Naturally his fame stood high, and he was first among the citizens.

It is a curious picture: Kimon was more provident than St. Martin, having, of course, a larger fortune to manage and a more critical public opinion to conciliate. It would never have done for the chief man in Athens to tear his own cloak in two or give it away to beggars and come home γυμνός.

[1] Fr. 89 (89 H).

A *stratêgos* who acted in that way would not have inspired confidence.

In looking through the criticisms passed on Theopompus in later ages I have sometimes suspected that he was misunderstood, not merely in his general attitude towards history, but in one detail of style. Not realizing the Cynic strain in the man, late critics did not see when he was ironical. The later Greek critics are always missing points of this sort; they have so largely lost the fresh movement of mind.

The test case is a passage cited and condemned by Longinus on the ground that it begins with a description of really magnificent things and then condescends to such mean details that it spoils its own effect. It describes the march of Xerxes:

Fragment 263 (283a H). What city or what race in Asia did not send embassies to the king? What fruit of the earth, what rare and beautiful product of art was not brought to him as a gift? Abundance of precious tapestries and cloaks, crimson and variegated and white, tents of gold with all their furniture, robes of state and expensive couches? Then came silver plate and wrought gold and goblets and mixing bowls, some studded with jewels, some exquisitely and expensively wrought. Then countless myriads of pieces of armour, Greek and foreign, mules and asses beyond number, fatted beasts for butchering, gallons upon gallons of sauces, and bags and sacks and paper for books and other necessaries. And such masses of pickled meats of every kind, piled in heaps, that people approaching from a distance thought they were mountains being rolled against them!

This seems to me to have a tone of intentional satire, with its oceans of sauce and its mountains of pickled meat.

Again, you will remember the description of Philip and the creatures by whom he was surrounded. Polybius complains that Theopompus says,[1] 'Europe has never produced such a man as Philip son of Amyntas.' Yet immediately after, both in the introduction and throughout his whole

[1] Fr. 27 (26 H).

history, he shows him utterly dissolute. Would not Theopompus have answered: 'Well, I only said there was nobody
like him. Nor there was.'

I recognize a similar tone in a story about a war-profiteer:

Fragment 192 (189 H). The ancient Spartans, wanting gold to gild
the face of Apollo of Amyclae, by the advice of Delphi went to
Croesus the king of Lydia and managed to get it. Later on Hiero in a
similar predicament went to Architeles, a Corinthian army contractor.
He easily produced the whole sum, and threw in a couple of handfuls
extra!

Lastly, both from the extant fragments and from the voice
of tradition, we know that Theopompus had another peculiarity. He liked to insert myths and fables into his narrative;
and indeed gave up one whole book, the eighth, to this kind
of matter. We find quoted from that book an account of a
sort of Golden Age; of an island of piety and an island of battle;
stories of Pherecydes foretelling an earthquake by the taste
of a certain well, of Epimenides falling asleep for fifty years,
like Rip van Winkle; of Midas and Silenus and others. Myths
of this sort were not, I think, in the ordinary practice of the
historians; they were of course thoroughly in that of the
philosophers. Antisthenes himself composed a large number
of myths, just as Plato did. It is here perhaps that the philosophers seemed to themselves chiefly to discover truth,
among the things which ἐγένετο μὲν οὔποτε, ἔστι δ' ἀεί.[1]

I think, therefore, that this rather enigmatic figure falls
into his place in the development of Greek literature when
once we conceive of him as a writer who learned his style
from Isocrates, as an Ionian intellectual in revolt against an
age in which neither intellect nor Ionia had much place, and
lastly as an historian who took his view of life and public
affairs from the Cynics. The streams did not easily combine.
Theopompus the Cynic broke the rules of Isocrates by using
odd and un-Attic and even violently coarse words; the

[1] 'Which never happened but always are.' Sallustius, περὶ θεῶν καὶ
κόσμου, iv Nock.

Isocratean broke the rules of the Kunosarges by the mere act of giving so much attention to the past futilities and crimes of this vain world. Yet he did achieve a style which induced the world to listen, and he did apply to the current coin of history a relentless Cynic *paracharaxis*.

All the fourth century is touched by this feeling of disillusion that goes with a lost cause. Athens had failed; the Greek *polis* had failed, with all its ambitions, its pieties, and its ideals of public duty. Things bigger and more brutal now possessed the world. In the beginning of the fourth century Plato has turned his civic enthusiasm away to utopias or to the other world; Antisthenes to contempt of all objects of admiration or desire except personal virtue; Aristippus to the rejection of all imaginary values, all, indeed, outside the actual pleasures and pains of the individual. The new philosophies had perhaps hardly acquired clear shape till the old age of Theopompus. The ferment took at least a generation to work. By that time we find the Epicureans treating public life not as a duty, but as a temptation that deludes fools to their ruin; the Stoics, though they admit the duty of serving the world, preaching the absolute nullity of all its prizes, and most of all Diogenes, the chief follower of that Antisthenes whom our historian so greatly admired, insisting with a fierce humour and a narrow intensity of vision which partly explain his astonishing success, that nothing, nothing matters except the soul, and that the soul is only trammelled, not helped, by all the conventions of this world. The way to true life was to deface all the current coin, for at present it was all wrongly stamped. The things called good and precious were worthless. The men called kings were really slaves. Art, learning, riches, and the like were all a prison and a blinding of the eyes. The pride of life itself was the *Vanitas vanitatum*. The true freedom was to have no wants, the true happiness to be at peace with God. Our brothers the animals show us the true way. Diogenes himself would have liked to have as few needs as a dog or a rat, but found he could not get on without four things: a blanket for warmth, a bowl for his food, a wallet for his worldly possessions, and a stick to keep off dogs and bad men.

Now the truth is that history cannot afford to look on things in this way. Dealing with the fortunes of a world largely based on the struggle for life, and the doings of those who come to the front in that struggle, she starts by accepting the world's current standards of what is important and unimportant. She regards wealth and power and territory and armies as undoubted goods. She studies character as it has practical consequences, but is terribly apt to ignore what the Greeks would call 'the soul' altogether, and to proclaim men great merely by their results. When questioned closely about such things as virtue or religion or philosophic truth, she is apt to turn cross or negative or frankly anarchic.

Apply to history the standards of Antisthenes or Zeno, not to speak of those of the New Testament, and it appears like a chaos or a bedlam. Carlyle among historians has a dash of the Cynic and sometimes applies these standards with much effect; but at heart, though a satirist, he is a worshipper of force and success, so he is at home with Cromwell and Frederick and Danton. A more real Cynic—in the ancient sense of course—is Tolstoy. On the rare occasions when he deals with history the effect is devastating. Some few passages in *War and Peace* and above all his matchless description of the Franco-Russian festivities at Toulon leave exactly this bedlamite impression. The great pageant becomes false and sordid and hollow: the overfed misshapen men in the beautiful expensive uniforms, the expressions of ardent affection between persons who are known to dislike one another, the alcoholic enthusiasm, the lying parade of religiosity, and in the background the contractors, armament-makers, and speculators rejoicing over their gains. It is all a farce, and a strangely cruel one. For behind it is oppression and misery, the knout, the prison, the gallows, and the torture-chamber, and eventually, in the background, war. It is like one of those plays in the Roman circus where criminals were made to take part in spectacular tragedies culminating in their own deaths, where the kings and crowns were sham kings and sham crowns but the shrieking victims and the famished wild beasts who tore them were good, solid, sentient flesh and blood. In a certain mood there seems to be no way out except the road taken by the Cynics and Stoics and certain Christian saints: to carry your rejection of earthly values one step farther and deny that pain is an evil. Pain is not either goodness or badness; and only goodness and badness are good and bad.

Tolstoy or Diogenes or St. Francis could never have made good, sober historians. You must believe a little in the seriousness of Vanity Fair before you can devote your life to chronicling its fortunes.

Had Theopompus been a true Cynic he could never have ploughed his way on through forty-eight books describing the solemn follies of mankind. But he was not altogether a philosopher; only a man of letters, oppressed by the ill fortunes of his country, and his whole age, and fascinated by a particular philosopher of strong character and great powers of persuasion. It is hard to judge from our scanty evidence, but supposing the papyrus to be his work and comparing it with the quotations, I should guess that he treated his narrative normally as the serious record of a momentous historical achievement; only when he stood back from the work and reflected did he feel the impulse to throw a sudden searchlight of piercing truth on a monument of lies and delusion. The papyrus does seem to be an exact, thoughtful, and detailed piece of historical writing.

As to the judgements he passes on individuals, no doubt our fragments do injustice to Theopompus. They consist largely of quotations made by Athenaeus and others who were interested in scandal. But one may doubt whether the Cynic school—until it was transformed by Stoicism—was capable of a sane moral criticism of public men. It denied all public social values: and it is by public social values that the work of a statesman must chiefly be judged. The Cynics cared only about the man himself. Had he the cardinal virtues? Was he just, brave, wise, and temperate? And, since justice to them was a very negative matter, since courage consisted in endurance of hardship and wisdom in rejecting the world, an altogether disproportionate stress came to be laid on temperance. Many of the ancients were apt to judge a statesman or philosopher as Indians to-day are said to judge a missionary. If he lives on rice in the bazaar and practises meditation he is a godly man; if he lives with the Sahibs, eats and drinks as they do, and has to play games to keep himself in health, then it is no good pretending that he is a godly man: he is something quite different. It was the later Stoics, I think, who redeemed this Cynic narrowness by regarding a statesman as one who had taken upon him a great service and who should be judged broadly by the way in which he had discharged it.

Doubtless the coins of history need a different stamping. But the task was harder than Theopompus realized, nor was he quite the man to carry it successfully through. It would need the faith of a great philosopher or mystic to conceive of a history in which all the secondary values were melted away and only the spiritual values left. It would need the insight and imagination of a great dramatist, or else the knowledge of a better-equipped psychologist than the world has yet seen, to depict in a history the movements of the human souls behind the phenomena. It is well that the conventional stamp of the coin should from time to time be challenged and denied, but it seems to live on, not much modified by all the challenges and denials. People sometimes suggest that there is always a deep, unspoken wisdom behind the established tradition. That may or may not be so, but there is at any rate a great toughness of vitality. Neither the Sophoclean *paracharaxis* of the fighting man and his wife, nor the Euripidean *paracharaxis* of the values of war and conquest, nor the Theopompan *paracharaxis* of the values of history have at all superseded the traditional images and superscriptions as you may see them, say, in the House of Commons or *The Times* or in Plutarch; but they have all added to it a note of question, a warning that the label never tells the whole truth; we must look deeper and think and understand. And it is interesting for us Greek scholars to realize that if we cleave firmly to the tradition, the tradition is Greek, and if we side with the spiritual rebels, that rebellion of the spirit is Greek also.

1928.

IX

THE BEGINNINGS OF GRAMMAR, OR FIRST ATTEMPTS AT A SCIENCE OF LANGUAGE IN GREECE

GRAMMAR is an unpopular subject nowadays. And the reasons for its unpopularity are, in part at least, interesting. We speak an almost uninflected language. Except in the pronouns we have practically no distinctions of case and gender, and our verbs appear to a medical eye to be in an advanced state of phthisis. The question has been raised by Jespersen, whether in course of time the English colloquial language will not consist of a few hundred monosyllables— the longer words having gone out of use—which will all indifferently play the part of noun, adjective, or verb according to their position in the sentence. *Black* is an adjective, but if you black the boots of a black it becomes both noun and verb. *Boot* in itself is a noun; but in 'boot polish' it is an adjective, and to 'boot' a man is a verb of at least two authorized meanings.

It is hard for us to realize either the difficulties or the delights of speaking a fully inflected language. We utter without mental discomfort sentences like: 'Whenever he met him he removed his hat', which, as Professor Sonnenschein has pointed out, may bear eight different meanings; and in time, perhaps, we shall drop even the remaining inflections *him* and *his*, and say simply, 'When 'e met 'e 'e remoov 'e 'at.'

And meantime the grammatical terms of this uninflected and amorphous language are all derived from one of the most beautifully constructed and highly inflected languages known to science. A great authority has pointed out that the various nations which spoke Indo-European languages differed widely in race, in build, in climatic conditions, and in most other things. They only agreed in speaking different forms of a language so precise, flexible, and rich in varieties of form, that no one could use it who had not considerable brains and some capacity for taking constant trouble. That is perhaps, he suggests, the reason for the extraordinary success of these nations in the battle of life and their general superiority over their neighbours.

Progressive science is always ungrateful. As unimaginative economists deride Mill, and biologists Darwin, as journalists who have dipped into Einstein treat Newton as a peculiarly incompetent mathematician, so the modern geometer warns us against Euclid, and the philologist against the concepts of Greek grammar. Yet not only does the whole science of language stand on a Greek basis; the actual achievement of the Greeks in the analysis of language is, if once we make the necessary imaginative effort to understand their meaning, both brilliant in itself and, I think, actually helpful to the modern inquirer. But we must first realize the meanings of the words we use. They have all changed. *Grammatikê* is not grammar, nor *rhêtorikê* rhetoric; and more important still, the angle from which the Greeks approached their problem is different from ours.

Ancient *grammatikê* was a τέχνη, an art or craft, a study aiming at practice; modern philology is not a τέχνη but a physical science. It takes the world-wide phenomenon of human speech as its object, and is concerned merely to ascertain and co-ordinate the facts. It is particularly interested in the variety of languages and the variety of their special methods. Up to the middle of the eighteenth century the languages known to European philologists were principally Greek, Latin, and Hebrew; all of these were alike in being inflected languages. Hebrew, it is true, was Semitic, and might have been immensely instructive by reason of its peculiarities; but these were largely obscured, or treated as mere anomalies, because it was studied according to the rules that had grown up for Latin and Greek. Then towards the end of the century came the great discovery of Sir W. Jones,

that Sanskrit was akin to Latin and Greek; a discovery made
significant by Bopp and followed, up to the present day, by
ever-widening discoveries of different types of languages,
some with new affinities of their own, and some with no dis-
coverable affinities.

The ancient Greeks used, no doubt, various languages
for purposes of commerce, but we have no evidence that
they studied them scientifically. And even in commerce, it
looks as if it was usually the foreigner who was compelled, if
he wished to do business, to learn Greek, as the peoples of the
Far East have now to learn pidgin-English. Thousands of the
Greeks in the Hellenistic period knew Hebrew well; but the
knowledge seems to have had no effect on their conception
of grammar. The Greek grammarians, as far as I know,
never notice that in Hebrew the verbs have masculine and
feminine forms, like Greek adjectives; that they have seven
voices but no tenses; that if you wish to say, 'a proverb of
Solomon', instead of dividing it *proverbium*, 'a proverb',
Salomonis, 'of Solomon', in Hebrew you alter מָשָׁל, 'a proverb',
into מְשַׁל, 'a proverb of'—and add Solomon with no case-
mark.

This is the sort of fact that specially interests the modern
student of grammar; it did not interest the ancient *Grammatikos*, because it was of no importance to his practice.
Similarly, if you read modern writers like Sayce or Jespersen,
you find a constant striving to get away from the current
grammatical tradition. They delight in the polysynthetic
languages, such as those of the Red Indians in North
America. We are told that in Delaware a word *kuligatchis*
means 'Give me your pretty little paw', but that no separate
part of it means 'little', or 'pretty', or 'paw'. Similarly, in a
Canadian language, a certain word means 'to throw a slippery
object far away', though no part of the word means 'throw',
or 'slippery', or 'far'. And in Cherokee there is no word
meaning 'to wash', but—beware of hasty conclusions—there
are thirteen words, apparently unconnected, each denoting

a different kind of washing. In the island of Rossel in the
north Pacific serious administrative trouble arose because
there was no one word meaning 'to kill'. The Government
wished to forbid murder, and thought it had done so, but
it really only succeeded in forbidding a number of particular
kinds of killing, and put the law-abiding natives to considerable trouble in devising other and more recondite ways
of putting their enemies to death. Almost the opposite of
this type of language is the Isolating type, like Chinese,
which makes its sentences of strings of monosyllabic roots,
all of them—except a few so-called 'hollow words'—possessing their definite meanings, while their grammatical relations are determined chiefly by their position in the sentence
—like 'boot' and 'black' in the examples given above.

The majority of the languages of the world, says Sayce, if
we put aside the North American dialects, belong to the
agglutinative class, of which the ancients knew nothing.[1] A
very convenient system it would seem to pursue. Thus in
Turkish *sev* is love; *mek* denotes the infinitive; *sev-mek* is
to love, *sev-in-mek* to love oneself, *sev-ish-mek* to love one
another, *sev-il-mek* to be loved, *sev-me-mek* not to love; and,
by joining several forms together, *sev-in-dir-il-me-mek* 'not
to be made to love one another', expressing thus in one word
the desire of many nations. It is clear from these examples
that the problem presented by the Science of Language, as
such, even without taking account of the extraordinarily
divergent phonetic systems which have grown up throughout
the world, and which could not possibly be represented
by the Greek alphabet, is something completely different
from that which the Greeks faced in their formation of
Grammatikê. And further, the rules and conceptions of
Greek *Grammatikê* were not meant to suit, and do not
suit, the formation of such languages as the Ural-Altaic or
Athapascan.

The phenomenon that lay before the Greek *grammatikoi*

---

[1] Possibly the Scythian language was agglutinative.

was not all human language. It was the *Logos*: the Logos, both as it existed in their own daily speech and records, and also as it ought to exist if ever it was to fulfil its ideal *Φύσις* (*Physis*), as a thing of beauty and of revelation. The early Greeks had, so to speak, discovered the Logos. Not 'the word', exactly—it is *oratio* rather than *verbum*—but the 'thing said'. They had discovered that often instead of fighting you could say something, and the thing said would make both sides agree. If people were bewildered or puzzled, they could say something, and the thing said would make them understand. There was even perhaps a Logos in the world; something which the Kosmos was saying, if only you could catch the words. There was a Logos of God, something that He was saying, the true Logos of the universe. And meantime, there were the Logoi of wise men and poets, things wonderfully august and beautiful when they were rightly spoken, and capable of ugliness or folly when they went wrong.

If we may anticipate our conclusions, I think some weak and strong points in the ancient Greek analysis of language may be noticed at once. First, the actual analysis, both logical and psychological, was extraordinarily acute, and it is natural that in spite of all the changing centuries we should use the greater part of it still in our current speech. Secondly, to these problems as to others, the Greeks on the whole brought to bear a real spirit of Rationalism. They thought hard and soberly, and the great *grammatikoi* treated language in a philosophic spirit. Indeed, in a sense they were too rationalist. It is very interesting to note how, in the third century and after, two contrary weaknesses appear in the ancient treatment of language as soon as the firm grasp of the classical Greeks has relaxed. We find on the one hand an outbreak of all sorts of mysticism and superstition about words and names, and on the other an excessive degree of analysis, of artificial rules, and of the isolation of word from word. From excess of meditation and reasoning the grammarians began to take the word as a unit, and to forget the Logos, i.e. the sentence or the 'stream of expression'.

The third characteristic I hesitate whether to attribute to Greek idealism or to the mere over-excitement and excessive hopefulness natural to all beginners. From first to last, the Greeks were not content to observe merely what happens, or what people do. They wanted to know what *ought* to happen and what they themselves, when using the Logos, *ought* to do. One knows, of course, how often ignorant people, as soon as they learn anything at all about language, turn all its laws from the indicative to the imperative. Everything is wrong or right, and usage is hardly admitted as a criterion. (You must not say 'available' or split your infinitives; you must not begin a sentence with 'But' or 'And'; you must always say, 'If it be'.) This consideration may explain the tone of Protagoras and Prodicus, the founders of Grammar. But it will hardly explain the persistent interest in *Rhêtorikê* and the *Krisis Poiêmatôn*, the constant effort not merely to analyse language as it is spoken, but to make it or keep it as beautiful a thing and as fine an instrument as it can be made. That is part of the regular Greek devotion to ἀρετή.

Let us consider the first steps of Greek language study. The great Protagoras of Abdêra, one of the most original and sane minds of the fifth century, wrote a book περὶ ὀρθότητος ὀνομάτων or περὶ ὀρθοεπείας, *On Correctness of Names* or *On Correct Speech*. We know very little about it, but we can see that the idea of correctness, or of right and wrong, is prominent. We may perhaps conclude from the word ὀνομάτων that Protagoras made the first great division of the Logos into its parts—into μέρη λόγου or 'parts of speech'—which we meet with in Plato. Speech falls into Names of things, and Things Said about them: Ὀνόματα, and Ῥήματα. *Nomina et Verba*, Nouns and Verbs, they eventually become; but at this stage they are more like Subject and Predicate. A name, and a statement about it. In Σωκράτης φιλεῖ, 'Socrates loves', and Σωκράτης σοφός, 'clever fellow, Socrates', σοφός is a ῥῆμα as much as φιλεῖ. In Plato's *Cratylus*[1] Δίφιλος is an ὄνομα, Διὶ φίλος a ῥῆμα, a thing said.

He also divided the Logos into four bases or πυθμένες, Εὐχωλή, Ἐρώτησις, Ἀπόκρισις, Ἐντολή: Prayer, Question, Answer, Command, a classification which shows that there was as yet no division between *rhêtorikê* and grammar. Protagoras divided nouns into Ἄρρενα, Θήλεα, καὶ Σκεύη, Males, Females, and Things. The last class was called by Aristotle μέσα, 'Middles'; it settled down eventually as οὐδέτερα, belonging to neither class, Neuter. If the untrustworthy evidence of Comedy is true, it would seem that Protagoras actually looked on words with feminine meanings but masculine terminations as irregularities which might well be abolished, and Aristotle says he criticized Homer for 'commanding' the Muse in the imperative, when he ought to have 'prayed' to her. Ἡ κάρδοπος, ἡ ὁδός might as well be made masculine or else turned into ἡ καρδόπη, ἡ ὁδή; and he seems also to have argued that words of such unfeminine character as πήληξ, helmet, and μῆνις, wrath, might be made masculine. I see nothing incredible in this. It was left for a much later age to say, 'Tu, Caesar, civitatem dare homini potes, verbo non potes.'

If Protagoras believed that the gender of words might be changed by agreement, κατὰ συνθήκην, it seems to follow that he thought language was a matter of Νόμος, not of Φύσις. The names of things were given them by Agreement or Convention; not given by God or fixed by the immutable nature of the things themselves. The controversy on this subject raged throughout the fifth century, being part of the whole great dispute between Φύσις and Νόμος, Nature and Convention. The other great Abderite, Democritus, as we might expect, gave solid reasons for believing that language came about τύχῃ, ἀλλ' οὐ φύσει, by Chance, not by Nature. They were all drawn from the actual imperfections of

[1] 339 b.

A a

language as it exists. (1) The same word has different meanings (box, post); (2) many different words have the same meaning (horse, steed); (3) the names of things sometimes change (bowler, Derby); (4) there are some things which have at present, or had till lately, no name. Hence, language cannot be regarded as a perfect image of Φύσις. To these arguments other writers added the variety of languages and dialects. It is easy enough to refute or at least to make ridiculous the notion that language is the work of God or of an unerring Φύσις; but the contrary notion that it is mere convention is equally false. Plato in the *Cratylus* first argues that, since it is possible to name a thing wrong or right, or at least to name it well or badly, there must be some element of Φύσις behind the mere convention. Whether at first the gods named things and taught the names to men, or whether some human lawgiver named them, he acted on some principle or other. This principle Plato finds in the elements out of which the names are made, whether other words or significant syllables or, in the last resort, particular στοιχεῖα or elements of sound, which he identifies with letters, with their phonetic suggestions. For instance, R suggests rapid motion or violence, as in ῥῆγμα, θραύω, ῥοή, τρόμος, τρέχω, κρούω, ἐρείκω, θρύπτω. There is some truth in this, as far as it goes; but it does not in practice carry one very far. As a whole the dialogue, with all its cleverness, seems to me—though I speak with deference to higher authorities—to illustrate a fatal weakness in Plato's thought. The mischief lies in his suggestion that, since language is meant by the lawgiver or the god to indicate the real *physis* or *ousia* of the objects named, it follows that if we only think hard enough about the names we shall discover the nature or essence of things. That is not only, as far as I can see, an error like another; it is an error which has at times acted like poison on the human mind, and is responsible for much childish superstition in later Greek philosophy. In public affairs it made people feel that God, who had named certain people

Πέρσαι or a certain city Ῥώμη, must have meant the first 'to destroy' (πέρσαι) Hellas, and the second to be the very embodiment of 'strength'. In philosophy it left them wallowing in allegories and false etymologies instead of trying to find out facts.

However this may be, late Greek and early Christian thought became drunk with mystical etymologies: Zeus was he 'through whom all things are', the First Cause, because his accusative was like the preposition διά, through, Hera was ἀήρ, as becomes clear if you repeat her name continuously ηραηραηραηραηραηρ, and so on, just as Ἑλένα was so called because she was by nature ἑλέναυς or, in Doric, ἑλένας.

It is a surprising, but not an absolutely illogical, proceeding when these mystical etymologists carry their *etyma*, or 'true meanings', across the borders of Greek into other languages. Plutarch points out that the name Osiris really means ὅσιος ἱερός, 'Holy Sacred'. No doubt the Egyptians who so called him could not know the real meaning till they learnt Greek. But the gods of course, who were the true authors of the name, knew Greek from the beginning, and were only hiding the truth behind a veil in their usual way when they expressed it in a strange language. Rather different is the odd attempt to remake, as it were, in a new language a series of *etyma* which were already extant in an old one. Reitzenstein points out that as ἠΐθεοι (youths) was interpreted as meaning ἦι θεοί, 'like gods', so in Latin *caelibes* (unmarried youths) was derived from *caelites*, celestials. Since οὐρανός = ὁ πᾶσιν ὁρώμενος καὶ φαινόμενος, it follows that *caelum* is derived from *celare*—by opposites, as *lucus a non lucendo*.

Aristotle, it is comforting to find, pays no attention to these *etyma*. He remarks definitely (*De Interpr.* ii) that τῶν ὀνομάτων οὐδὲν φύσει ἐστίν, no word is 'by nature'. If the elements of sound, the στοιχεῖα, were natural symbols of παθήματα τῆς ψυχῆς, states of mind, then all men would speak the same language, which is not the case. Λόγος is a φωνὴ σημαντική, a significant utterance, κατὰ συνθήκην, by convention. It is not in the least an ὄργανον (instrument) for naming the essential nature of a thing, as Plato had pretended.

In Aristotle the Μέρη Λόγου (Λέξεως) have grown to four: ὄνομα, ῥῆμα—which now have the definitely grammatical, not the logical sense—and two difficult anatomical terms which mean 'ligament' and 'joint', σύνδεσμος and ἄρθρον. We also meet, for the first time, the important technical term πτῶσις, Latin casus, 'Case' or 'Declension'.

The two anatomical terms are a little obscure. The sentence is still conceived as being a ῥῆμα about an ὄνομα, but obviously these propositions are in various ways tied together and turn, as it were, on pivots or joints. The ligament, σύνδεσμος, is not exactly a conjunction. It covers regular connecting particles like καί, δέ, κ.τ.λ., and also mere emphatic particles or expletives, like δή, τοι, μέν. The ἄρθρον is a joint, articulus, but it is not by any means what we call an article. We are told by Aristotle that in a sentence it marks the beginning, the end, or a division. Bywater conjectures that the ἄρθρα are the conditional and causal conjunctions, if, because, the relatives, which, when, the final and illative conjunctions, in order that, therefore, and lastly the disjunctives, either, or. The seven 'parts of speech' now current are due to the Stoics.

Ptôsis, or 'Declension', Latin casus, is a new and very important conception. A noun in the nominative singular like ἄνθρωπος, or a verb in the present indicative like λέγω, is conceived as standing straight. Then it falls, or is bent, or declines into various positions. Ptôsis covers the oblique cases of nouns, ἀνθρώπου, ἀνθρώπῳ; the various forms that show a distinction of gender, like οὗτος, αὕτη, τοῦτο; the derivative adjectives, like χαλκοῦς, from χαλκός, χρυσοῦς from χρυσός; comparatives and superlatives from the positive; adverbs from adjectives as δικαίως from δίκαιος. Also the past and future tenses of the verb; and, what is very curious and interesting, words pronounced in a peculiar tone of voice, e.g. the verb βαδίζει pronounced as a question is a πτῶσις of the same word pronounced as a statement. Also in certain circumstances the nominatives singular and plural may be *cases* when they specially mean 'one' or 'many'.

These uses illustrate curiously the length of time and the minuteness of thought that were necessary to the building up of a systematic Grammar of the Greek tongue. *Tantae molis erat* . . .

The complete system of Grammar, as it was eventually developed in Greece, principally by the work of the Stoic philosophers, has come down to us chiefly in two books: the brief Τέχνη Γραμματική of Dionysius Thrax (late second century B.C.), and the Περὶ Συντάξεως of Apollonius Dyscolus. Dionysius' *Technê* was one of the most successful school-books in the world, which remained the basis of Greek grammar till well into the nineteenth century, and was actually used in Merchant Taylors' School, London, when a great-uncle of mine was a boy there. Dionysius Thrax was a pupil of the great Aristarchus, and his work consisted in putting together in a clear and concise form the results of some centuries of work upon the analysis of language. He did for Grammar what Euclid did for Geometry, and his text-book has lasted almost, though not quite, as long as Euclid's.

The *Syntax* of Apollonius Dyscolus (second century A.D.) is a much more thorough and scientific work, but is rendered more difficult than it originally was by the loss of Apollonius' other works, as well as those of his celebrated son, Herodian. He was invited from Alexandria to Rome by M. Aurelius.

Both these books strike a modern reader as overcrowded with technical terms, just as do the ancient books on metre. The fault is natural. The Greeks started with no technical terms and felt desperately the need of them. The demand produced the supply, and the unusual facility of Greek for coining words made the supply abundant and perhaps excessive. But let us try to conceive the difficulty that lay before these exact thinkers in finding names, and correct names, for the immense wealth of nice psychological distinctions which lay before them in the Greek verb. Even the noun had its difficulties. Λόγος, λόγου, λόγῳ, λόγον, λόγε. How was one to name and distinguish these forms? They were πτώσεις, falls or declensions of the original word. Well, λόγος was straight; it was simply the name form, ὀνομαστικός, *nominativus*. Λόγε was obviously the πτῶσις for calling some one, κλητική, *vocativus*. But λόγου? Well, it was the name of the father; Νικίας Νικηράτου meant 'Nicias, son of Niceratus'. Call it πατρική. But it was the case of the possessor, οἶκος Νικίου, 'the house of Nicias'. It was κτητική, *possessivus*. It was also the form to denote the class or genus; it was γενική. And the Romans, who were not strong in abstract matters, called it *genetivus*.

Λόγῳ was comparatively easy: δίδωμί σοι, ἐπιστέλλω σοι. It was the case that belongs to giving or commanding, the δοτική or ἐπισταλτική; and the Romans got it right with *dativus*.

But what about λόγον? We are accustomed to speak of it as denoting the object of a transitive verb, but that is a highly abstract and recondite conception, and the Greeks had no word for object, and were not, I think, quite at home with the notion of transitive. (They speak of διάβασις, the transition of the action of a verb; and τὰ ἐν διαβάσει τοῦ προσώπου ῥήματα are transitive verbs, and there is a regular word διαβιβαστικός for transitive; but the idea seems still difficult to Apollonius.) They had a word ὑποκείμενον, *subjectum*, which meant the matter in hand or the thing spoken about; it might, according to the context, denote either the subject or what we call the object of the sentence.[1] But the *object* as opposed to the *subject* is one of the very few philosophical terms which are Latin and not Greek. In the philosophic sense it had to wait for its birth till Duns Scotus (thirteenth century), and his use of it was completely different from that which is now current.

[1] For example, in active verbs ἡ ἐνέργεια ὡς πρὸς ὑποκείμενόν τι διαβιβάζεται. Apollonius, Συντ. iii. 148 Uhlig.

What, then, were the predecessors of Dionysius or Apollonius to say of λόγον? Somewhat oddly, it seems to us,
they said it was the case that indicated Cause. It follows
the preposition διά. Διὰ σέ, διὰ τὸν λόγον, 'Because of you',
'Because of the word'; it is the case that goes with the causal
preposition. And further, if you try to analyse the relation
of this case to the verb in φιλῶ σε, μισῶ σε, it is not such a bad
shot to say that it means φιλῶ 'I love', σε 'because of you';
'you are the cause of it'. The Romans translated αἰτιατικὴ
πτῶσις as *casus accusativus*, as if it came from αἰτία, an
accusation, though the term *causativus* is also found. They
may have been misled by the curious technical use of κατη-
γορεῖν in Greek for a definite or 'categorical' statement.

The school of Aristarchus had re-mastered the meaning of
the dual, though previous generations had forgotten it. It
had disappeared long since, apparently, from all dialects
except the Attic, and the early Alexandrian poets, including
even Apollonius Rhodius, took the duals in Homer to be
merely older forms of the plural, and made, e.g., dual participles agree with plural nouns, and the like. Philologists
tell us that they were in principle right. The dual was only
a first attempt at denoting plurality as opposed to one, when
our ancestors had not begun to distinguish the various kinds
of 'many'. One may compare a plural like that of the Bush-
men who say *tu* for mouth and *tutu* for the plural, mouths.
But, of course, in the earliest Greek the dual was specialized
into meaning 'two', and Dionysius duly denotes it as the
δυϊκὸς ἀριθμός.

But the Verb: how were you to distinguish, for example,
λέγω, λέγεις, λέγει? I, thou, he. By a clever metaphor the
Greek grammarians thought of the three actors on the stage,
and described these forms as the three Πρόσωπα or Characters
(Masks), and the Romans kept the same word, *personae*.

And the Tenses: they saw that certain forms of the verb
differed in point of χρόνος or time. Τύπτω denotes the ἐνεστὼς χρόνος, *tempus instans* or *praesens*, the time that is now

upon us. Τυπτήσω is μέλλων, the time that is going to be. But there is a kind of action that is present before us but already completed; it is like a dish prepared and cooked and laid on the table; it is παρακείμενος, served up ready, or sometimes more exactly, ἐνεστὼς συντελικός, present perfect.

There is also the action that is past, παρεληλυθώς, παρῳχημένος, Latin *praeteritus*, gone by: and it may take two shapes. It may be παρατατικός, stretched out alongside some other action. The word ἔτυπτον for example implies, according to the scholia to Dionysius, that, at the particular moment of time envisaged, I did beat, I had been beating before, and I was going to beat in the future, at any rate for some little time. But past action may also be ἀόριστος, not determined in any way except that it refers to the past.

So far we are in the region, not indeed of tangible things, but of distinctions with which we are more or less familiar in daily life. But what are we to say of the distinctions between τύπτω, τύπτω, τύπτοιμι, τύπτε, τύπτειν, τύπτων? The last can be got rid of; it is not really part of the verb, it has no persons, it is an adjective (or, as Apollonius said, a noun); at best it is a μετοχή, a participation in both the noun and the verb, *participium*. But the other four? They are not cases, πτώσεις: they are something different, ἐγκλίσεις, and an ἔγκλισις is an inflexion of the voice κίνησιν ποιὰν τῆς ψυχῆς ἐμφαίνουσα, ἢ ὁριστικήν, ἢ προστακτικήν, ἢ εὐκτικὴν ἢ διστακτικήν, indicating some sort of movement or mood of the mind, either of Definition, or Command, or Desire, or Deliberation or Dubitation. It needed a great deal of close abstract thinking to arrive at that conception of the 'mood'.

Λέγω, λέγεις, λέγει is ἔγκλισις ὁριστικὴ ἢ ἀποφαντική (*definitivus, indicativus*). The attitude of mind is one of defining or demonstrating. Curious to speak of defining; it shows how much Greek professional thought was still ruled by the ὅρος or definition. Of course all definitions have to be in the indicative, but we should hardly think of making that the characteristic of the mood.

Next comes, according to Apollonius, τύπτειν, ἡ ἀπαρέμφα-τος. Παρεμφαίνω is to make a secondary suggestion or impli-cation; and the word means 'without secondary characteris-tics'. The Latin *infinitivus* is rather a bad shot. Ordinarily a verb has person, number, and 'mood' or attitude of mind; the form τύπτειν, λέγειν, has none of these. It has no 'secondary attributes'. It is κυρίως ῥῆμα καθαρόν, οὐσίας μὴ καταμειγνυμένης, 'strictly the pure verbal idea with no admixture of matter'.

The form λέγοιμι, λέγοις, λέγοι is simply the prayer-form, expressing pure desire, or εὐχή, as distinct from command, ἐντολή. It is εὐκτική, *optativus*.

The forms λέγε, λεγέτω are προστακτικαί: they denote commands, hence there is no first person. No one gives com-mands to himself, except by metaphor.

What we call the subjunctive was the subject of a special treatise by Apollonius, now lost. We know that he objected to the term διστακτική, *dubitativus*. It suits the deliberative subjunctive,τύπτω; Am I to strike? and fairly suits ἐὰν τύπτω, If I strike, but it does not work well for the commonest uses of this mood, ὃς ἂν τύπτῃ, ἵνα τύπτῃ, and Apollonius prefers the name ὑποτακτική, *subjunctivus* or subordinate. This depends on a theory that, while the indicative, optative, and imperative can form complete sentences, the subjunctive cannot do so except in dependence on some other verb. It occurs almost always in subordinate clauses. The holders of this view probably explained the deliberative and hortative subjunctives as involving an ellipse.

Let us now leave Accidence and Syntax and turn to another side of *Grammatikê*, which culminated in the great Glos-saries and Lexica. (The Greeks, though they paid little attention to other languages, obtained something of the same mental training by studying the ancient monuments of their own.) As so often with the Greeks, the principal motive force of this study is the love of beauty. They loved Homer because the poetry was so good, as well as for other

reasons, and therefore wanted to understand him. Even as
early as the fifth century we find scholars explaining Homer
to classes. We find that words which seem to us simple,
ἀμενηνὰ κάρηνα and the like, were unintelligible to contemporaries of Aristophanes. Hence the need of interpretation.
The beginnings of this art of exegesis are as faulty and feeble
as the beginnings of other arts. Notes in the Homeric scholia
make reference to some of the absurdities of these early
Γλωσσογράφοι, or interpreters of the hard words in Homer.
It seems odd that while τοιοῦτος, τοσοῦτος were common
words in Attic, the simple forms τοῖος, τόσος were apparently
unintelligible. The Glossographi, dealing with such a passage
as τοίην γὰρ κεφαλὴν κατὰ γαῖα κάλυψεν, 'Such a head the
earth had covered', explained that it meant 'a good head', and
therefore concluded that τοῖος meant 'good'. Τόσος, τόσσος,
on the other hand, in their opinion, meant 'a body'. This
mistake came from two passages—and perhaps others now
lost—where τόσον is used adverbially in the sense of 'just
so much', or 'nearly'. A horse is mentioned ὃς τὸ μὲν ἄλλο
τόσον φοῖνιξ ἦν, ἐν δὲ μετώπῳ λευκὸν σῆμ᾽ ἐτέτυκτο,[1] 'The
rest of him, so much, was red; but on his forehead was a white
mark.' But the glossographers took it, τὸ μὲν ἄλλο τόσον,
the rest of his body. This interpretation was supported by a
certain amphora in the hands of Hephaistos' servants:[2] οἱ δ᾽
ἤδη τόσσον μὲν ἔχον τέλος, οὔατα δ᾽ οὔπω ... 'They were just
finishing, but the ears were not yet put on.' The glossographers took it, 'They were finishing the body, but the
ears ...'

One can to some extent follow the growth of the art
of interpretation from these bewildered beginnings, which
actually imposed on Aeschylus, on Callimachus, and even on
the later Homeric poets themselves, to the extraordinary
delicacy and exactitude with which it was invested by
Aristarchus (160 B.C.). We have great numbers of his notes
preserved calling attention to the differences between the

[1] *Il.* xxiii. 454.   [2] *Il.* xviii. 378.

meaning of the same words in Homeric and later Greek. φόβος in Homer never means 'fear', which is δέος, but always 'flight'. Τρεῖν never means 'to tremble', always 'to retire'. Θῦσαι never 'to slaughter' (σφάξαι), always 'to burn incense' (θυμιᾶσαι). Φράζω never means λέγω, 'to say', but always 'to point out'. Τλήμων never is 'unhappy', always 'patient'. Σχεδόν never 'nearly', but always 'near'. Πάλιν always 'back', never 'again'. Σῶμα is never used of the living body, δέμας, but always means a corpse. And so on.

The number could be largely increased. These are observations which show such acute observation and such delicate sensitiveness to language that I believe they were all of them new to scholars when the scholia containing them were first published by Villoison in 1788. Ancient scholarship had lost hold of them, and modern research not discovered them again till Aristarchus' old notes were found.

Such interpretations of the rare words (γλῶσσαι) or the peculiar ways of speech (λέξεις) in Homer were, of course, accompanied by similar interpretations of other authors: of Aristophanes, Pindar, the Tragedians, Hesiod, the Orators, and so on. Aristarchus wrote his notes in the form of a commentary on the continuous text, so that you found the explanation when you came to the hard word. An easy development from this was to take the hard words by themselves, and arrange them in alphabetical order, with the interpretations attached. This gave you the Λέξεις Ὁμηρικαί, Λέξεις τραγικαί, in separate books. Similarly, you might have a collection of proverbs, or riddles, or peculiar sayings. The next step is conveniently described in the Letter to his Companion Eulogius, which is prefixed by Hesychius to his great lexicon (fifth century A.D.).

'Many of the ancients have collected *lexeis* in alphabetical order; but some have only treated those from Homer, like Apion and Apollodorus; others have treated the comic and the tragic *lexeis* separately, like Theon, and Didymus, and others. Not one of them has treated all the *lexeis* in Greek together. But more recently a certain Diogenianus, a man of ability and taste, has collected the above-mentioned books and all the other *lexeis* he could find scattered throughout literature, and arranged them in a single alphabetical series. I mean the *lexeis* in Homer, in comedy, in tragedy, in the lyric poets, and in the orators; and furthermore those in the medical writers and the historians. In sum, he did not omit a single *lexis*, either from ancient writers or from contemporaries.'

Diogenianus, he tells us, carried the alphabetical principle so far as to take into consideration not only the first letter, but the first three or even four. He also collected all the proverbs he could find and added them, and then entitled the whole book *Periergopenêtes*—'The Industrious Poor', meaning thereby that by his book even the poor could attain education if they took the trouble. Hesychius goes on to explain that he found certain points to criticize in this remarkable work of Diogenianus: (1) He left the proverbs without explanations of their subject; (2) he did not give the authors and references to the ordinary glosses; (3) he did not adequately discuss the words that had several meanings. These defects Hesychius sets himself to remove in his own great dictionary.

It is a great work, and one of recognized utility to any Greek scholar. But it differs in a striking way from a modern dictionary. It gives only the 'hard words', the peculiar λέξεις ἢ γλῶσσαι; that is to say, it gives only the explanation of those words which an ordinary reader might fail to understand. Its object is to help the student to understand the old literature. A modern dictionary, from Dr. Johnson to Littré or Sir James Murray, tries to give all the words in the language. Its object is not merely to help a student of literature with his hard words; it is to give a full account of the existing state and history of the language itself as an object of science.

Etymology; grammar; lexicography: we have seen the study of language branch out from its first spring into these three main currents. We might follow other lines which lead to the great dictionaries of literature, like those of 'Suidas' and Harpocration; or the technical encyclopaedias, like that of Pollux. Those we can let be. But we cannot well forget that right from the beginning there has been another study of the Logos in process; the study of the Logos not as a phenomenon to be investigated, but as an art to be developed. If we find the fully developed Greek grammar a little mechanical, with its study of each word separately, its elaborate analysis and definition, we should remember that all the time there was flourishing the study of the Art of Speech, which saw speech as an organic and growing whole, with its own ἀρετή of clearness and beauty. Besides γραμματική, the technical grammar which we have been considering, besides even the wider γραμματική, or Art of Letters, which could read the *Grammata* and turn them from the scratches on paper which they now are back to the living words which they were in their first life, there was also ῥητορική, the Art of Speech itself.

The numerous handbooks on Greek rhetoric are weary reading to us. They come from an unoriginal age. They deal with a subject-matter in which we have little taste or keenness of perception. And they start by encountering a strong prejudice in the modern mind. We associate rhetoric with flashy ornament, falsity, exaggeration, and bombast, and indeed with most of the special faults which Greek rhêtorikê set itself to eradicate. We also make the profounder error of not seeing the immense practical use of rhêtorikê in later antiquity. We have, in fact, two things to realize before we can see the meaning of ancient rhêtorikê and the immense importance attaching to it.

First, an aesthetic point. We have to realize the existence of a sensitiveness of ear and stylistic sense which is apparently far beyond our modern capacities. There is a parallel in Chinese. There, on the one hand, there are in ordinary cultivated speech four different tones of voice, and on occasion eight tones, which we 'foreign devils' can neither reproduce nor properly appreciate, but which are absolutely essential both to the lucidity and the beauty of good Chinese; and on the other hand, there are points of style, apparently rousing the greatest enthusiasm among connoisseurs, to which our western sense is practically dead. Read Philostratus' *Lives of the Sophists*, and you will again and again be met by the same difficulty of understanding. Multitudes flocking to hear a particular Sophist because he can pronounce Greek in the old way, with the proper attention to quantity and the proper rise and fall of musical tone according to the accents; large audiences affected to tears or wild delight by what seems to us a rather ordinary trope or a rather pleasant effect of rhythm. That is one of our blind spots.

But we also forget that the Greek Empire lived on for over a thousand years by the use of an artificial language. The mixed races of the Eastern Empire needed a common language; it was necessary that their officials should understand one another's speeches or dispatches. They needed the consciousness of a common heritage, a common culture and tradition and patriotism; and they found them all in the great literature which was not only their pride and their bond of union, but remained their practical daily possession, just because they kept up the knowledge of Attic Greek and the practice of Attic style as the natural birthright of all who aspired to be Hellenes.

It is not easy to say whether in the long run the price paid for this great possession of a continuous language was more than could be afforded; whether it would have been better for the Byzantines to let the official language merge freely into the colloquial, and to cease to be able to understand Plato or Demosthenes as they had already ceased to understand Sappho or Aeschylus. And perhaps it is not our business as scholars to make any such judgement. It is our business as γραμματικοί or men of letters to try to understand sympathetically not only in general the great adventure of the human soul which we call history and can read in the literatures of the world, but quite particularly the great spiritual and intellectual efforts which the human mind has often made for the sake of some end which we now hardly recognize or appreciate, and the peculiar recompenses of delight or triumph which it has often received, paid in strange coin which is no longer current among us, and of which we can hardly read the superscription. That is where the imaginative aspects of scholarship come in, enabling us to see things that would otherwise be unseen, and to rescue from death or oblivion things that have inspired mankind.

1931.

X

GREECE AND ENGLAND

THE old classical tradition, with all its weaknesses, has deep roots in England.

Two members of the House of Commons were once discussing why it was that Mr. Gladstone, when compared with such highly able and industrious colleagues as Joseph Chamberlain and Sir Charles Dilke, seemed to tower above them by a sort of 'greatness' of mind and character. 'One thing is', said one of them, 'that Mr. Gladstone spends his spare time reading Homer and Plato and Dante and the Bible, whereas Dilke and Chamberlain mostly read bluebooks.' Bluebooks, of course, seemed far more business-like; bluebooks taught them the facts and statistics which they wanted to know, and in the end bluebooks tended to make the furniture of their minds. Mr. Gladstone could get up the facts and statistics when they were wanted, but for a permanent possession he preferred to carry about with him the greatest thoughts of poets, saints, and philosophers. And when he spoke, that possession coloured his language; when he faced a political problem, those ideas formed his background.

There is something peculiarly British in this attitude of mind. I am sure neither Bethmann-Hollweg nor Stresemann, not to speak of the present usurpers of power in Germany, would ever have spent their leisure in reading Homer and Plato and the New Testament. They would have listened to music; they would probably have drunk beer; but read Greek—the very idea would have seemed ridiculous. University professors were paid to do that. In France it would be different. There would be quite as much literature, but not so much classics. M. Herriot, an omnivorous reader, might be caught with Dante or Vergil, and Marshal Pétain with the *Imitatio Christi*; but Laval, Briand, and the majority of ex-Prime Ministers—I think not.

Among English statesmen of the older tradition, a weakness for great literature, and in particular for Greek literature, has been almost endemic. Charles James Fox is a striking instance. It is always difficult for us moderns to understand the enormous affection and admiration which Fox inspired. To us he seems a courageous and eloquent but singularly unsuccessful statesman. But listen to the opinion of a contemporary, not actually a member of Fox's party; to Sir Francis Burdett he was 'the man who is universally acknowledged to be the greatest character in this country, whose virtues and abilities are so transcendent as to hold him out to the whole world as an object of esteem and admiration'. Was not his secret the same as Mr. Gladstone's? He was not very diligent about bluebooks; Pitt easily beat him there. He read great literature and his mind was full of the kind of thoughts that inspired the greatest writers of the past. He was quite an authority on Euripides. He seems to have been at home in great literature everywhere. Once at Rogers' breakfast table he was suddenly asked what was the greatest work of imagination produced in Italy in the eighteenth century. Most of us, I think, would have felt rather at a loss or at least have asked for notice of that question. But Fox was not taken aback; he suggested at once 'Metastasio's *Death of Adam*'.

Burke, Gladstone, Peel, Lord Derby, Asquith, Bryce, Baldwin—and may we add General Wavell?—all carried on the tradition, not merely a tradition of classical scholarship, but something far deeper—a conviction, held as an obvious and indisputable truth, that however pressing a particular crisis, and however important the immediate financial or electoral interests involved, there are always other considerations more permanent, considerations of wisdom or honour or magnanimity or maybe of eternal right and wrong. Burke summed up this point of view in a memorable sentence: 'Small minds and a great empire go ill together.' I fear some of our political business men will be impatient of this habit of mind. I know many foreign statesmen and diplomats will consider the habit deplorably amateurish. What business has a hard-working Foreign Minister to sit reading Plato like Lord Halifax, or even Wordsworth like Sir Edward Grey? Above all, what right has he to mix up his policy with considerations of morality? Policy is one technique practised by statesmen; morality is another, practised, or at least expounded and recommended, by clergymen. To confuse them is simply a trick of the well-known and detestable English hypocrisy!

It is quite possible to argue that a more professional and less amateurish—or shall we say less 'gentlemanly'?—attitude towards politics would be more effective in serving the interests of the country. 'You will always be fools and we shall never be gentlemen' is the saying attributed to a German diplomat. It may be argued that statesmen are the solicitors of the nation; and solicitors are engaged to look after their clients' interests, not to indulge in unselfishness on their behalf or to secure them a reward in heaven. But hitherto, wisely or unwisely, the British people has not inclined to that way of looking at things. It wants a leader whom it can admire, who can appeal to its higher nature, its courage, its sense of honour, its magnanimity, its great traditions. It likes statesmen who have drunk at the eternal springs. Even short of that, I believe the English public—especially that Backbone of England represented by 'the Nonconformist Conscience'—greatly prefers its political leaders to be not entirely absorbed in their politics, to have other interests, to be sportsmen like Lord Rosebery, cricketers like the Lytteltons, bird-lovers like Sir Edward Grey, or even philosophers like Mr. Balfour. To be nothing but a politician, they think, somehow turns a man stale or sour. I remember that when Mr. Neville Chamberlain was Chancellor of the Exchequer, M. Flandin, the French Minister of Finance, came over to consult with him. On his arrival Flandin opened *The Times* and saw that it contained a letter from

Mr. Chamberlain. He eagerly turned to it and found to his bewilderment that it had nothing to do with finance. It was to say that the Chancellor had found on his lawn the previous day a particular kind of water-wagtail, that the time was unusually early for that species, but he was sure he was not mistaken. A French Finance Minister who wrote such a letter to the press, said M. Flandin, would immediately be visited by two alienists.

Is this British quality or weakness at all particularly Greek? I think it is. None of the great Greeks of the fifth century were specialists; they were σοφοί, skilled, and their σοφία, skill, fed itself on the whole of μουσική, 'Music', or the realm of the Muses. They were φιλόσοφοι, φιλόλογοι, φιλόκαλοι, lovers of wisdom, lovers of words, lovers of beauty; all the names they use seem to denote the lover, the amateur, the man who does a thing because he likes it, rather than the hard-faced, efficient professional.

A few years ago an amiable and incredibly learned Austrian came to deliver some lectures in Oxford. He addressed our learned societies and overpowered them with the extent and minuteness of his erudition. Then he was good enough to accept an invitation to an undergraduate Classical Club, where a student was reading a paper on the poets of the Greek anthology. It was a lively meeting, and a hot argument took place, backed by quotations, between various young students about the merits of their favourite Greek poets. Our learned visitor was staggered. He said afterwards that he did not believe such a scene was possible in any other university in Europe. Our men were not at all erudite; they were only φιλόσοφοι, they liked scholarship. They were φιλόκαλοι, they cared for beauty. They happened to love Greek poetry and carried it about in their minds and their pockets. To a German professional scholar they would be mere amateurs, *unmethodisch*, almost *unwissenschaftlich*; that is how we seem to like them.

The anecdote illustrates the curious way in which Greek

culture has soaked unconsciously into the English tradition, at least into that small but influential part of it which finds its centre in the old universities. Like the Greeks, we combine 'music' with 'gymnastic'. We all play games as a matter of course; a comparatively small number shoot and hunt, but everybody plays cricket, tennis, football, or something similar. And we play as amateurs, for the fun of the game, not with the grim determination of one who regards the game as his life-work or his means of livelihood. We play games as the Greeks played them. We are islanders and seamen, traffickers of distant seas, a nation of shopkeepers, if you like, but very adventurous shopkeepers, just as the Greeks were. We have a way of seeking our fortunes abroad and settling down on strange coasts just as the Greeks had.

Perhaps some of these qualities are superficial, but there are others that go deep. Freedom, free speech, toleration, and that willing acceptance of the law which is the usual corollary to freedom, are qualities as characteristic of Britain among the nations of Europe as they were of Greece among the nations of antiquity. The causes which led to this freedom were, I think, different in the two cases; of Greek freedom I will speak later, but our English freedom is, I believe, almost entirely the result of our long insular security, that precious possession which has been ours for centuries and which the generation now living has lost, and perhaps lost irretrievably. The Great Powers of Europe have lived always in danger; they are militarist because they have armed enemies just across that imaginary line that is called a frontier; they are despotic because they have to be militarist; they are suspicious and repressive towards their own people because under a despotism people are apt to be discontented and because despotisms have often for strategic reasons annexed territories inhabited by alien and hostile races. We, surrounded by our blessed barrier of sea, have been almost free from these ugly necessities. Our public life has been comparatively free from fear. Παρρησία, ἐλευθερία, ἰσονομία, Free Speech, Liberty, Equality before the Law, all the familiar Greek watchwords are our watchwords also.

The International Federation of League of Nations Societies once held its annual meeting in Wales. The discussions were friendly and vigorous. And at the end the audience suddenly broke out enthusiastically into song, into Welsh song. A distinguished German statesman, now dead, who was present, clutched at the arm of a friend of mine. He suspected an outburst of Welsh nationalist sedition. 'What are they singing?' he asked. 'Only "God Save the King" in Welsh', was the answer. The incident perhaps illustrates in some degree the wisdom of British statesmanship, but far more it illustrates the extraordinarily happy results of prolonged insular security. We tolerate all kinds of vagaries which in continental countries would be suppressed, not because of any special overdose of natural virtue, but because with us such things are not dangerous; in other countries they are. Anyone who likes may mount upon a chair in Hyde Park and advocate the abolition of the monarchy or the adoption of polygamy or any other cause he likes; anyone may listen or interrupt. A policeman in the neighbourhood will see that nobody is hurt. Many years ago a friend showed me a Russian handbook for the use of Russian exiles in England; one of its cautions was a warning not, when in England, to kill a policeman, even if you found one alone. The populace would be against you if you did. In this odd country the police were protectors, not enemies! When Russian revolutionaries wished to be free from the dictatorship of the Czar, all they could do was to substitute the 'dictatorship of the proletariat'. In Germany, after years of struggle against the dictatorship of the Kaiser, there emerged at last the dictatorship of a political clique. An Englishman says instinctively, 'Why dictatorship? Why not freedom and law?' and echoes of ancient Greece come back to one's mind. 'There are only two ways of governing a city,' says Plato, 'either compulsion or persuasion. You need a little of both, but the more persuasion and the less compulsion the better.'[1] It might be an English county councillor speaking. 'Who is the Master of this land?' asks the foreign herald in a play of Euripides. 'Seek no Master here', answers the Athenian Theseus. 'The people itself is its own master, obedient to the law.'[2] 'How can your Greeks stand up to me in battle?' asked Xerxes, 'when they are all free with no Master to compel them?' 'Free as they are,' answered the Spartan, 'they have one Master over them called the Law, whom they fear more than thy servants fear thee. And he commands them never to turn tail in battle.'[3]

If European civilization as a whole is a child of the Greco-Roman tradition, it is roughly true that at home England is Greek, in the Empire she is Roman. In the balance between compulsion and persuasion, order and freedom, the safe course and the ideally best course, the first alternative counts for most in the administration of the Empire, where there are dangers, and the second at home where things are safe. I must not be led aside into a discussion of the Roman side, the imperial side, of British civilization. The rule of one race or nation over another is always a fearful problem. When the ruling nation is a democracy the difficulties are greater. I often remember the angry cry of Cleon in Thucydides: 'It has been proved again and again that a democracy cannot govern an empire.'[4] But I am inclined to think that if under a democracy the difficulties are greater, the hopes of a successful issue are greater too. I think we may even claim that democratic Britain is the only empire known to history which has deliberately pursued the policy of training her dependencies to become independent. At home we are idealists, perhaps rather muddle-headed, rather sentimental, but still idealists. They call us hypocritical. Of course we

[1] *Laws*, iv. 722 a and b; *Rep.* 548 b.   [2] Eur. *Suppl.* 399 ff.
[3] Hdt. vii. 104.   [4] Thuc. iii. 37.

are hypocritical; that is a characteristic not of English human nature but of human nature itself. The human heart may not be quite what the psalmist says of it, 'deceitful above all things and desperately wicked', but certainly it is terribly prone to indulge in wishful beliefs, convenient blindnesses, and self-flattering explanations. And many a man who would be sharply on his guard against the illusions of mere personal selfishness accepts almost with open arms the illusions of patriotism. We must fully admit that in Pericles' eulogy of Athenian freedom, as in Lord Baldwin's rhapsodies about England, there are a good many bubbles which might be pricked. Yet it is worth remembering that one of the first acts of the British people, when it got into power after the Reform Bill, was to tax itself £20,000,000—a very large sum in those days—in order to set free all slaves in the British Empire. As for the alleged English 'muddle-headedness', it seems a singularly un-Greek quality; but does it not only mean that we are slow to make up our minds, shrink from being positive, and, like the Greeks, are extraordinarily tolerant of different opinions? In France politicians of opposite views seldom chat with one another, but compensate for that reserve by frequently making the most lurid statements about one another. In Germany, Russia, Spain, those in power condemn those not in power to absolute silence, under pain of torture or death. In England, as in the ancient Athenian *ecclesia*, ὁ βουλόμενος ἀνίσταται, 'whoever wishes stands up', and people are expected to listen to their opponent's argument. In Athens, our ancient authorities tell us, the desire to hear both sides of every question amounted to a positive taste, a taste which showed itself in the high development of drama, and the invention of the philosophic dialogue. There are no mere villains in Greek tragedy, such as abound on the Elizabethan stage; every character has his case to state, his intelligible point of view to defend. And similarly in the philosophic dialogues, no point of view is merely silly; none so certainly wrong as not to deserve a hearing. Plato, the most characteristic of Greek philosophers, never likes to assert his own doctrine without first trying to understand the view which he thinks false.[1]

A spirit of the same kind seems to show itself in public affairs. When we observe how often in England political opponents are united by personal friendship, how they dine together and argue, we are reminded of that famous dinner in ancient Athens where Aristophanes, the comic poet, sat with Socrates at a friend's table till early morning discussing the nature of love—Aristophanes, who was reckoned, in public matters, to be Socrates' most dangerous enemy. Yes, at home and in peace-time we Britishers, in spite of enormous external differences, are very Greek in our ways.

In time of war we come even closer to the Greeks. That is inevitable. War flattens out the differences between persons and nations; when people in thousands and millions are trying to kill you, all other interests yield to the one uniform effort not to be killed. That effort unites the civilized man and the savage. Still, even amid the general flattening out, the Greeks in many ways seem closer to us than other warring nations. The war of Athens against Philip of Macedon is rather grim reading for us to-day. The *Philippics* of Demosthenes, delivered in vain to a sluggish and wishfully-thinking Assembly, remind one constantly of Mr. Churchill's 'Arms and the League' speeches which so long failed to stir the Baldwin and Chamberlain Governments. The Athenian Assembly evidently hated the thought of plunging into war, just as our Parliament did, and they allowed that laudable aversion to blind them to important facts and make them forget awkward responsibilities. Also, whether by corruption or flattery or pure deceit or otherwise, Philip had provided himself with a valuable group of partisans in Athens—many of them probably honest, and therefore the more influential. The majority of the Assembly argued that there was no necessity to plunge the country

[1] Cf. 'Hellenism', p. 15.

into war; Philip's proceedings and principles might not be
what most Athenians approved, but he had not made war on
Athens. He had not attacked any direct Athenian interest.
He had got possession of one state after another, true; but
he had generally done it by threats and diplomacy, not by
war. In all such states there were parties which favoured
him. No doubt he had upset democracies and put in their
place dictatorships dependent on Macedon. He had divided
Thessaly 'according to race', and so broken its power. But
none of this amounted to war. He had sent troops into some
states; was that not war? No, he always explained that he
had sent them in kindness to protect the country against
possible enemies. And, after all, how could Athens interfere?
In most of the countries the leaders of the anti-Philip party
had been imprisoned or 'beaten up', and sometimes killed.
Such countries would not welcome Athenian interference.
It was much fairer and wiser to try to understand Philip and
appease him; there was even the chance of persuading him
to involve himself in a war against his very large neighbour
to the East, the Persian Empire. 'Every State', cried Demosthenes, 'congratulates itself on being safe while Philip destroys
its neighbour. They never see that they must unite for the
common security, that their only chance of security is by
union, and that meantime he is growing stronger and stronger
till he will be irresistible.' When accused of warmongering,
Philip has said: 'I am at peace with all who listen to me.'
Is Athens to accept that claim—that peace is only to be
had by obedience? 'Not all Hellas nor all the rest of the
world will satisfy that man's ambition', cries Demosthenes.
'He has proclaimed his contempt for religion and for justice
between nations. Whatever the rest of Hellas may do,' he
concludes, 'we at least will fight for freedom.' And so at
last, when it was too late, Athens girded herself to war and
was beaten. There was no American arsenal then to redress
the balance in support of democracy.

Then there was the earlier war in the fifth century between

Athens and Sparta, each with her respective allies, about which we have such abundant first-hand evidence from Thucydides and Aristophanes. Just as in 1914 or 1939, a rich democratic sea power with a naval empire, full of interest in all forms of social, artistic, and intellectual life, was pitted against a reactionary militarist land power, which had sacrificed most of its earlier culture to stark efficiency in war. The broad similarity is obvious, and it leads to similarities in detail which are at times almost fantastic. At one time, for example, the Spartans, their blockade baffled by the Athenian command of the sea, decided to sink at sight every ship they found afloat, of whatever nationality.[1] Admiral Tirpitz's 'unrestricted submarine campaign' was evidently not entirely his own invention.

The Peloponnesian War, as it is called, exhibited many of the horrors and almost all the inconveniences which are usual in war-time, but what makes it seem specially familiar to us is the accident that we hear it spoken of in no less than eleven contemporary comedies. Aristophanes lived right through it and shows us how the Athenians took it: with abundant humour, apparently, with much cheerful grumbling, and almost without hatred—very like Londoners, in fact. Aristophanes himself was anti-war from the beginning; he hates warmongers wherever they come from, but naturally attacks the Athenian warmongers most. There are constant jokes about various hardships of war, about the scarcity of food, about the trade prohibitions which closed every market. The hero of one play contrives, by divine help, to establish peace and free trade for himself and his family while the rest of the world is at war. He receives a trader from Boeotia, that fat and happy land which has not been invaded or blockaded, a man who comes laden with every kind of game: 'ducks, choughs, francolins, coots, wrens, divers, geese, hares, moles, hedgehogs, weasels, brocks, martens, otters, and— incredible luxury—Copaic eels.'[2]

---

[1] Thuc. ii. 67.   [2] *Ach.* 870 ff., 910 ff.; *Vesp.* 250 ff.

Not very appetizing food for the most part, but when there is nothing else to eat no doubt foxes and otters are fairly tasty. And the list ends with a real luxury—eels from Lake Copais. The sight of that beloved eel produces a burst of lyrical enthusiasm. How can Athens pay for such treasures? She has no farm product which is not far more abundant in Boeotia; but there is one manufactured article which will be a rarity in Boeotia while in Athens it is as common as mud—a paid informer! Shall we call him an officer of 'M.I.5', or imagine some parallel to an oppressive Air Raid Warden looking for lights? They catch one informer, small, but guaranteed full of vice, and post him away to Boeotia, labelled 'WITH CARE', upside down. In another play an opponent of Cleon, in order to interrupt a debate in the Assembly, announces that a shoal of sardines has arrived off the coast of the Piraeus. In a half-starved city that is more exciting news than any reports from the front. The whole assembly rushes to the harbour and the Minister of War is left addressing empty benches. Even hunger can be a joke; yet it is a joke through which there sometimes shows a gleam of tragedy. A boy in one play is to have a prize. His father promises him a nice set of knuckle-bones to play with. But he does not so much want to play; he wants to eat. Could he have some figs? 'Nonsense,' says his father, 'how can I buy figs? I have only my pay to buy bread and firewood for the three of us.' And the boy cries. But the famine had grimmer depths than that. Megara was really starved, and starved by the deliberate policy of Athens. Aristophanes gives us a scene where a Megarian farmer tries to sell his two daughters in a sack, pretending that they are pigs; sheer farce of course, but farce with tears of pity in its eyes. The scene ends in giving them all a good feed, the sort of feed that everyone could have if it were not for this stupid war! Fuel, too, was a constant difficulty. Oil was precious, every drop of it. It was hard to buy wood. A man who sees a whole sack of charcoal rushes to embrace it like a lover. Then debts and reluctance to pay them, and what we should call overdrafts, were a universal joke; and almost more universal, as was suggested above, the nuisance of the informers. Though they had no motor-cars and no blackouts, there seem to have been innumerable ways of breaking small regulations and getting yourself fined. And of course there was the evacuation of exposed places and the fearful overcrowding of the town of Athens, with refugees camped on every bit of open ground and sleeping in every cave or hut or sentry-box or cellar. The authorities expected it would lead to an epidemic; and sure enough it did. It led to the great plague. And I confess that on that one subject I find no jokes in comedy.

Aristophanes was a bold and determined opponent of the war. It is astonishing that he should have dared to speak so freely against it, and still more astonishing that, except for one violent brush with Cleon, he was allowed to do so. The normal man has, I think, mixed feelings about war. He hates war, but he admires the soldier. It is senseless and brutal for men to spend all their powers in killing and hurting one another; yet it is a splendid thing to face wounds and death for one's country. The Greeks certainly had both feelings. They were without doubt very fine soldiers. Not without reason has 'Marathon become a magic word', and Thermopylae, the lost battle, a word of even greater magic. Later on the Greeks were the crack professional mercenaries of the Mediterranean. They fought as their descendants are now fighting, with the same skill as well as the same heroism. Yet here again the Athenians have a likeness to our modern Western democracies. Savage peoples often fight well, Maoris and Zulus and of course Nazis, who purposely make themselves savage. But savages like war and live for it, as the Spartans did. The Greeks as a whole honoured the soldier but certainly they hated war. They loved beauty and freedom and human learning and the eternal effort to build 'a good life for man', and war is the negation of all these things. Even in Homer the War-god, Ares, is hated and despised by the rest of the Olympians. He is the only god who is a bit of a coward and a bully. The earliest of the three tragedians, Aeschylus, who fought at Marathon, had himself seen some savage conquests. He prays, 'May I never be a Sacker of Cities'—using the particular title of honour, πτολίπορθος, which was reserved for military glory at its highest and cruellest, —'nor yet be the captive in a conqueror's hands.'[1] Euripides, the latest of them, has left us, in his *Trojan Women*, a drama which is perhaps the most tragic denunciation of war in European literature, war when the fighting is over and nothing remains but to wait and think. As we of the British Commonwealth fight our great battle to-day, we might well take as one of our mottoes the words of Aristotle: 'We make war that we may live in peace', and add to it a war-cry used by the present Greek armies, 'For the victory of all men!'

War was fierce in ancient times because life itself was hard. Close outside the civilized area of ancient Greece there were vast tracts of barbarism; and close behind it lay the memory of a Heroic Age or Time of Troubles in which the old Minoan civilization, centred in Crete, was broken down by invading nomads and pirates. What a tale is told by the existence of an old proverb like, 'A fool is he who kills the father and spares the sons'! It speaks of a time when the blood-feud was the only law. Even in the height of Athenian civilization the long strain of the Peloponnesian War led to savage reprisals and atrocities disguised as precautions. We should remember that our record is probably misleading— the facts true but the proportion wrong. History, as Gibbon warns us, is mostly a record of 'the crimes, disasters and follies of mankind'. When there is no crime, disaster, or folly to write about, the Muse is mostly uninterested. Like a modern newspaper, history records what is exceptional, the breach of custom, the thing that shocks, and thereby gives things in a false ratio.

It is not the occasional outbreak that is characteristic of

[1] *Ag.* 472.

Greece; it is the Law, the Νόμος, the Moderation, the Σωφροσύνη, against which such outbreaks are offences. For example, after the capture of Plataea the Spartans put their prisoners of war to death, apparently on the ground that in taking the side of Athens against Thebes they had committed high treason against their native Boeotia. But all Greece was shocked. The Plataeans' claim is plain: 'We surrendered, and it is the universal Greek law that those who surrender must not be put to death' (Thuc. iii. 58 f.). The incident illustrates the demoralization on which Thucydides comments in iii. 82 ff. In Euripides' *Heraclidae*,[1] the deeply wronged Alcmena proposes to kill the cruel enemy of her children, Eurystheus, but is at once forbidden. It is against the law of Athens. 'What, do they not kill their enemies?' 'Not any whom they have taken alive in battle.' When the raging old queen insists, the answer is firm: 'No man living shall kill this prisoner.' A passage in Diodorus xiii. 28 is interesting. The Syracusan Nicolaus pleads the cause of the Athenian prisoners. He states the law of Hellas, and continues: 'But, you will say, certain of the Greeks have, as a matter of fact, on certain occasions killed their prisoners. What then? If they are praised for it, good; let us imitate them. But if you your-selves are the first to condemn them, you cannot do the same.'

No less strongly forbidden was any mishandling of a dead body, or any offering of insult to a fallen foe. The famous line of Odysseus in the *Odyssey*,[2] 'Unholy is the voice of loud thanksgiving over slaughtered men', marked his refusal to exult over enemies who had done him unforgettable wrongs. And it represents the dominant feeling of classical Greece. One may think of the tone of Aeschylus' *Persae* towards a brave conquered enemy—intense relief and thank-fulness, but not a word of insult. Or again one may think of the strange scene in Euripides' *Electra*[3] where the dead body of Aegisthus is brought on, and that morbid heroine,

[1] 960 ff.   [2] xxii. 412.   [3] 900 ff.

embittered by long years of suffering, longs to do the for-bidden thing, νεκρους ὑβρίζειν, to insult the dead. There is none to prevent her; she tries to utter the insults and finds that she cannot.

One cannot but contrast with this attitude of mind the practice of the Roman triumph, in which, amid every possible sign of glory and exultation, the captives were dragged in bonds behind the conqueror's chariot up to the Capitoline Hill, whence the leaders were taken down to the Mamertine prison and strangled.[1] Still fiercer was the Hebrew custom. Saul was actually rejected from the kingship because he had not killed the captive Agag; Samuel in cold blood remedied the omission.[2] David, after taking Moab, killed two out of every three prisoners; after conquering Ammon he put 'all the children of Ammon under saws, axes of iron, harrows of iron and made them pass through the brick-kiln'.[3] As for the Assyrian practice with their prisoners of war, one need merely glance at the long rows of reliefs in the British Museum and their descriptions in the Guide Book. 'Troops of prisoners, piles of heads, tortures, &c.', is one entry; others are, 'Military operations connected with a siege, the impaling of prisoners, &c.': 'The slaughterers of the prisoners offering decapitated heads to the musicians and bowmen': 'Asshur-bani-pal receiving the Armenian ambassadors; officers pointing out to them the tortures inflicted on the Elamite prisoners.' The Egyptian records are less ferocious, but come nowhere near the humanity of the Greek.

Even more significant of a moral feeling far above the average of antiquity or the Middle Ages was the Greek custom of marking the site of a victory by a trophy and nothing more. A trophy was a plain wooden cross with a suit of captured armour on it. And by Greek law it must be made of wood only, not of stone or metal; it must never be repaired by the conqueror nor yet pulled down by the conquered. It must simply be allowed to fall to pieces and

[1] Cf. 'Hellenism', p. 3. [2] 1 Sam. xv. [3] 2 Sam. viii. 2, xii. 31, 1 Chron. xx. 3.

disappear as the memory of the old strife disappeared. The reason is given in several passages. 'It is the law', says Nicolaus in Diodorus, 'to set up trophies not of stone but of ordinary pieces of wood. It is well to preserve for ever the goodwill we feel towards our friends, but to let our hatred of our opponents die.'[1] Plutarch discusses the reason why trophies alone of all offerings to the gods are never repaired. 'It would be invidious and malignant that we men should ourselves repair and renew the monuments of hatred towards our enemies when time is making them dim.'[2] Cicero has a story that the Thebans after the victory of Leuctra set up a bronze trophy over the Spartans, and were accused before the Amphictyonic Council of breaking the law and erecting *aeternum inimicitiarum monumentum*.[3] The trial is probably fictitious, but the story shows that the law was recognized.

The essential humanity or moral sensitiveness in Hellenic civilization is shown by another crucial test. When gladiatorial games, already the chief delight of the Roman mob, began to spread through the cities of the empire, they found resistance only in Greece. Despised by Cicero, reprobated by Seneca as a sign of *morum perversitas*, this hideous form of entertainment spread like wildfire among the dregs of the subject populations and the magistrates who wished to imitate Rome. Antiochus Epiphanes, for instance, introduced the games, *Munera*, as they were called, in Syria but found that his people hated the bloodshed. He contrived, however, gradually to lead them to a more masculine and Roman attitude by first stopping the battles at the first shedding of blood, and later letting them go on to the death. At Corinth they did get a footing. At Athens a proposal was made to introduce them, but Demonax the Cynic moved an amendment that before admitting gladiators they should 'tear down the altar of Pity in the market-place'.[4] That settled it! The references to the *Munera* not merely in philosophers, but in

---

[1] Diod. xiii. 24.   [2] *Aet. Rom.* 37.   [3] *De Invent.* xxiii.
[4] Lucian, *Demonax* 57. Plutarch, *Praecepta Reipublicae Gerendae, passim.*

writers like Plutarch and Lucian, are all in the same tone. The whole thing is θηριῶδες καὶ δεινῶς σκαίον, 'bestial and horribly perverse'. The magistrates who provide such shows δημαγωγοῦσι μᾶλλον δὲ δημοκοποῦσι, 'are demagogues or rather deceivers of the people'; 'such things are like the tricks of a prostitute to inveigle the mob'. 'Drive them out of the city', cries Plutarch, 'or, if that is impossible, shun them and fight against the mob which demands them.' It is a grim indication of the tastes that develop like ill weeds in unregenerate human nature to see how spectacles of mere blood and torture—fights, executions, tortures of heretics, autos-da-fé—almost always have attracted crowds of spectators; almost always, but not in classical Greece. Humanity or, as they called it, τὸ φιλάνθρωπον, love of humanity, remains a central characteristic of Hellenism.

If one looks for the cause of this humanity it is worth observing that the Greeks themselves connected it with the freedom of their institutions. Cruel punishments, beheadings, mutilations, tortures, are things that belong to barbarian countries, especially to the despot-ridden East. In the *Eumenides* of Aeschylus[1] Apollo drives the Furies away from his temple into barbaric lands:

> This floor shall be no harbour to your feet.
> Are there not realms where Law upon her seat
> Smites living head from trunk? Where prisoners bleed
> From gougèd eyes? Children with manhood's seed
> Blasted are there; maimed foot and severed hand;
> And stonings; and a moan through all the land
> Of men impaled to die.

And it seems true that there is a definite connexion between despotism and cruelty, as between freedom and regard for the human person. One of the most obvious differences between Hellenic civilization and the other great civilizations of antiquity is that in Greece there was no divine Great

[1] 185 ff.

King, such as there was in the Babylonian and Egyptian and
even the Roman empires. For one thing, Greek city-states
were all on a small scale and surrounded by neighbours of
more or less equal importance. For another, as I have said
elsewhere, Greek potentates are always sharply—and to our
minds almost monotonously—warned that they are not gods
and will suffer for it if they imagine they are. The law is
always above them. The gods are jealous when mortals
become too proud; and *Hubris* brings its sure punishment.
It is significant that even in the somewhat debased Hellenism
which spread through Asia under the Seleucid Empire a
sharp difference was made between the towns, which had
Greek law, with autonomy in municipal affairs and personal
freedom for the individual, and the country-side, which
lived in the oriental tradition.

Just as there was no divine king, there was also no authoritative and overmastering system of religion. Religious fanaticism was quite unknown; and that, next to despotism, is
perhaps the most dangerous source of man's inhumanity to
man. There was no orthodoxy, no uniform body of taboos
and rules of behaviour, such as we find for instance in the
Book of Leviticus or the Laws of Hammurabi, and such as
are normally found in almost all primitive tribes. As Greece
became more of a conscious unity, there grew up a certain
fairly uniform undogmatic piety, which might be directed
towards the major Olympians or to some local deity or to
some particular Healer or Saviour whom the individual chose,
or merely to 'God' or 'The Divine', unnamed and undefined.
Every small community inherited its own gods; if you
travelled into strange countries it was well to pay some
attention to the gods of the place and observe the peculiarities of their worship. Otherwise choice was fairly free. There
was no persecution until the classical Greek atmosphere had
long passed away. Individuals were even free to reject the
canonical legends, like Hecataeus[1] who began his history, 'I

---

[1] Cf. 'Hellenism', p. 11.

write as seems to me true, for the legends of the Greeks are contradictory and absurd' (πολλοὶ καὶ γελοῖοι), like Xenophanes, the philosophic *rhapsôdos*, who rejected all the anthropomorphic gods and their too human adventures, remarking that if cattle or lions had gods they would probably have the shape of cattle or lions. The spirit of discovery, the search for truth, was a stronger feeling and a more effective force than either the fear that dreads the supposed effects of unorthodoxy or the narrowness that cannot bear contradiction.

I have spoken to you for nearly an hour, mentioning point after point that seemed to me interesting or characteristic in that small shining island of human achievement which we call Hellenism. Yet I seem to have said nothing of the qualities and doings that have chiefly made the fame of ancient Greece and left the deepest mark upon the world. To many students ancient Greece really means Greek art. They think of the builders of the Parthenon and the Erechtheum, of the reliefs at Olympia, of those priceless marbles brought by Lord Elgin to the British Museum, and now waiting hidden under piles of sandbags while the bombers come and pass. Most of my fellow-scholars at Oxford think chiefly of Greek philosophy, of Plato and Aristotle, those still unexhausted treasure-houses of luminous thought; of Epictetus and Marcus and Epicurus, still helpful as guides to life. For my own part, Greece to me means chiefly Greek poetry in all its wide variety, Homer, Euripides, Aeschylus, Aristophanes, Sappho, and all that great company long since departed whose words have still the magic secret of beauty. I remember, twenty or thirty years ago, poring in the Laurentian library at Florence over a manuscript that was blurred and hard to read and troublesome, until suddenly I caught the opening words of a lovely lyric that I had long known: Αὖρα ποντιὰς αὖρα, 'Wind, wind of the deep sea . . .', when the walls of the library seemed to disappear and that poet, dead for two thousand years, spoke straight and unhindered to my heart.

I have said nothing, or almost nothing, of all these sides of Greek culture, the sides that are most living and that stir the imagination most. I have dwelt by preference upon aspects that are less widely known. My purpose, of course, was not to give a complete description of ancient Athenian life—a task far beyond my powers—but to call attention to some similarities between the ancient Greek and the modern English attitude to life, similarities due partly to our traditional study of Greek letters, partly to geographical and historical facts. The differences no doubt are greater than the similarities, and in any case it is rash to interpret confidently the fragmentary evidence about ancient Greece, or even Athens, that has come down to us. The picture one makes of it is very incomplete. An impression comes to us of external conditions, rude and almost primitive, of pervading beauty, of amazing intellectual power and unexampled spiritual energy, but the impression is surrounded by great silences and void spaces, which a man fills up out of his own imagination by conjecture and historical analogy. In my own mental picture I do not doubt that there may be an element of illusion, the sort of illusion that is inseparable from love and sometimes reveals a truth that only love can see.

1941.

XI

HUMANE LETTERS AND CIVILIZATION

THE Greek and Latin classics, which for ten eventful years I helped to teach in this University, owe their place in modern education to a long historical tradition. For many centuries Latin was a sheer necessity to educated men. Not only were most serious books written in Latin, but Latin was the common language of daily intercourse among educated men throughout Europe. It has lasted on in this sense rather longer than most of us realize. An uncle of mine who was a war correspondent in the Polish insurrection of 1863 found Latin the most convenient language to talk, and was only a little confused by the Poles' complete neglect of quantity. A Pole to whom he commented on this replied, if I may use a barbarous phonetic, 'Ego Pollŏnus et nos Pollŏni non curămus de quantittăte syllabbărum.' Some Catholic priests still speak Latin freely. I have noticed in the Assembly of the League of Nations that whereas a quotation from Shakespeare or Dickens gets nowhere, and one from Racine or Goethe has little effect, a line from Vergil or a tag from Cicero obtains a universal welcome.

But it is not that aspect of the classics about which I wish to speak. Throughout the ages following the break-up of the Roman Empire, when the lights, one after another, went out in our Western world, Latin was cherished as a sort of life-line by which a people broken into weak and disordered fragments could keep connexion with a great, wealthy, and well-organized civilization. Latin letters were cherished not because they were necessary but because they were 'humane' or because they were 'liberal'. The late Colonel Casson has reminded us that the Romans left England well supplied with roads, but after they had gone there were no good roads till the eighteenth century.

'Humanitas' was a word coined by Cicero to translate the Greek ἀνθρωπότης, 'man-ness', itself a coinage of Posidonius or some other philosopher. It was invented to denote the essential quality by which Man differs from what he arrogantly calls 'the brutes' or, a shade more politely, 'the lower animals'. A starving man, a terrified man, a man entirely absorbed in the struggle for life, differs from them very little. He is a beast like another, a gregarious beast, of course, so that inside his group the struggle is either done away with or greatly eased, but in this he does not differ from the other gregarious animals. Only as he becomes civilized does his 'man-ness' begin to assert itself. And civilization, as Professor Toynbee has taught us, is the process by which a group or society lifts itself above the struggle for life and controls its environment. Before civilization the group is absorbed in the struggle, afraid of its enemies, afraid of starvation, possessing no reserve, no surplus of wealth or energy or time. Civilization brings it that reserve or surplus. To the Greeks civilization begins when men live in a *polis*, and a *polis* is originally—unless I am mistaken—merely a circuit-wall. Behind the wall he begins to be safe; for the time at least his enemies cannot touch him. He can wait and think. He can store his property. He has leisure, and for the first time can begin to do what he wants to do, and not simply what he must do in order to live. The Greeks were fond of distinguishing between τὸ ἀναγκαῖον, the 'necessary', the thing you must do because you are compelled, and τὸ καλόν, 'the beautiful', as we clumsily translate it; the thing that looks good, that you desire for its own sake. In a civilized society man is free to pursue the life that he really desires: he can live a freer, nobler, and more generous life, now that he is not oppressed by poverty and fear. He can follow learning and science, he can try to think out the primordial puzzles of life and steep himself in philosophy or religion; he can create objects of beauty, he can make verses and books. And as he does all these things his ἀνθρωπότης, his *humanitas*, comes out more clear and unmistakable. His time is spent on 'humane studies'.

One sees why they are called humane studies, but why are they 'liberal studies'? For much the same reason. *Liberalis* is simply the adjective from *liber*, a free man. Civilization, when it goes right and not wrong, sets man free to live the life he really desires, to study the things that really interest him, and not merely the things which other people compel him or pay him to do.

Now if you look back to the seventeenth or eighteenth century, you find that the learned men of those times made more or less successful attempts at covering the whole of liberal knowledge. Newton, the mathematician and astronomer, wrote on theology and studied his Greek Testament. Musgrave, the editor of Euripides, was a doctor of medicine. Even in the late nineteenth century, though a large gap was growing between letters and physical science, a man like Macaulay or Mr. Gladstone covered, almost as a matter of course, a variety and extent of knowledge which makes most of our modern savants seem narrow specialists. There are exceptions: Professor Toynbee, in his great *Study of History*, starts in the old way from a wide and minute knowledge of Greek and Latin literature, and then spreads his net wider and wider till all the recorded doings and thoughts of man for the last 5,000 years become relevant to his subject. Bergson again, with a very considerable knowledge of literature, kept his eye on the developments of all the sciences. But for the most part our knowledge has so vastly increased that our savants are forced to specialize. This makes a problem about humane studies. To be a mere specialist— to know all about some part of philology, or some part of economics, or chemistry, or physics and have no interests beyond—does not constitute a liberal education. On the other hand, no one can possibly cover the whole of knowledge. I think there is a rough practical solution of the difficulty which consists in trying to know some one subject really well—how large a subject will depend on individual taste or powers—and then, while recognizing the limits of your own knowledge, keeping your sympathy and intelligence alert for things that are moving in that much vaster sphere where you can be nothing but a listener. Any subject, almost, will do as a centre; but no doubt different subjects differ greatly in fruitfulness. What of our subject from this point of view—as a centre of *liberalitas*, of *humanitas*?

You and I belong to a great civilization, in space covering most of Europe, America, and Australia and parts of Africa, in time reaching from dim beginnings in the barbarian invasions that destroyed the Roman Empire up to some unknown time, perhaps far distant, perhaps imminently close, in the future. But historically the most marked characteristic of this civilization is that it is descended from another: from that Hellenic or Greco-Roman civilization which reached from the barbarian inroads which destroyed the Minoan civilization in the fifteenth century B.C. to those which destroyed the Roman Empire. There have been other civilizations in the world, the Chinese, the Indic, the Islamic, the Mexican: Professor Toynbee counts twenty-two of them; but none is associated with ours at all as closely as is the Hellenic or Greco-Roman. That society produced on a vast scale what Aristotle calls 'a good life for man'; it produced security, law, art, science, philosophy, and religion, expressed in a very extensive and magnificent literature. That is why we call it a civilization and a great one. More important still, it is ours. We are its children and its pupils. We have inherited its ways of thought, in politics, in art, in religion, in literature. Amid all the unparalleled variety of world-wide contacts which we now possess we can seldom escape from the spell it has cast upon us, and when we do we mostly become uncivilized. At least, I think most people would agree that in so far as nations like Russia and Germany in various ways turned their backs on the normal Greco-Roman tradition of western Europe and reverted to the supposed worships of their proto-heroic ancestors, all were in their degrees slipping away from civilization. To substitute the will of a party leader for the rule of law; to use the resources of the law chiefly against political opponents, not against criminals; to kill out, as the leaders of these governments have both preached and practised, those who by intellect or character or courage might become centres of thought in the nation; to subject all publications and sources of information to the censorship of secret police in order to shut out the knowledge of inconvenient truth and bolster up the faith in propagandist myth—all these tendencies are not, as some would have us believe, bright, new, creative ideas, but merely backslidings into the slough from which western civilization, based on its Greco-Roman predecessor, had raised Europe, as some of us thought, for ever.

This matter of civilization has a vivid interest for us who are now living. Before 1914 you could send a letter safely to almost every part of the world, thanks to the well-established International Postal Union. You could travel almost anywhere without fear of robbers, and of course you travelled almost everywhere without passports. In 1920 in Europe there was a fairly safe postal service as far as Vienna, but not much farther, except to the ports. The Ukraine, much of Poland, Russia, and Turkey could seldom get letters. If they arrived at all, their contents had been examined and, if valuable, stolen. Large stretches of country were dominated by robbers. The law did not run. Everyone who crossed a frontier was suspected and examined. The Postal Union is a good material test. In the realm of psychology I would take another. Nothing in a society is so traditional, so intimate and characteristic, as its religion. Now in 1914 one would have said that two of the most stable institutions in the world were the Orthodox Church in Russia and the Moslem religion in Turkey. Few had any doubts of the secure position of the Christian churches in Germany. The first we have seen collapsing like a pack of cards. The second bullied and made submissive by soldiers and politicians. The third treated with contempt and deprived of influence as compared with 'the Party'. The war taught mankind a dangerous lesson: that it is possible for one nation or one mass of men to impose their will by violence upon others, and that in that enterprise such things as justice, morality, truth matter little: what matters is to have a machine-gun and be ready to use it. As Dr. Goebbels phrased it, the important thing is not who is right but who wins. We ourselves came, after the war, and largely through the war, near enough to a real collapse of civilization to be able to cast a glimpse down into the gulf beyond the precipice. Whether or no the dominant forces of the world have learned enough from that glimpse to make them not merely desirous of peace and law, but resolute to uphold peace and law, may be still uncertain; but I believe—differing here from various of my revolutionary friends—that mankind as a whole has learned the enormous and inestimable value of the civilization built up by centuries of bold progress and spiritual adventure, which we came so near to losing or seeing cast down.

Hence comes the special interest, I might say the tragic interest, of the study of Humane Letters. The story of this great civilization from which our own civilization is drawn lies before us as a whole. It is of manageable compass, comprising an immense variety of human experience recorded in a small number of books and records, each one of them containing, if I may so put it, an extraordinary amount of matter to the square inch. It is a story of great experiments, social and psychological, made in conditions somewhat like those which face ourselves but far less intricate and complex, presenting problems fundamentally the same as our own but always the same with a difference. It gives us access to regions of much greatness of thought and spiritual effort; to the awakening, in Canon Scott Holland's words, of those 'dead heroisms' with which 'the paths of our civilized life

are paved'; to a beauty of literature and art which many
generations have thought supreme and which is at any rate
unique and irreplaceable.

How can we best attack this study, or seek to deserve the
name of scholar or Hellenist? The ordinary Oxford course,
in which I taught for some twenty-eight years, illustrates
rather well the double task that lies before us. There for the
first year and a half a man studies the languages and reads
the poets and orators; for the next two and a half he works,
with a maturer mind, at the historians and philosophers.
Naturally enough, he reads the poets and orators chiefly with
a view to their form, the historians and philosophers with
a view to their subject-matter. And the peculiarity of the
Oxford Greats School is that in studying Herodotus and
Thucydides, or still more perhaps Plato and Aristotle, for
their subject-matter, you also study that subject-matter
itself by any means in your power. You get light on the
history from recent excavations or theories of economics;
on the philosophy from Kant and Bergson and Alexander,
and arguments with your tutors or contemporaries. In the
Scottish universities much the same attitude towards this
work is carried on by the great Scottish national tradition.

It is easy to see why some division of this sort is made.
You cannot understand the civilization unless you know the
two languages in which it is shrined; that is what makes the
classical course so difficult; and it follows that the language
is best learnt on material where, so to speak, the form is more
important and the subject-matter less.

Here we strike one of the great mistakes which we classical
teachers have been apt to make, and which have filled various
intelligent students with a disgust for the classics. I am sure
that many of us at school were chiefly taught to construe,
or construe and parse; and if we did that, we did not
much bother about either appreciation or understanding. I
remember myself, though I did in a sense appreciate and
immensely enjoy my Vergil and Homer, I generally read

them sentence by sentence, phrase by phrase, noting and feeling the beauty of language in detail, but without any consciousness of the long sweeps of composition or construction. I knew the *Agamemnon* by heart years and years before I thought of asking myself what it was about. It may not be entirely true that we were taught to concentrate our attention on the fact that Thucydides was 'a poor hand at grammar' without noticing that he was 'a great genius at history', but I should be inclined to admit that we did read ancient literature, much as Longinus or Denys of Halicarnassus read it, either as mere 'language' or as *belles lettres* and no more.

I can remember being a good deal bored by various Greek orators, and even by Demosthenes, because I was somehow led to regard it as oratory pure and simple. If that was the point, I wanted rhetoric, purple patches, sentiment, or invective; the sort of thing you get in Burke or Cicero; what the Greeks called ἐπιδεικτικὸς λόγος. I wanted: 'Contempsi Catilinae gladios; haud pertimescam tuos.' Or: 'He resolved in the gloomy recesses of a mind capacious of such things to make the whole Carnatic an everlasting monument of vengeance. . . .' And one hardly ever got them: even the magnificent close of the *De Corona* is not quite in that style. Demosthenes' public speeches are not epideictic; they are συμβουλευτικοὶ λόγοι, speeches of counsel, whose effect depended partly no doubt on their form, but whose value lay chiefly in the value of the advice which they gave. The difference is vital. The epideictic speech is a purely artistic effort; its object is to impress, amuse, interest. It is what Thucydides would call an ἀγώνισμα ἐς τὸ παραχρῆμα. Cicero's second *Philippic* can be read with enjoyment as a mere *epideixis*; a splendid invective, never actually delivered. The *Philippics* of Demosthenes only begin to be interesting when you understand the political problem with which they deal, when you know what the crisis was, what was at stake, and what policies were possible. You may well admire the clarity and simplicity of the form, but you must if you want to understand it at all read it for its content, its subject-matter.

The same thought applies even to poetry. Take the end of the first *Georgic*: the account of Caesar's assassination, the wickedness of the deed, the resultant wars and disorders, the signs and portents and the judgement, as it seemed, of God:

> Ergo inter sese paribus concurrere telis
> Romanas acies iterum videre Philippi.
> Nec fuit indignum superis, bis sanguine nostro
> Emathiam et latos Haemi pinguescere campos . . .

The world like a chariot out of control is rushing to its destruction:

> et frustra retinacula tendens
> Fertur equis auriga, neque audit currus habenas.

Those lines I learnt at school; but their meaning only came to me suddenly, one day when I was a Delegate at Geneva, after the Great War, and I recalled Vergil's cry to the gods about Octavianus:

> Hunc saltem everso iuvenem succurrere saeclo
> Ne prohibete!

True enough; we classical teachers need the correction and we accept it. But there is something to be said on the other side. How far is criticism on these lines going to carry us? Many an ancient historian will tell us that we students of language and literature have been reading all our books in a childish, external way. He will tell us to turn aside from all that; not to bother about *belles lettres* but to think entirely of history. He will bid us read Aristophanes simply in order to fix various dates and incidents in the Peloponnesian War and just afterwards. He will even set us the task —fairly hopeless, as well as unedifying—of reading the great tragedies in order to discover references to contemporary politics: of searching the sublimest parts of Plato in order simply to get allusions to the friction between Plato and Isocrates. Here, I think, we must check him, and ask him what he really means by history.

He will mean in the first place, you may be sure, political and constitutional history. Think of the ordinary school text-book of history of the abbreviated sort, which, without going quite so far as *1066 and All That*, has left out all that is superfluous. The remainder will be, presumably, the essentials: dates of kings, wars, battles, treaties, revolutions, and constitutional changes. Almost all is political, though of late years economics have been forcing their way into history as into everything else. Almost all is about king, parliament, army and navy, and trade.

Are these things really the essentials? Is this the knowledge that Lord Acton meant when he said of the study of history: 'it is a continuous development, not a burden on the memory but an illumination of the soul.' No, such things are only pegs on which to hang your study of history, pegs almost meaningless and valueless until they are draped.

Let us consider, then, the history of the word 'history'. Ἱστορίη in Greek means simply research or inquiry.[1] Pythagoras, for instance, used it to describe his researches into mathematics. But the two great Greek 'historians', as we call them, have had the decisive influence. Ἡροδότου Ἁλικαρνησσέος ἱστορίης ἀπόδεξις ἥδε, it is thus he begins: 'This is the setting forth of the inquiry of Herodotus of Halicarnassus.' It is the publishing of his inquiry; and he had inquired, during a varied and extremely intelligent life, into everything that had interested him. Geography, anthropology, comparative religion, political and social history in our modern sense, biographies and anecdotes about individuals, all come in; but all are subservient to his chief aim, the aim that gives unity to his wonderful book, an inquiry into 'the great deeds of the Greeks and the Persians in the war which they waged against one another'. It has often been remarked that Herodotus' conception of history is really more philosophic than that of the far more scientific historian, Thucydides. Modern history is turning rather

[1] Cf. 'Prolegomena to the Study of Greek History', p. 45.

away from Thucydides and back to Herodotus. But Herodotus himself by the special importance he gave to the war
between Persians and Greeks really launched history on the
course it was afterwards to take. Thucydides, following this
lead, definitely narrows the range of his inquiry. His *historiê*
is a history of the war, a political and military history in the
strict sense, and the fashion of 2,000 years has followed him.
As a rule, unless otherwise qualified, history means political
and military history.

And why so? Simply because people inquire into what
interests them, and on the whole the doings of kings, statesmen, and armies are what interest people, or at least worry
people, most. If you can only manage to learn a little about
the surface of the past, that is probably the best thing to
learn. But suppose you want to go deeper, suppose you want
not merely to know but to understand, what then?

The most illuminating suggestion that I have met with,
is found in the ancient definition not of *historiê* but of
grammatikê (I have quoted it in my *Religio Grammatici*).
Man, *Homo sapiens*, as they call him, finding something in
his experience, some fragment of life, which he wished to
live on and not be forgotten, invented *grammata*.[1] He made
scratches or marks—we call them 'letters'—on some durable
material, and the marks had meanings. They reminded him;
and in course of time they were improved and made clear
enough to remind other people. He wrote down what he
wanted known or remembered, so that ever so long afterwards someone else could come and read those apparently
dead *grammata* and turn them back into *logoi* or living speech.
If the reader was a really good *grammatikos* he would be able
to say them exactly as the writer had meant them to be said.
He would call back the live speech that seemed long ago to
have passed out of the world, and thereby enable people to
live again the fragment of life which, ever so long before,

[1] Cf. Rutherford, *A Chapter in the History of Annotation*, pp. 10 ff. and
Isocrates v. 10.

had seemed particularly worth preserving. In the second part of *Faust* there is a question whether there will ever come to the hero a moment of life to which he can deliberately say: *Verweile doch, du bist so schön,* 'Stay, thou art so beautiful.' The *grammatikos* does not exactly say to the moment, 'Stay'; but he does say, 'Return again, thou art so beautiful.' Beautiful? Well, beautiful or interesting or instructive or funny—or in some way desirable to live again.

Now is not that exactly what the true historian wants to do? He wants to know and understand and feel and relive the past, or rather some few selected fragments of it. He will relive it very imperfectly in comparison with the people who actually experienced it, but there is something else which he can do and which the people of the time never could. He can see that particular piece of life in its historical connexion, and so compare and judge and understand. He can see the triumphs which turned to ashes: the despairing heroisms which seemed folly at the time and bore their fruits afterwards: the confident theories which turned out to be mere gropings towards some result which would have shocked the theorists.

The sort of thing that we popularly call history is for the most part just a scaffolding for reaching that 'illumination of the soul' of which Lord Acton spoke. The historian's field ranges of course far outside mere literature. A good archaeologist, to take one instance, will study some foundations of buildings and a mass of broken pots, and out of them will make good history. He will show what the completed buildings must have been like and what purpose they served, and why the pots were that shape and not another. He will even know a great deal about the way in which the inhabitants of the houses spent their time. Think how much we already know, almost entirely from archaeological remains, about Minoan Crete, and, chiefly through such remains, about ancient Egypt and Assyria. The work done in rediscovering and re-creating those remote societies is not only wonderful in its skill and accomplishment; it also does succeed in its purpose. It rouses our imagination. It gives us what we want to know. And yet, consider for a moment how far it fails.

It fails just where our knowledge of the past of savage nations fails; where, curiously enough, a great part of our knowledge of the Middle Ages fails. We know how the people dressed, when and where and why they fought each other, what their weapons were, and who won. But the thing we really want to know is not told us, because they have in the one case left no literature, and in the other comparatively little self-expressive literature.

'A good book', in Milton's famous words, 'is the precious life-blood of a master spirit, treasured up to a life beyond life.' It holds his actual thought and feeling preserved; and a good *grammatikos* knows how to re-create that thought and feeling so as to live it again. (Not perfectly, of course; not exactly as it was lived before, but nevertheless to live it.) Now, if you are a historian and, studying some past age, wish to get really inside it in imagination, there is no way in which that miracle can be performed half so well and effectively as by steeping yourself in its literature. The literature tells you, *ceteris paribus*, even more than the art, though the art no doubt comes next. The only condition is that the literature must be free and expressive literature. There are many societies which, though they did produce books of a sort, sometimes even very long ones, did not succeed in really expressing themselves in *grammata*, just as others, though they left monuments and works of art of a sort, never succeeded in expressing themselves that way. It so happens that the Greeks and Romans did succeed admirably in both ways, and inspired their followers to do the same.

Suppose, for example, we go back to Demosthenes and consider his policy. It was, on the face of the matter, a failure. For him it meant exile and suicide. For Greece it meant incessant warfare on the part of a number of small states, occupied with many diverse and sometimes conflicting interests, against a big military monarchy which was able to conquer them all piecemeal, and, being comparatively uncivilized, had no particular interest in doing anything else except conquering people. Many persons, then and now, have thought Demosthenes very foolish for making so much trouble instead of capitulating to Philip on the best terms he could get. And his only real defence, in which he believed to his death, and which the Athenians still upheld when it had led them to utter disaster, was—roughly speaking—that it was better to fight and be crushed than willingly to allow a higher civilization to be swamped and destroyed by a lower. And how are you to know what that higher civilization was? By reading dictionaries of antiquities or text-books of history? No: you will never get there that way. By reading the *Oresteia*, and the *Troades*, and the *Oedipus*, and Thucydides and Plato and even Demosthenes himself. Take the *Philippics* and *Olynthiacs*, or the *De Corona*, for that matter, and ask yourself how often in the world's history it has been possible to address a vast open-air audience of ordinary citizens with long speeches so free from showy rhetoric or comic relief, so full of sustained and severe political argument, so destitute of false sentiment or 'high-falutin', and—one may add—so consistently addressed to high motives? Could you do it now? You might in parliament, but certainly not to an open-air audience. We are not quite sufficiently civilized or serious.

But that by the way. My main contention is that if you want to understand Greek civilization you can do so by reading. If you want to feel what it was like to be a Greek, read the books they have left, and read them with your imagination alert. You cannot of course succeed completely, but you can succeed sufficiently to obtain an extraordinarily rich and inspiring experience. Of course you must try to take in their art also; to take in all that you can find of the work and expression of free Greece in the region of what they

called τὸ καλόν. Τὸ καλόν is that which you love for its own
sake, and which you naturally seek as soon as you are free
from the grip of ἀνάγκη, and therefore it is in the pursuit of
τὸ καλόν that a man best expresses himself.

You see to what conclusion the argument is leading us.
Granted that it is a matter of intense import to us to know
the great civilization of which we are the children and the
successors; granted that to reach that knowledge is the work
of a historian, that the knowledge we want is history pure
and simple; the argument shows us that such history, if it is
to attain or approach its goal, must call in the help of scholarship, scholarship in the linguistic and imaginative sense of
the word. Scholarship is of all instruments the most deep-
reaching if you would really make your ancient history into
an intelligent whole. Your task, as a historian, is to know
what life in Athens was, and you will know it best by re-
living the highest and most characteristic parts of it. Do not
let anyone persuade you that questions of scholarship and
style and grammar are childish things, of the sort that we
leave behind when we leave school; that only inscriptions, and
excavations, and archaeological research are really 'scientific'
and worthy of serious study. If you read Cicero's *Letters* you
want not merely to know the facts and dates and intrigues
about Caesar's assassination. You want to know what Cicero
was like, what various of his correspondents and contemporaries were like: and your knowledge of them will often
depend on the humorous or kindly turn of a phrase, or even,
if they are poets, on the self-revelation that comes with some
impetuous metaphor or delicate rhythm. How much you
learn of the faults and qualities of Roman society from the
first half-dozen lines of Propertius or from Catullus' farewell
to his brother! That is where the value of composition comes
in. There has been, of course, an excessive worship of Greek
and Latin composition in Oxford and Cambridge and the
great public schools on which they used so largely to depend;
but composition has its importance for history. It has been

said that a man who can write good Greek has got more
intimately inside the mind of a fifth-century Athenian
than many a man who has read tomes and tomes of Pauly–
Wissowa, and in looking back over my education I sometimes
wonder whether the most educative, the most mind-training,
subject I was ever taught may not have been the writing
of Greek prose. It taught one to get beyond the word to the
thought behind it, and set one free from the domination of
ambiguities and catchwords.

I took earlier in this address a passage at the end of the
first *Georgic* as an instance of poetry charged with history,
poetry which does not yield up its secret until we set it in
its historical environment. But let me go farther. What
would you say of the long passage about Orpheus and Eurydice at the end of the fourth *Georgic*? As pure poetry it is
perhaps the most beautiful thing Virgil ever wrote. In a
sense I am tempted to call it one of the most exquisite
achievements in the technique of lovely verse which the
world has ever seen. But to the historian is it any use at all?
It is a mere mythological idyll, about things that were never
done by people who probably never existed, with no reference
to historical fact from one end to the other. Taking this
passage as a test case, a literary scholar—a 'mere scholar', as
he is called—will aim at thoroughly mastering and enjoying
it, feeling its special beauties of rhythm and language, and
the innumerable associations which radiate from every line
of it, reverberating as it were again and again before they
cease. 'All very well', you may say: 'he may get as much
enjoyment and inspiration from it as he likes, but that will
not make him a better historian. A purely imaginative
account of something that never happened nor could have
happened is not history.' Let us try to answer that argument.

'Not a burden on the memory but a continuous illumination of the soul.' Remembering those words, let us ask ourselves, was not the writing of that idyll a great historical
event? When General Wolfe said he would sooner have

written Gray's *Elegy in a Country Churchyard* than have taken Quebec, he was expressing a judgement which may or may not be right, but is certainly not absurd. What we study in history is the Rise of Man, the upward climbing of human life. Of course the rise is not a continuous process, and the phrase I have used may be highly inadequate and inexact; but if there is any sense in the long record of man's life on earth, if it is not, in a satirical phrase of the late Lord Balfour, merely 'a brief and discreditable episode in the life-history of one of the minor planets', it must be a process in a direction, a story with a plot, and roughly speaking it seems to be a constantly repeated effort after the bettering or ennobling of life. Now, if that is so, the writing of Gray's *Elegy* may well be a more significant fact than the taking of Quebec. A great piece of poetry is a piece of very noble living—that is, of high, intense, and beautiful experience—and a source of noble living afterwards to those who read it. It is a great achievement. A historian can say of it, 'Here for the first time, in its centuries and millennia of struggle, the spirit of man reached such-and-such a height. . . .' And obviously he cannot say that with understanding unless he understands the achievement itself—unless he feels the poem.

Compare a more obvious piece of noble living. You remember the tradition, true or false, that the Roman gladiatorial shows were stopped eventually, after many protests, when the monk Telemachus rushed down into the arena and got himself killed in preventing the slaughter. A similar story was told of two philosophers of the Cynic school. Most men, no doubt, still enjoyed the sport of seeing their fellowmen butcher one another; some men so hated it that they gave their lives to prevent it. Surely the world moved a step upward when that was done. It was a fact of far greater historical importance than many which bulk ten times as large in our histories.

But now notice a difference between these two pieces, as I have called them, of noble living. You can feel a thrill of admiration at the heroic deed of Telemachus; you can be made braver and stronger by it. But you cannot relive it, you cannot share the experience. But when, with imagination really alert, you read the *Orpheus and Eurydice* you are able actually to share an experience with Augustus and Maecenas and the rest of them, and that a very intimate and characteristic experience. Of course no two people get fully and exactly the same experience from reading the same poem : obviously not. But a great part of the experience is the same. In great literature, when the dead *grammata* come alive and speak, you can recapture the great moments of the past. Without literature it is very difficult or impossible. You would like to know how Caesar felt when he heard of Pompey's murder on the sea-shore; how Brutus felt when he made up his mind to the *praeclarum facinus*; how the crowd felt when Antonius addressed them over Caesar's body. You cannot do it except by a feat of imaginative guessing. But you can feel just as various contemporary Romans felt when they heard or read Vergil's Idyll about Orpheus. The best part of your experience, at least, is not very different from that of a Roman who heard Vergil read and came away with his mind full and his ears ringing with the last cadences:

Eurydicen vox ipsa et frigida lingua,
Heu miseram Eurydicen, anima fugiente vocabat,
Eurydicen toto referebant flumine ripae.

Historical records can tell you about things that happened long ago; but great works of art or poetry, and, I would add, great works of philosophy, are themselves the things that happened. I have taken my example from a piece of pure literature, but my argument applies far more widely. Our records, our power of expression, our sense of spiritual values are all miserably imperfect; but at times, here and there, during its long pilgrimage the Spirit of Man has been able to say to a given moment of life, *Verweile doch, du bist so schön.* Through the study of Humane Letters, as through the study of Art in all its forms, we relive those moments, we keep them from disappearing, we understand and interpret them, and thereby we minister to that great spiritual adventure of mankind which we call Civilization.

1937.

PRINTED IN
GREAT BRITAIN
AT THE
UNIVERSITY PRESS
OXFORD
BY
CHARLES BATEY
PRINTER
TO THE
UNIVERSITY